J. WILLIAM FULBRIGHT

J. WILLIAM FULBRIGHT

A Bibliography

Compiled by
Betty Austin

Bibliographies and Indexes in Law and Political Science,
Number 22

GREENWOOD PRESS
Westport, Connecticut • London

Library of Congress Cataloging-in-Publication Data

Austin, Betty.
    J. William Fulbright : a bibliography / compiled by Betty Austin.
       p.   cm.—(Bibliographies and indexes in law and political
science, ISSN 0742–6909 ; no. 22)
     ISBN 0–313–26336–1 (alk. paper)
     1. Fulbright, J. William (James William), 1905– —Bibliography.
I. Title. II. Series.
Z8318.22.A97   1995
[E748.F88]
016.9739′092—dc20   94–38435

British Library Cataloguing in Publication Data is available.

Library of Congress Catalog Card Number: 94–38435
ISBN: 0–313–26336–1
ISSN: 0742–6909

First published in 1995

Greenwood Press, 88 Post Road West, Westport, CT 06881
An imprint of Greenwood Publishing Group, Inc.

Printed in the United States of America

The paper used in this book complies with the
Permanent Paper Standard issued by the National
Information Standards Organization (Z39.48–1984).

10 9 8 7 6 5 4 3 2 1

For
Gene
and
Jenny

Contents

Preface

Much literature has been written about Senator J. William Fulbright, ranging from undergraduate honors papers to biographies. Recently, two more books have been published, one by a journalist in Japan and the other, a biography, by a scholar from the former Soviet Union. Several Fulbright works are under way, among them two biographies. The growing number of studies undertaken in the Fulbright Papers reflects a continuing interest in Senator Fulbright and illuminates his role in postwar America. This accelerating pace of scholarship indicated the need for a bibliographical guide for published, secondary, and primary sources. The purpose of the guide is to provide information for persons interested in the existing literature and for prospective researchers in the Fulbright Papers and major complementary collections.

Using bibliographical information from the University of Arkansas Libraries as a starting point, I set out to assemble a basic bibliography of works by and about the senator. Materials have been gathered from some fifty indexes to periodicals and guides to literature. The Fulbright Papers themselves have also provided many clues.

Because scholars and students will be the primary users, comprehensive treatment has been given to literature in the popular press and careful attention devoted to scholarly articles, dissertations, master's theses, and books. Contributions by Fulbright to the publications of others are another important category. These contributions take several forms: introductions, prefaces, forewords, epilogues, and essays. Significant pieces about Fulbright in collections of essays and books which feature him prominently or which include salient information are another important category.

Certain groups of materials were excluded for reasons of time, space, and relevance. Those consist of most foreign publications, newspaper stories, most government documents, audiovisual items, juvenile literature, fiction, conference papers, and most articles in Sunday supplement magazines. Some of those materials, such as major newspapers and many government documents, are already adequately indexed.

A consideration of space dictated the omission of materials regarding the Fulbright exchange program, except for pieces by Fulbright and pieces about the program which focus significantly on the senator, biographically or philosophically. Again, a concern for space precluded the incorporation of items in most university publications and university alumni magazines other than those of the University of Arkansas. Most book reviews were left out; only reviews which were developed into major critical articles have been included.

The book itself consists of two parts, a short biographical sketch and an annotated bibliography. The narrative concerns Fulbright's early background and political career, with special attention given to his encounters and endeavors in public life. The focus of the study is on the annotation of the existing literature, slightly fewer than thirteen hundred entries.

The annotated bibliography is in two parts, primary sources and published and secondary works. Primary sources include only the senator's papers and major complementary collections in the area of international educational exchange. Smaller manuscript collections and oral history interviews were omitted, again for considerations of space. The annotations for the first part are arranged alphabetically and include information on the kinds of documents, subjects, dates, size, and research access. The annotations for the second part are organized in a chronological subject arrangement. Both parts are supported by an author and subject index. The entries are numbered sequentially throughout the book, with the entry numbers keyed to names and subjects in the index.

Because speeches and articles by Fulbright were widely reprinted in popular periodicals, scholarly journals, and anthologies, ad hoc entries were developed to show the publication history of those pieces appearing in more than one place. Titles that differ from the title in the main entry are included in the additional citations. The annotations primarily concern content and the author's perspective and do not include many editorial comments. Assessment of the literature is best left to the reader.

Fulbright scholars are making significant contributions to historical research. Because the senator's career is closely associated with the course of American foreign policy from the early forties, his story is also a chronicle of mid-century U.S. history. This rich and growing corpus of Fulbright literature serves to confirm his place in the annals of the postwar period.

Acknowledgments

A number of people have been important in this undertaking. I gratefully acknowledge Michael J. Dabrishus, head of the Special Collections Division, University of Arkansas Libraries, for supporting the project from the beginning; the late Samuel A. Sizer, former curator of Special Collections, for giving me the opportunity to work with the J. William Fulbright Papers; and Ann Waligorski for giving me the idea. Endless thanks to Věra Ekechukwu and Nan Lawler of Special Collections for setting the text and, once more, to Nan Lawler for page makeup and production of final camera-ready copy. Without their expertise and warm support, the project would not have been possible. Special thanks to my editor, Mildred Vasan, for her guidance and patience. My thanks to the Interlibrary Loan Department of the University of Arkansas Libraries for securing materials for my research, especially Monica Doman, Catherine Kilgore, and Susanna Price, and to Andrea Cantrell of Special Collections and Nan T. Ernst of the Library of Congress for helping me in the final stages. I am grateful to Patsy Moore of the Circulation Department of the University of Arkansas Libraries for locating materials for my project. Special thanks to Martin Manning of the United States Information Agency, Dulcie Schackman of the Institute of International Education, and Kim Scott of Special Collections for their assistance with the chapter "Manuscript and Record Collections." I am especially indebted to my husband Gene. I could not have completed the book without his help and encouragement. Finally, my appreciation to Senator Fulbright, whose distinguished career is the inspiration for the literature in this bibliography.

Chronology

1905	Born in Sumner, Missouri, on April 9, the son of Jay and Roberta Waugh Fulbright.
1906	Moved with his family to Fayetteville, Arkansas.
1920	Entered the University of Arkansas, Fayetteville.
1924	Received a Rhodes scholarship in December to study at Oxford University, Oxford, England.
1925	Graduated in January with a B.A. degree from the University of Arkansas and began his study at Pembroke College, Oxford, in the fall.
1928	Graduated in June with a B.A. degree from Oxford.
1928-1929	Traveled on the continent, settled in Vienna for a time, and traveled with foreign correspondent Marcel William Fodor.
1931	Received an M.A. degree from Oxford in April.
1932	Married Elizabeth Kremer Williams on June 15; two daughters, Elizabeth and Roberta.
1934	Graduated in June with an L.L.B. degree with distinction from George Washington University, Washington, D.C.; also admitted to practice before the Bar of the Supreme Court.
1934-1935	Served as special attorney, Antitrust Division, U.S. Department of Justice.
1935-1936	Accepted a position as instructor in law at George Washington University, Washington, D.C.
1936-1939	Accepted a position as lecturer in law at the University of Arkansas, Fayetteville; also helped with the family businesses.
1939-1941	Became president of the University of Arkansas on September 18, 1939, and served until June 9, 1941.
1943	Began his term in the U.S. House of Representatives in January; assigned to the Foreign Affairs Committee. Drafted the Fulbright

resolution favoring U.S. participation in a postwar international peace-keeping organization.

1944 Served as chairman of the American delegation to the Allied Ministers of Education Conference in London in the spring.

1945 Began his first term in the U.S. Senate in January. Became a member of Phi Beta Kappa, Arkansas Alpha Chapter, in May.

1946 On August 1, President Harry Truman signed the Fulbright Act authorizing the scholarship program bearing the senator's name.

1947 Introduced a resolution in March that would have secured congressional support of the political unification of Europe.

1949 Assigned to the Senate Foreign Relations Committee; also became Honorary Fellow of Pembroke College, Oxford University.

1950 Began the Banking and Currency Committee's investigation of the Reconstruction Finance Corporation.

1953 Awarded honorary Doctor of Civil Laws degree from Oxford University.

1954 Nominated by President Dwight D. Eisenhower as a Representative of the United States to the Ninth Session of the General Assembly of the United Nations; also cast the only dissenting vote against appropriations for Senator Joseph R. McCarthy's Permanent Investigations Subcommittee.

1955 Became chairman of the Senate Banking and Currency Committee.

1956 Signed the Southern Manifesto.

1957 Clashed with Secretary of State John Foster Dulles over U.S. policy in the Middle East.

1958 Introduced legislation on February 24, 1958, authorizing the construction of a National Cultural Center for Washington, D.C., which became the John F. Kennedy Center for the Performing Arts; also filed a brief, Amicus Curiae, *Aaron v. Cooper,* with the Supreme Court in August urging a delay in desegregation.

1959 Became chairman of the Foreign Relations Committee on February 6.

1961 Delivered a memorandum to President John F. Kennedy advising against the invasion of Cuba at the Bay of Pigs; sent a memorandum to the president and Secretary of Defense Robert S. McNamara alerting them to educational and propaganda activities of the military; introduced legislation consolidating and expanding the educational and cultural exchange program (Fulbright-Hays Act).

1963 Traveled to Moscow for the signing of the nuclear test ban treaty.

1964 Delivered his "Old Myths and New Realities" speech in the U.S. Senate on March 25; also introduced and managed President Johnson's Gulf of Tonkin resolution in the Senate in August.

1965 Delivered a speech in the U.S. Senate on September 15 criticizing U.S. intervention in the Dominican Republic, a move that precipitated his break with President Lyndon B. Johnson.

1966	Launched hearings before the Foreign Relations Committee in January and February on the conduct of U.S. policy in Vietnam; also delivered the Christian A. Herter Lectures at Johns Hopkins University in the spring on the "arrogance of power."
1968	Reelected to the U.S. Senate for fifth and last term amid the Vietnam War controversy.
1969	Reintroduced his 1967 national commitments resolution. The Senate passed the resolution in June.
1974	Defeated by Governor Dale Bumpers in his reelection bid for a sixth term.
1975	Became counsel for Hogan and Hartson, Washington, D.C.; also delivered the first R.B. McCallum Memorial Lecture at Oxford University.
1983	Testified in November before the Senate Foreign Relations Committee on U.S.-Soviet relations.
1985	Elizabeth Williams Fulbright died on October 5.
1990	Married Harriet Mayor in March. Traveled in June to Oxford University for the naming of a quadrangle at Pembroke College in his honor and to Moscow State University for an honorary degree.
1993	Received the Presidential Medal of Freedom in May; the first J. William Fulbright Prize for International Understanding was awarded by the Fulbright Association on October 1 to Nelson R. Mandela.

Biographical Sketch

James William Fulbright was born on April 9, 1905, in Sumner, Missouri, the fourth of six children of Jay and Roberta Waugh Fulbright. The following year the Fulbright family moved to Fayetteville, Arkansas, where William Fulbright, the senator's grandfather, had retired. Jay Fulbright quickly established himself as a successful businessman, acquiring a number of business interests. Young Fulbright's summers were spent working for his father and later taking summer school classes at the University of Arkansas for high school students. By attending summer sessions, he graduated from high school early and was admitted to the university in 1920 at the age of fifteen.[1]

All of Fulbright's formal education in Fayetteville was completed on the University of Arkansas campus, first in the training school conducted by the Department of Education and later in the College of Arts and Sciences. He achieved an academic record that subsequently earned him membership in Phi Beta Kappa. The university did not have a Phi Beta Kappa chapter during the twenties, but he became a member of the Fayetteville chapter in 1945.[2] His college career encompassed a wide range of activities outside the classroom, from the playing field to student government. He was president of the Associated Students, captain of the tennis team, halfback on the football team, a Sigma Chi, and a member of several organizations, including the Glee Club and the Periclean Literary Society.[3]

The unexpected death of his father in July 1923 forced him to drop out of school for a semester to help his mother with the family businesses. He returned to school in January 1924 and finished his undergraduate studies the following year, graduating with a B.A. degree in political science in January 1925. Earlier, he was awarded a Rhodes scholarship to study at Oxford University in England. His tenure at Arkansas also included enrollment in the law school as a part-time student, beginning in September 1924, where he took courses from Dwight Savage and a young professor from Harvard named Claude Pepper.[4]

In the fall of 1925, the twenty-year-old Fulbright sailed for England. He spent three years at Pembroke College and earned two degrees, a B.A. in 1928 and an M.A. in 1931, both in the Honor School of Modern History. Fulbright excelled at Oxford as a scholar and an athlete. He joined Oxford's academic clubs and societies and played the Oxford games—tennis, rugby, and lacrosse. His tutor was a young don from Scotland, Ronald Buchanan McCallum, who had a significant impact on his intellectual development. Another important tutor during his European period was the well-informed and scholarly journalist, Marcel William Fodor, whom he met in Vienna following his Oxford tenure.[5]

Fulbright returned to the United States in the spring of 1929 and soon settled in Washington, where he had met Elizabeth Kremer Williams of Philadelphia. They were married on June 15, 1932. He continued his law studies at George Washington University, graduating with distinction in 1934. Fulbright worked briefly in the Antitrust Division of the U.S. Department of Justice and then spent a year teaching law at George Washington University. In 1936, he returned to Fayetteville to manage the family businesses and to teach part-time at the University of Arkansas Law School.[6]

Fulbright's academic career took another direction in September 1939 following the death of the university president in an automobile accident. The thirty-four-year-old professor was appointed by the board of trustees to fill the vacancy. But the election of a political opponent of the Fulbright family, Homer Adkins, who took office as governor in January 1941, curtailed his career as a university administrator. He was summarily removed on commencement day in June 1941.[7]

The next year Fulbright decided to run for the U.S. House of Representatives in the third district and won easily. As a freshman member of the House Foreign Affairs Committee, he introduced a resolution of special importance for the future United Nations. The fifty-five-word resolution called for congressional support of U.S. participation in the creation and maintenance of a postwar international peace-keeping apparatus. It passed the House on September 21, 1943.[8]

In 1944, Fulbright successfully campaigned against several Democratic opponents, including Governor Adkins, and won his first election to the U.S. Senate. One of his earliest efforts in the Senate was to introduce legislation which would result in the academic exchange bearing his name. An amendment to the Surplus Property Act of 1944, the Fulbright proposal authorized the use of foreign credits from the sale of U.S. surplus war properties abroad for international educational activities.[9] On August 1, 1946, President Harry Truman signed the Fulbright Act establishing the Fulbright program for the exchange of teachers, students, professors, and research scholars between the United States and participating countries.

In the early fifties, Senator Fulbright was one of the few to oppose the tactics used by Senator Joseph R. McCarthy in his anticommunist campaign. The senator encountered McCarthy several times in hearings before both the Banking and Currency Committee and the Foreign Relations Committee. In early 1954, Fulbright was the only senator to cast a vote against appropriations for McCarthy's Permanent Investigations Subcommittee. Finally, he was instrumental in the successful movement in the Senate to censure the Wisconsin senator in December 1954.[10]

The senator maintained a high profile during the Eisenhower years as a result of his outspoken criticism of Secretary of State John Foster Dulles's foreign policies. He clashed with Dulles over issues related to the Soviet Union and the course of U.S. action in the Middle East.[11]

Besides his efforts in foreign affairs, the senator served as an advocate for Arkansas. His interests and accomplishments are reflected in the kinds of legislation that he introduced and sponsored in the areas of education, agriculture, water resources, forestry, urban renewal, and small business.[12] His position on civil rights generally supported the views of his constituents and the Democratic party in the South.[13]

In February 1959, ten years after he had been appointed to the Foreign Relations Committee, Fulbright became the chairman, a position he would hold longer than any other senator in U.S. history. His tenure as chairman spanned more than fifteen years during a critical time in American history and included five administrations, from Eisenhower to Ford.[14] He was the second senator from Arkansas to hold the post.

The first, Ambrose H. Sevier, served as chairman from 1846 to 1847 during the Polk administration.[15]

In the spring of 1961, the senator delivered a memorandum to President John F. Kennedy advising against the invasion of Cuba at the Bay of Pigs.[16] He sent another memorandum to the president and the secretary of defense the same year alerting them to educational and propaganda activities of the military.[17] In the Senate, he marshalled support for the nuclear test ban treaty, which was ratified by a vote of 80-19 on September 24, 1963. Earlier, he had traveled to Moscow for the signing of the treaty.[18]

In October, Fulbright traveled to Arkansas with the president on a campaign trip, which included the dedication of a dam at Greers Ferry. It was one of the last times that he would see Kennedy. Lyndon B. Johnson became president on November 22, 1963, and his friend, Bill Fulbright, was among the first people to meet with him when he arrived in Washington.[19]

But the progression of events in Vietnam would permanently alter the Fulbright-Johnson friendship. On August 6, 1964, Senator Fulbright introduced the president's Tonkin Gulf resolution in the Senate and acted as floor manager. The Senate passed the resolution by a vote of 88-2, with Wayne Morse and Ernest Gruening casting dissenting votes. Fulbright would later acknowledge his handling of the resolution in the Senate as a grave mistake.[20]

As the war escalated in Vietnam, Fulbright became increasingly outspoken. His dissent from Johnson administration policy also included a critique of U.S. action in the Dominican Republic in the spring of 1965. After holding Foreign Relations Committee hearings on the Dominican situation the following summer, he delivered a speech in the Senate criticizing U.S. intervention, a move that precipitated his break with President Johnson.[21]

As Fulbright's relationship with Johnson deteriorated, he launched hearings before the Foreign Relations Committee in January and February of 1966 on the conduct of U.S. policy in Vietnam. He continued his off-and-on investigation for a number of years, using the Foreign Relations Committee as a forum on the question of U.S. involvement in Southeast Asia.[22]

In 1974, Senator Fulbright returned to Arkansas for his most formidable campaign since the one in 1944, when he was first elected to the Senate. He was defeated by Governor Dale Bumpers in the Arkansas Democratic primary. Shortly before his departure from the Senate, President Gerald Ford offered him the post of ambassador to Great Britain.[23] Fulbright declined the offer and later became counsel for the legal firm of Hogan and Hartson in Washington, D.C., an association which lasted eighteen years, from 1975 until 1993.

NOTES

1. J. William Fulbright, interview by Dean Albertson, 20 April 1956, interview #1, "The Reminiscences of J. William Fulbright," transcript, Oral History Research Office, Columbia University (hereafter cited as "Reminiscences").

2. Ibid. Fulbright incorrectly identifies the date as circa 1951. The date on his Phi Beta Kappa certificate is May 1945.

3. For a complete record of his activities, see the *Razorback* yearbooks for the years 1921-1925.

4. "Reminiscences," 20 April 1956, interview #1; 6 August 1956, interview #3. Although Fulbright does not say specifically that he stayed on for the spring 1925 semester, he is listed as a graduate student in the university's catalog.

5. "Reminiscences," 2 July 1956, interview #2.

6. "Reminiscences," 6 August 1956, interview #3.

7. "Reminiscences," 6 August 1956, interview #3; 2 October 1956, interview #4.

8. H. Con. Res. 25, J. William Fulbright Papers, series 89, subseries 2, box 4, folder 5. Special Collections Division, University of Arkansas Libraries, Fayetteville (hereafter cited as JWF Papers).

9. "Reminiscences," 6 May 1957, interview #7.

10. J. W. Fulbright, *Against the Arrogance of Power: My Personal History* ([Tokyo]: Nihon Keizai Shimbun, [1991]), 67-70. This work consists of a series of thirty interviews conducted by Michio Katsumata and first published in the *Nikkei Financial Daily* in Tokyo in May 1991. These Fulbright reminiscences were later published in book form with both English and Japanese texts.

11. For a good treatment of this subject, see Kenneth W. Grundy's article, "The Apprenticeship of J. William Fulbright," in the summer 1967 issue of the *Virginia Quarterly Review*.

12. See series 89 in the JWF Papers for the legislative files of bills and resolutions introduced or sponsored by the senator. The series also includes his congressional voting record.

13. Fulbright discusses his civil rights position in his book with Seth P. Tillman, *The Price of Empire* (New York: Pantheon Books, 1989), 88-94.

14. Robert C. Byrd, *Historical Statistics, 1789-1992,* Vol. 4 of *The Senate, 1789-1989* (Washington, D.C.: U.S. Government Printing Office, 1993), 546-48.

15. Ibid., 547.

16. Memorandum, "Cuba Policy," 29 March 1961, JWF Papers, series 48, subseries 14, box 38, folder 1.

17. Memorandum, "Propaganda Activities of Military Personnel Directed at the Public," n.d., JWF Papers, series 4, subseries 19, box 25, folder 4.

18. Newsletter, *Bill Fulbright Reports from the United States Senate,* 25 September 1963, JWF Papers, series 48, subseries 5, box 20, folder 4.

19. Haynes Johnson and Bernard M. Gwertzman, *Fulbright: The Dissenter* (Garden City, N.Y.: Doubleday and Company, 1968), 183-84.

20. Fulbright with Tillman, *Price of Empire,* 104.

21. Carl M. Marcy, interview by Donald A. Ritchie, 19 October 1983, interview #5, "Fulbright Breaks with Johnson," transcript, Senate Historical Office, Washington, D.C.

22. For a scholarly treatment of Fulbright and the war, see Lee Riley Powell's book, *J. William Fulbright and America's Lost Crusade: Fulbright's Opposition to the Vietnam War* (Little Rock, Ark.: Rose Publishing Company, 1984).

23. William C. Berman, *William Fulbright and the Vietnam War: The Dissent of a Political Realist* (Kent, Ohio: Kent State University Press, 1988), 194.

Part I
PRIMARY WORKS

1

Manuscript and Record Collections

1   Bureau of Educational and Cultural Affairs. Historical Collection. Special Collections Division, University of Arkansas Libraries, Fayetteville, Arkansas 72701-1201. (501) 575-5577; FAX (501) 575-6656.

The historical collection of the Bureau of Educational and Cultural Affairs (CU), formerly the Division of Cultural Relations, documents the development of U.S. international educational and cultural exchange activities, including the Fulbright program. Organized in 1961 within the Department of State, the bureau was responsible for administering the principal provisions of the Fulbright-Hays Act. It functioned as a part of the State Department until 1978 when it merged with the United States Information Agency. The basic collection consists of papers generated while CU was in the State Department, from 1938 until 1978. The remainder consists of papers produced after CU moved to USIA in 1978. The collection was presented to the University of Arkansas by the United States Information Agency in the spring of 1983.

The collection comprises over 500 linear feet of correspondence, reports, studies, minutes, photographs, publications, audiovisual materials, and other records concerning various international exchange programs, dated circa 1938-1983. Files pertain to academic exchanges; the international visitor program for foreign leaders in government, communications, education, and labor; cultural presentations for both the performing arts and athletics; and private agencies cooperating with CU.

Significant portions of the collection pertain to the Center for Cultural and Technical Interchange Between the East and West (East-West Center) and the National Review Board, an advisory and review body concerned with the programs and operations of the EWC; the U.S. Advisory Commission on Educational and Cultural Affairs; the Government Advisory Committee on International Book and Library Programs; the Cultural Presentations Program, including tour files of American performing artistic and athletic groups and figures; the American Specialist Program; the Teacher Development Program; the Teacher Exchange Program; the "Brain Drain"; the CU-USIA reorganization in 1978; and the CU budget.

The report files are an integral part of the collection and support many projects undertaken in the collection. They include evaluation reports regarding the exchange program for the fifties, sixties, and seventies; annual post reports on educational and cultural programs; American and foreign grantee reports, lists, and statistics; CU weekly activity reports; printed reports authorized by the Fulbright Act and the

Smith-Mundt Act; reports of the U.S. Advisory Commission; and general reports, chronological summaries, statistics, and bibliographies of the history of the State Department programs.

Another historically significant set of files concerns the Fulbright academic exchange program for students, teachers, professors, and research scholars. The files include program legislation and agreements; Fulbright Binational Commission and Foundation correspondence, annual reports, minutes, and annual program proposals; and Board of Foreign Scholarship materials. Other important files pertain to the early programs with Latin America and Germany and the exchange program with the former Soviet Union.

The collection includes the files of assistant secretaries and deputy assistant secretaries of state for CU, their predecessors in charge of educational exchange, and other CU officers. Important correspondents are Jacob Canter, C.A. Chapman, Joseph D. Duffey, J. Manuel Espinosa, William K. Hitchcock, Frederick Irving, William B. Jones, Katie Louchheim, Francis P. Miller, David L. Osburn, Eleanor Reams, John Richardson, Jr., and Richard Straus. The collection also includes papers of Francis A. Young, executive director of the Committee on International Exchange of Persons.

Finally, the collection includes materials regarding the CU History Project. The CU History Office was established in the fall of 1972 for the purpose of writing the history of the international educational and cultural exchange programs of the Department of State and for maintaining a core collection of documents on policy and program development. The Bureau of Educational and Cultural Affairs published three monographs on the exchange program in Germany, China, and Latin America. The first volume in the series, *America's Cultural Experiment in China, 1942-1949*, by Wilma Fairbank, was published in June 1976. The second, *Inter-American Beginnings of U.S. Cultural Diplomacy, 1936-1948*, by J. Manuel Espinosa, appeared in February 1977. The third, *Cultural Relations as an Instrument of U.S. Foreign Policy: The Educational Exchange Program Between the United States and Germany, 1945-1954*, by Henry J. Kellermann, was released in March 1978.

Although the collection is not completely processed, access is available through a folder-level inventory. To facilitate their work, researchers who wish to use the collection are advised to write or telephone the Special Collections Division in advance.

2 Council for International Exchange of Scholars. Records. Special Collections Division, University of Arkansas Libraries, Fayetteville, Arkansas 72701-1201. (501) 575-5577; FAX (501) 575-6656.

The records of the Council for International Exchange of Scholars (CIES) document the role of the organization in facilitating international educational exchange activities in higher education. Established in 1947 by the Conference Board of Associated Research Councils, CIES is a private agency cooperating with the U.S. government in the administration of Fulbright scholar grants for advanced research and university teaching. CIES, formerly the Committee on International Exchange of Persons, recommends American scholars for university lectureships and postdoctoral research abroad and manages the Fulbright-Hays program for visiting scholars in the United States. It also provides administrative services for visiting scholars and organizes conferences which familiarize them with cultural, educational, and social institutions in the United States. In addition to the Fulbright program, CIES administers the Indo-American Fellowship Program, the Spain Research Fellowships, and the NATO Research Fellowship Program. In 1986, CIES named the University of Arkansas Libraries as the official repository for their records.

The collection comprises more than 200 linear feet of correspondence, memoranda, reports, minutes, publications, program proposals, and other records documenting the program histories of participating countries in six geographical areas: Africa, Latin America and the Caribbean, Near East-South Asia, East Asia, Western Europe, and Eastern Europe. Files of the CIES archives reflect the geographical organization of the agency and include final reports of American and visiting scholars in which they describe and evaluate their experiences; annual program proposals; annual reports from Fulbright Binational Commissions and Foundations; grant authorization documents; and CIES, Department of State, and International Communication Agency memoranda regarding the nomination and selection of Fulbright scholars. Dates range from 1947 to 1993.

The collection also contains CIES publications and outreach materials, including directories of American and visiting scholars and files of regional and medical conferences, Washington conferences, and the Metropolitan Area Program. Other historical materials include lists and log books concerning visiting and American scholars receiving awards under the Fulbright, Smith-Mundt, and Fulbright-Hays acts and the early files of the Conference Board of Associated Research Councils. Some files pertain to the Asian Professor Project, Asian Scholars-in-Residence, the NATO Visiting Professorship Program, and the Occasional Lecturer Program. Other files concern the American Council on Education and the Board of Foreign Scholarships. The collection also includes fiscal and budget materials and the minutes of the CIES annual board meetings for the years 1948-1993.

Although the CIES records are not completely processed, access is available through folder-level inventories. To facilitate their work, researchers who wish to use the collection are advised to write or telephone the Special Collections Division in advance.

3   Fulbright, J. William. Papers. Special Collections Division, University of Arkansas Libraries, Fayetteville, Arkansas 72701-1201. (501) 575-5577; FAX (501) 575-6656.

The Fulbright Papers document the public career of J. William Fulbright, former Democratic senator from Arkansas. Fulbright was in Washington for thirty-two years, from 1943 until 1975, and was chairman of the Senate Foreign Relations Committee for the last fifteen years. The collection consists of 1,400 linear feet of constituent, official, and personal correspondence, memoranda, legislative bills, speeches, photographs, and other records, all related to the governmental, political, and diplomatic activities and issues in which he was involved or interested. Some of the files concern his tenure in the U.S. House of Representatives from 1943 until 1945, and others pertain to the Fulbright family. The collection also includes postsenatorial papers regarding his activities and interests since 1975. The papers contain materials which document the internal workings of Congress and its relationship with the other branches and with government agencies. An important component of the papers concerns Fulbright's committee work, particularly his tenure on the Banking and Currency Committee and the Foreign Relations Committee. The papers also support research in Arkansas studies, providing information regarding state politics and personalities and subjects with a regional focus, like the Buffalo National River, Beaver Dam, and the University of Arkansas.

The uniqueness of the Fulbright Papers comes from the character, concerns, and contributions of the senator in international education and foreign affairs and is reflected in the kinds of materials in the collection. One special set of files is the personal correspondence between the senator and family members and close friends. This personal correspondence contains substantive and thoughtful remarks on a variety of subjects. An outstanding example is the correspondence between Fulbright and his Oxford mentor, Ronald Buchanan McCallum. These letters reflect a lifelong friendship in which they advised each other on contemporary British and American political issues. Another important file is the correspondence between the senator and Marcel William Fodor, the scholarly journalist who introduced Fulbright to Vienna and the Balkans in the late twenties. Written from Europe by foreign correspondent Fodor, these letters and lengthy memoranda contain intimate accounts of postwar political developments on the continent.

Other files that are historically significant for researchers are the Fulbright letters with colleagues and government officials. These include correspondence with other senators and congressmen, the president and his cabinet, state political leaders, ambassadors and other embassy officials, and members of foreign governments. Although some of this correspondence is routine, letters of record on important subjects are included. One example is the memorandum which the senator wrote to President John F. Kennedy in the spring of 1961 cautioning him against the Cuban invasion at the Bay of Pigs. Another eminently important series documents the close working relationship between the senator and Carl Marcy, chief of staff of the Foreign Relations Committee from 1955 until 1973.

The legislative files are useful for several reasons. These files document the senator's participation in the legislative process, his major legislative interests and accomplishments, and his interaction with his constituency. These papers also provide insight into Fulbright's skill as a parliamentarian in soliciting support for imaginative and innovative legislation in the areas of foreign policy and international education. Additionally, the files document the relationship of a legislator primarily interested in foreign affairs with a constituency primarily concerned with domestic matters.

The speech files are an integral part of the papers and enhance many research projects undertaken in the collection. The files document not only his contribution to congressional debate but also his role as an independent thinker.

Fulbright's special interest files add another dimension to the collection. These files contain materials regarding the origin and administration of the Fulbright exchange program, the progress of the program in participating countries, and letters of appreciation from American and foreign scholarship recipients.

The collection also includes materials on the Fulbright resolution of 1943, the senator and McCarthyism, U.S. policy toward the Middle East, Fulbright's 1961 memorandum on military propaganda, U.S. relations with the Soviet Union, the Vietnam War, foreign aid, and the senator's political campaigns.

A comprehensive index of significant correspondents in four volumes exists for the first accession of the papers (1942-1960) and locates correspondence at the folder level. Significant correspondents are selectively noted in series and subseries descriptions for the second accession of the papers (1960-1975).

The senator presented his papers to his alma mater in two installments, in 1972 and 1974. Since the papers were opened, scholars have visited the collection from throughout the United States and around the world. The research constituency represents institutions in more than twenty-five states, the District of Columbia, and twelve foreign countries. Some have come from as far away as the former Soviet Union, Japan, and Israel. Most of the researchers have concentrated on U.S. political history and mid-twentieth century foreign policy. However, Fulbright's intellectual ties with people outside politics allow researchers from a variety of disciplines to make productive use of the papers.

The Fulbright Papers are processed and open to researchers. Access is available through an unpublished twelve-volume finding aid. Restrictions limit access to some files. To facilitate their work, researchers who wish to use the papers are advised to write or telephone the Special Collections Division in advance.

4 Institute of International Education. Annual Reports. IIE Library, 809 United Nations Plaza, New York, New York 10017-3580. (212) 984-5418; FAX (212) 984-5358.

The annual reports of the Institute of International Education document the role of the organization in facilitating international exchange in higher education. Established in 1919, IIE is a private, nonprofit organization cooperating with the U.S. government in the administration of Fulbright scholar grants for graduate students. IIE, the oldest educational exchange agency in the country, also administers programs sponsored by governments, foundations, corporations, universities, and international organizations.

The annual reports provide information about IIE's management of programs associated with the interchange of students, scholars, leaders, technicians, and specialists. The reports also include information regarding the educational and support services provided by IIE to professionals in higher education. To facilitate their work, researchers who wish to review the reports are advised to write or telephone the IIE Library to make an appointment to use the materials.

5 NAFSA: Association of International Educators. Records. Special Collections Division, University of Arkansas Libraries, Fayetteville, Arkansas 72701-1201. (501) 575-5577; FAX (501) 575-6656.

The records of the National Association for Foreign Student Affairs (NAFSA) document the development of the association and its role in facilitating international educational exchange in higher education. NAFSA is a nonprofit membership association providing educational and support services to professionals in the area of international education, including consultations, workshops, in-service training, national and regional conferences, information services, and liaison with U.S. government agencies and other educational associations. Among those served by NAFSA are directors of international offices, deans of international education, campus administrators, admissions officers, teachers of English as a foreign language, faculty members, foreign student advisers, community volunteers, and directors and advisers of study abroad programs. Created in 1948 as the National Association of Foreign Student Advisers, the organization changed its name to the National Association for Foreign Student Affairs in 1964 to more adequately reflect the scope of its responsibilities and activities. Another recent change resulted in the present form. In 1987, NAFSA named the University of Arkansas Libraries as the official repository for their records.

The collection consists of approximately 200 linear feet of correspondence, minutes, reports, publications, proceedings, photographs, and other records concerning NAFSA's involvement in the administration of exchange programs and services, dated circa 1948-1990. Eight major record categories make up the NAFSA archives.

The first group consists of the association's official records and includes minutes, reports, and other documents of the board of directors and the executive board; some of the records pertain to the business meetings of the sections and their executive committees. Other special documents are reports to the Ford Foundation, regional guidelines, materials regarding NAFSA's name change in 1964 and its reorganization in 1972, and membership files of foreign institutional and individual members of NAFSA as well as foreign contacts working with the organization.

Another important category consists of the association's central office files and includes correspondence, memoranda, reports, and other materials regarding NAFSA's interests, activities, task forces, special projects, and liaison with governmental and private agencies and organizations for the period 1949-1980. Other historically significant materials are the association's annual conference files, including files predating the establishment of NAFSA in 1948. Significant portions of the collection concern NAFSA's link with the Agency for International Development and the association's Government Regulations Advisory Committee. Another group consists of files related to the administration and activities of the Field Service Program, NAFSA's first major program funded by the U.S. government. The collection also includes the files of the association's Community Section (COMSEC).

The final group consists of publications of the association and includes early annual reports of the board of directors; annual conference reports; directories; research and other reports of general and specific interest; NAFSA Newsletters; publications related to the NAFSA constitution and bylaws; reference guides on foreign student affairs; NAFSA guidelines for working with foreign students; the TESL program; U.S.-China Educational Clearinghouse; NAFSA Admissions Section; NAFSA Community Section, including the COMSEC Newsletter; and publications which were cooperative ventures with other groups and organizations.

The NAFSA records are processed and open to researchers. Access is available through an unpublished one-volume finding aid. To facilitate their work, researchers who wish to use the collection are advised to write or telephone the Special Collections Division in advance.

Part II
PUBLISHED AND SECONDARY WORKS

2

Fulbright Writings

6 "Address by the Honorable J.W. Fulbright Before the American Bar Association on August 26, 1943, at Chicago, Illinois." *International Conciliation,* No. 395 (1943): 606-15. (Adapted for *The New York Times Magazine,* 17 October 1943, 9, 38-39, under the title "'Power Adequate to Enforce Peace'"; and *The Journal of the National Education Association* 32 [November 1943]: 217-18, under the title "Congress and the Peace"; reprinted in *Representative American Speeches: 1943-1944,* edited by A. Craig Baird, 83-95. The Reference Shelf. Vol. 17, No. 4. New York: H.W. Wilson Company, 1944, under the title "America and Internationalism.")

In a speech to the American Bar Association, the freshman congressman asserts that "our only hope for security is in collective action." Fulbright discusses House Concurrent Resolution 25, his proposal calling for U.S. participation in a postwar international peace-keeping organization, and outlines the steps necessary to implement the proposal. His remarks include an explanation and a defense of his concept of sovereignty.

7 "America in an Age of Revolution." *The Progressive* 30 (February 1966): 18-20.

Fulbright discusses the effects of the Vietnam War on our relations with communist countries and on our policies toward Latin America. He focuses on the reluctance of the United States to support the forces of political and social reform in the world, noting the profound differences between the American Revolution and contemporary social upheavals in the Third World.

8 "The American Agenda: Evaluation of Our Society." *Vital Speeches of the Day,* 15 June 1963, 520-26. (Adapted for *Saturday Review,* 20 July 1963, 15-17, 62-63, under the title "The American Agenda.")

In an assessment of U.S. society, the senator asserts that the problems facing the country emanate from past political and economic successes. His concern is whether the nation uses its accumulated power and wealth as ends or as means to enhance the lives of its citizens. He maintains that the country's extensive concern with power has distorted its national priorities, resulting in pressing needs on the domestic front, particularly in education. It is this issue—the problems and tasks confronting education—that he addresses in the last of his three William L. Clayton Lectures on May 1, 1963, at the Fletcher School of Law and Diplomacy at Tufts University.

9 "The American Character: We Must Revive and Strengthen It." *Vital Speeches* *of the Day,* 1 January 1964, 164-67. (Also published in *University: A Princeton Magazine,* No. 20 [1964]: 9-13, under the title "The Strain of Violence"; and *Speech in Personal and Public Affairs,* by Virgil L. Baker and Ralph T. Eubanks, 364-75. New York: David McKay Company, 1965, under the title "The American Character"; condensed version in *The Annals of America.* Vol. 18, *The Burdens of World Power, 1961-1968,* 206-11. Chicago: Encyclopaedia Britannica, 1968, under the title "Violence in the American Character"; the Industrial Union Department, AFL-CIO, Washington, D.C., issued a reprint of the speech as Publication No. 58.)

This speech, delivered at the Rockefeller Public Service Awards luncheon in Washington on December 5, 1963, is a thoughtful consideration of U.S. society in the wake of President John F. Kennedy's assassination. The senator examines the importance of the country's Puritan heritage and its frontier experience in shaping the national character and concludes with a prescription for overcoming the effects of those forces on a democratic society.

10 "The American Example." In *Readings in American Foreign Policy.* 2d ed., edited by Robert A. Goldwin and revised by Harry M. Clor, 694-97. New York: Oxford University Press, 1971.

The senator discusses the importance of the American example in the world and the consequences of the loss of our understanding of that concept in Vietnam. The article is excerpted from Fulbright's book, *The Arrogance of Power.*

11 "The American Experiment in Self-Government." *The Virginia Magazine of History and Biography* 63, No. 1 (1955): 151-60.

In commemorating the anniversary of Robert E. Lee's birth, the senator talks about Lee's importance as a historical figure. He turns from the past to the present with a discussion of McCarthyism and its impact on the country. His concluding remarks address two examples of the lingering vestige of McCarthyism: the debate over the Bricker amendment and the demand for U.S. withdrawal from the United Nations. The paper was originally presented at the annual meeting of the Virginia Historical Society on January 19, 1955.

12 "American Foreign Policy in the 20th Century Under an 18th-Century Constitution." *Cornell Law Quarterly* 47, No. 1 (1961): 1-13.

In a discussion of the importance of presidential power in the foreign policy process, the senator advocates giving the executive authority commensurate with his responsibilities in foreign affairs. He also addresses the reasons for inadequate presidential authority and closes with an examination of the methods associated with policy formation in the British parliamentary system and the totalitarian systems. The article is drawn from the senator's Robert S. Stevens Lecture at Cornell University on May 5, 1961.

13 "America's Place in the Postwar World." *Social Science* 18 (October 1943): 180-81.

Arguing for U.S. leadership in the postwar world, Fulbright discusses the necessity of changing American attitudes toward international alliances and persuading members of Congress of the importance of U.S. participation in an international peace-keeping organization.

14 "Anti-Poverty Program for Arkansas." *The Ozarks Mountaineer* 12 (March 1965): 15.

The senator discusses the educational benefits to be realized by the people of Arkansas from the Economic Opportunity Act of 1964. The *Ozarks Mountaineer* is a publication of the Ozarks Commonwealth, Branson, Missouri.

15 "Approaches to Understanding." *Institute of International Education News Bulletin* 28 (May 1953): 3-6.

The article consists of two parts: a review of the Senate committee study of the overseas information and educational exchange programs and an examination of the problem of favorably influencing opinion abroad to harmonize with U.S. foreign policy objectives. The senator looks at both democratic and totalitarian approaches.

16 "Arms Without End: Congress Must Take the Lead in Bringing Nuclear Arsenals Under Control." *The Progressive* 38 (September 1974): 22-23.

The senator calls for congressional leadership in bringing about a climate favorable to the conclusion of an arms control agreement with the Soviet Union.

17 *The Arrogance of Power*. New York: Random House, 1966. (Selections from the book are published in *Patterns in American History*. 2d ed. Vol. 2, edited by Alexander DeConde, Armin Rappaport, and William R. Steckel, 681-703. Belmont, Calif.: Wadsworth Publishing Company, 1970; and *Consensus at the Crossroads: Dialogues in American Foreign Policy*, edited by Howard Bliss and M. Glen Johnson, 245-59. New York: Dodd, Mead and Company, 1972, both under the title "The Arrogance of Power.")

In this critical analysis of U.S. foreign policy, the senator warns against the dangers of the practice of the "arrogance of power" in international relations and makes recommendations for new directions in foreign affairs. The book includes a perceptive examination of our relations with revolutionary movements in Latin America and Asia and an eight-point peace proposal for Vietnam. Other topics concern the relationship of patriotism and dissent in a democracy, the role of the Senate in foreign affairs, the internationalization of foreign aid, and development of policies and strategies for promoting better relations with the communist world, improving relations between Eastern and Western Europe, and refocusing energies toward reconciliation and reconstruction on the domestic front. He concludes with a look at the two Americas (see Fulbright entry titled "A New Look at an Old Problem: The Two Americas"). Although the book is based on a development of the senator's three Christian A. Herter Lectures at Johns Hopkins University in the spring of 1966, it incorporates new materials and topics.

18 "'The Arrogance of Power'—A Clash over U.S. Policy." *U.S. News and World Report*, 23 May 1966, 113-22.

This is the complete text of Fulbright's third Christian A. Herter Lecture at Johns Hopkins University on May 5, 1966, in which he criticizes the direction of U.S. foreign policy and warns against the dangers of the practice of the "arrogance of power" in international relations. In an assessment of our attitudes toward other peoples and cultures, he examines manifestations of arrogance in the behavior of American tourists abroad and in the disruptive economic and cultural impact of American wealth and power on smaller nations, particularly Vietnam. Concluding remarks concern the application of psychological principles to international relations, specifically our relations with China. He returns to an important theme in his speaking and writing, Edmund Burke's idea of the power of the good example. Rejoinders are by President Johnson, Secretary of State Dean Rusk, and Mrs. Oswald B. Lord. The three Herter Lectures appear in expanded version in the senator's book, *The Arrogance of Power*.

19 "Balanced Growth: Arkansas' Hope for the Future." *Opportunities* 3 (1971-1972): 6, 8.

Fulbright discusses the importance of balancing the economic development of the state with the preservation of its natural resources.

20   "Beyond Coexistence." In *Beyond Coexistence: The Requirements of Peace,* edited by Edward Reed, 127-31. New York: Grossman Publishers, 1968.

Drawing on the thoughts of Konrad Lorenz, the senator discusses the importance of understanding human behavior as the first step in the development of a sense of community among nations. Fulbright made the remarks at a convocation organized by the Center for the Study of Democratic Institutions in Geneva, Switzerland, in May 1967. A discussion in which the senator participated begins on page 144.

21   "Beyond the Sinai Agreement." *Worldview* 18 (December 1975): 9-15.

The senator assesses our crucial interests in the Middle East, including a consideration of their order of priority and the reconciliation of conflicting interests. The second part concerns his appraisal of the Sinai agreement and includes a discussion of its shortcomings and the constitutional considerations of the U.S. role. Fulbright is featured on the cover. The article is drawn from an address before the Middle East Institute in October 1975.

22   "Bill Fulbright Reports from the United States Senate." *Arkansas Highways* 9 (July 1961): 2.

In a report to his constituents, the senator talks about problems created when the law fails to spell out the responsibilities of the state and the federal governments. He cites an example concerning the construction of Titan missile bases in Arkansas and gives the legislative history of an amendment that he introduced to correct the situation.

23   "Bill Fulbright Reports from the United States Senate: 'Urban Renewal' in Arkansas." *Arkansas Municipalities* 17 (September 1961): 6.

In his newsletter to his constituents, the senator discusses the accelerating urbanization of Arkansas and the growing participation of the state's cities and towns in the urban renewal program.

24   "Bipartisanship Is a Two-Way Street." *The Reporter,* 16 December 1954, 8-11. (Excerpts published in *Time,* 20 December 1954, 30, under the title "Bipartisan Policy Requires G.O.P. Changes.")

Fulbright outlines the requirements for a bipartisan foreign policy in the Eisenhower administration.

25   *Bridges East and West.* Arnold Foundation Monographs, edited by John M. Claunch, No. 14. Dallas: Southern Methodist University, Arnold Foundation, 1965.

The senator prefaces his remarks about U.S. foreign policy toward the communist world with a consideration of the merits of compromise. He proceeds to outline policies of accommodation for improving relations with Eastern Europe, the Soviet Union, and China. The remarks were made at Southern Methodist University on December 8, 1964.

26   "The Businessman and the Government." *New York Chamber of Commerce Bulletin,* December 1944, 202-9.

The senator talks to businessmen about what they can do to improve the government. His thesis concerns the application of business principles to the practice of government and the organization of the peace.

27   "The Case for a New Internationalism." *War/Peace Report* 11 (May 1971): 3-7.

In a discussion of U.S. policies in Indochina and the Middle East, the senator advocates a foreign policy designed to use the United Nations to solve international crises, particularly the Arab-Israeli conflict. He made the remarks at Yale University on April 4, 1971.

28 "The Challenge to American Education." *The Kansas Teacher* 71 (November 1962): 21, 23, 37, 43. (Excerpts published in *School and Society* 91, No. 2220 [1963]: 31, 47, under the title "Sen. Fulbright on U.S. Education.")

Introducing his remarks with quotations from Plato and Thomas Jefferson, the senator addresses the crisis in American education and focuses on the primary tasks facing educators in the nuclear age. He concludes with a discussion of the role of international education in foreign policy. The speech was delivered to the National Education Association's Department of Rural Education on October 13, 1962, in Wichita, Kansas. A related article on page 22 of this issue of the *Kansas Teacher* includes additional Fulbright remarks.

29 "Changing Swords into Scholarships." *The Optimist Magazine*, April 1959, 8-9.

Fulbright discusses the aims of international educational exchange activities.

30 "The Clear and Present Danger." *The Atlantic Community Quarterly* 12 (Winter 1974-1975): 413-25. (Also published in *Vital Speeches of the Day*, 1 December 1974, 102-7, under the title "The Clear and Present Danger: Middle East and the United States"; slightly abbreviated version in *Worldview* 18 [January 1975]: 19-24; abridged version in *The Washington Monthly* 6 [February 1975]: 23-27, under the title "Getting Tough with Israel.")

In an address at Westminster College on November 2, 1974, Fulbright discusses the economic and political effects of increased oil prices consequent to the discord in the Middle East. His thesis is that another Arab-Israeli conflict could escalate into a world crisis involving a confrontation with the Soviet Union. The senator suggests agendas for alleviating the inflationary problems on the domestic front and for negotiating a settlement in the Middle East, with the assistance of the Soviet Union and the United Nations. The remarks were delivered in Fulton, Missouri, on the centennial of Winston Churchill's birth.

31 "The Cold War: Its Effect on American Life." *Vital Speeches of the Day*, 1 May 1964, 422-27. (Condensed versions in *The Progressive* 28 [June 1964]: 28-31, under the title "The High Price of the Cold War"; and *The Debate over Thermonuclear Strategy*, edited by Arthur I. Waskow, 107-12. Problems in American Civilization. Boston: D.C. Heath and Company, 1965, under the title "The Cold War in American Life"; slightly abbreviated version in *The Triple Revolution: Social Problems in Depth*, edited by Robert Perrucci and Marc Pilisuk, 35-47. Boston: Little, Brown and Company, 1968, under the title "The Cold War in American Life"; and excerpt in *Arms, Industry and America*, edited by Kenneth S. Davis, 19-20. The Reference Shelf. Vol. 43, No. 1. New York: H.W. Wilson Company, 1971, under the title "Our Faith in the Military Is Akin to Our Faith in Technology.")

The senator discusses the enormous changes in American life brought about by the cold war, particularly the diversion of resources and attention from domestic needs to the military and space requirements of national security. Saying that "we have had to turn away from our hopes in order to concentrate on our fears . . . ," he cautions against excessive reliance on the military and technology and proposes a reassessment of our national policy priorities. The remarks were delivered at the University of North Carolina on April 5, 1964.

32 "Commentary." In *The Fulbright Fortieth Anniversary Washington Conference Proceedings: Minds Without Borders: Educational and Cultural Exchange in the Twenty-first Century,* edited by Anne Rogers Devereux and George Liston Seay, 172. November 16-19, 1986.

In concluding remarks, the senator recommends using available funding to maintain the Fulbright program in countries that participate in cost sharing. The front matter also includes a letter from Fulbright regarding the importance of the exchange program.

33 "A Common Purpose for the Free World." *American Bar Association Journal* 46 (November 1960): 1192-96. (Abridged version published in *Freedom and Union* 16 [January 1961]: 9-10, under the title "Closer NATO Unity 'Sure' to Come; Delaying Makes It 'More Costly.'")

In an address before the American Bar Association in Washington on September 1, 1960, the senator examines the frustrations and problems of the United States in the cold war era and calls, once again, for closer cooperation with Western Europe. He discusses the importance of establishing an international community of free nations and the requirements for creating such a community. Recognizing the problems associated with achieving unity, he concludes with a quotation from Salvador de Madariaga.

34 "A Concert of Free Nations." *International Organization* 17 (Summer 1963): 787-803. (Excerpts published in *The Atlantic Community Quarterly* 1 [Summer 1963]: 113-30, under the title "A Community of Free Nations.")

This is an abridged version of the second of Fulbright's three William L. Clayton Lectures delivered at the Fletcher School of Law and Diplomacy, Tufts University, on April 30, 1963. The senator discusses the Atlantic plan for a partnership involving the industrial democracies of the North Atlantic and the steps required to encourage cooperation and eventual unity. Included also is a treatment of Charles de Gaulle's plan for Europe and its effects on the Western Alliance.

35 "Congress and Foreign Policy." In *Appendices: Commission on the Organization of the Government for the Conduct of Foreign Policy, June, 1975.* Vol. 5, *Appendix L: Congress and Executive-Legislative Relations,* 58-65. Washington, D.C.: U.S. Government Printing Office, 1975.

The senator discusses the loss of congressional power to the president in the foreign policy realm, particularly the war and treaty powers. He focuses on the treaty power, noting the measures used by the executive to circumvent congressional involvement in the area of national commitments. Other remarks concern the role of Congress as protector of the people's liberties, drawn from a 1946 speech titled "The Legislator."

36 "Congress and Foreign Policy." In *Congress and the President: Allies and Adversaries,* edited by Ronald C. Moe, 197-209. Pacific Palisades, Calif.: Goodyear Publishing Company, 1971.

Fulbright discusses the constitutional imbalance between the legislative and executive branches and the importance of regaining congressional powers in the foreign policy realm. His primary focus is on the congressional role in foreign policy which concerns the advice and consent function. Other remarks regard joint resolutions, congressional briefing sessions, treaties, and commitments. The senator made the statement before the Subcommittee on Separation of Powers of the Committee on the Judiciary on July 19, 1967.

37 "Congress, the President, and the War Power." *Arkansas Law Review* 25, Nos. 1 and 2, Part 1 (1971): 71-84.

This is a treatise on the increased scope of presidential powers in the foreign affairs realm. The senator discusses the causes and the consequences of executive encroachment upon congressional foreign policy powers, particularly the war power, and possible causes of congressional inertia. A treatment of the Tonkin Gulf resolution of 1964 is also included.

38 "Congressional Investigations: Significance for the Legislative Process." *The University of Chicago Law Review* 18 (Spring 1951): 440-48.

The senator discusses the function of the congressional investigation and the factors and circumstances affecting an investigation. He calls the investigatory power "perhaps the most necessary of all the powers underlying the legislative function." The second part of the paper concerns the Senate investigation of Reconstruction Finance Corporation activities conducted by Fulbright in early 1950.

39 "Continuation of Hearings on Impoundment of Funds." *Limestone* 10, No. 35 (1973): 40-41, 81-87.

This is a statement by Fulbright before the Subcommittee on Separation of Powers of the Senate Committee on the Judiciary and the Ad Hoc Subcommittee on Impoundment of Funds of the Senate Committee on Government Operations on February 1, 1973. In making a case for the reassertion of congressional power in the area of appropriations, he mentions examples of impoundment of funds affecting programs important to Arkansas, including proposed Amtrak service to the state. His concluding remarks concern steps that congressmen can take to meet the challenge of the president.

40 "The Creative Power of Exchange." *International Educational and Cultural Exchange* 11 (Summer 1975): 4, 42-43.

The senator discusses the aims of international education. He made the remarks during a visit to the University of Oslo on the twenty-fifth anniversary of the Fulbright scholar program between the United States and Norway.

41 *The Crippled Giant: American Foreign Policy and Its Domestic Consequences.* New York: Random House, 1972.

The senator introduces the book with a discussion of the internationalist, ideological, and geopolitical conceptions of foreign policy but focuses on the second in this analysis. He examines the anticommunist ideology dominating postwar foreign policy and the effect of twenty-five years of cold warfare and crises on both foreign and domestic policies. Included is an analysis of the Truman Doctrine and a consideration of its long-term impact on U.S. foreign policies, particularly those related to relations with China and Vietnam. He also examines the mythology underpinning the conflict in the Middle East and offers an agenda for a negotiated settlement. The second part of the book concerns the constitutional imbalance between the president and Congress in the conduct of international relations, resulting from the war in Vietnam. He concludes with an assessment of U.S. society.

42 "Crisis—Academic and National." *College and University Journal* 7, No. 1 (1968): 19-23.

Fulbright, in remarks before the Senate on December 13, 1967, assesses the role of the military-industrial-academic complex in our society and includes a discussion of the special problems that the affiliation of the university presents. The second part concerns the significance of the U.S. example in the world and the loss of our understanding of that concept in Vietnam.

43 "Criticism and Praise for the [*sic*] Dulles's Views." *U.S. News and World Report,* 9 March 1956, 111-14, 116. (Excerpts published in *Foreign Policy Bulletin,* 15 April 1956, 116-18, under the title "Foreign Policy Forum: Two Views of U.S. Foreign Policy.")

Responding to John Foster Dulles's analysis of Soviet foreign policy, Fulbright leads the assault in the Senate on the secretary's views. He challenges Dulles's remarks before the Senate Foreign Relations Committee on February 24, 1956, on Soviet "setbacks" with questions about the effects of Soviet policies in Asia, Europe, and the Middle East. Senator H. Alexander Smith answers Fulbright's criticism. The Dulles remarks that inspired the debate begin on page 108.

44 "Current Crisis and Need for Education." In *Representative American Speeches: 1957-1958,* edited by A. Craig Baird, 157-61. The Reference Shelf. Vol. 30, No. 4. New York: H.W. Wilson Company, 1958. (Excerpts also published in *The Ozarks Mountaineer* 6 [February 1958]: 20, under the title "What Present-Day Education Needs"; and *Arkansas Alumnus,* n.s. 11 [March 1958]: 15, under the title "A Senator and Alumnus Says, The Real Challenge Is Education.")

In this excerpt from his Senate speech of January 23, 1958, Fulbright discusses the importance of education in the struggle with the Soviet Union. In addition to providing more money for the schools, the senator recommends rethinking our approach to education and learning and includes an outline of requirements for a sound educational program.

45 "Debate in Print: Should the Government Conduct Research for Small Business? Yes, Says Senator Fulbright; No, Says Major Putnam." *Modern Industry,* 15 March 1946, 130, 132, 135-36, 138, 140, 142.

In an argument for a research agency to assist small businesses, the senator outlines the objectives of his bill to create an Office of Technical Services within the Department of Commerce.

46 "The Debate on Vietnam and Its Meaning for the Class of 1966." *Arkansas Alumnus,* n.s. 19 (June 1966): 12-15.

In this commencement address at the University of Arkansas in Fayetteville in June 1966, the senator discusses the nature of dissent in a democracy, calling it an "act of faith." He examines the importance of free thought and open discussion in the foreign policy process and the purpose that it serves in the debate on Vietnam.

47 "A Decent Society Must Have a Moral and Religious Basis." *Front Rank* 56, No. 39 (1947): 8.

This is a statement prepared for the International Council of Religious Education, Chicago, supporting their seventeenth annual Religious Education Week, September 28 to October 5, in the United States and Canada.

48 "The Demands on the FSO Were Never Greater." *Department of State News Letter,* No. 39 (1964): 13.

The article commemorates the fortieth anniversary of the founding of the Foreign Service. It begins on page 13 but is not continued elsewhere in the issue.

49 "Department of Apologies." *The Nation,* 20 March 1954, 248.

In a letter to the editor, Fulbright corrects several statements in Edgar Kemler's article, "The Fulbright Fellow: An Arkansas Traveler," which appeared in the February 20 issue of the *Nation.*

50 "The Development and Decline of Federal Support." *The American Oxonian* 56 (April 1969): 73-78.

The senator examines the historical and legislative background of educational exchange programs in an effort to explain the severe cut in the exchange budget and to identify those responsible for the reduction.

51 "Dimensions of Security." *Foreign Service Journal* 46 (July 1969): 14-18, 45. (Abbreviated version adapted for *American Militarism 1970: A Dialogue on the Distortion of Our National Priorities and the Need to Reassert Control over the Defense Establishment,* edited by Erwin Knoll and Judith Nies McFadden, 132-42. New York: Viking Press, 1969, under the title "Epilogue: Dimensions of Security"; condensed version in *Congressional Digest* 48 [August-September 1969]: 202, 204, 206, 208, under the title "The Question of Curtailing the Executive Role in the Making of Foreign Military Commitments.")

In a discussion of ends and means in U.S. foreign policy, the senator argues that the United States is subverting democratic values by the pursuit of policies based on military considerations. His focus is on an examination of the economic, political, and moral costs of thirty years of erring on the side of the "security of means." The remarks are drawn from a speech at the National War College on May 19, 1969. The condensed version in the *Congressional Digest* also includes remarks from an address in the Senate on June 19, 1969, during debate on the senator's national commitments resolution.

52 "Education and Public Policy." *The Bulletin of the National Association of Secondary-School Principals* 49, No. 299 (1965): 3-13. (Also published in *Representative American Speeches: 1964-1965,* edited by Lester Thonssen, 157-69. The Reference Shelf. Vol. 37, No. 4. New York: H.W. Wilson Company, 1965.)

The senator examines the issue of federal assistance to education, including the problems associated with the formulation of an effective program. In a discussion of the responsibilities of education, he challenges educators to help bridge the gap created by modern technology and man's ability to use it wisely in international relations. He concludes with a reflection on the cold war in American life.

53 "Education for a New Kind of International Relations." *International Educational and Cultural Exchange* 2 (Winter 1967): 9-19.

In an address at the annual meeting of the Swedish Institute for Cultural Relations in Stockholm in December 1966, the senator describes the purpose of education in international relations as "the civilizing and humanizing of relations between nations." He examines the new concepts necessary to develop new methods and new attitudes for changing the way nations interact, specifically concepts regarding the nation and a community of nations. His concluding remarks concern the role of international education in achieving that goal.

54 "Education for the Professions." *Arkansas Dental Journal* 30 (September 1959): 4-6.

Focusing on the dental profession, the senator discusses the professional man's dual role in society as a practitioner of his specialty and as a citizen and leader.

55 "Education in International Relations." *Colorado Quarterly* 15 (Winter 1966): 209-16. (Abbreviated version published in *International Educational and Cultural Exchange* 2 [Fall 1966]: 1-4, under the title "Twenty Years of the Fulbright Act.")

In this Fulbright speech at the University of Colorado, Boulder, on the twentieth anniversary of the Fulbright Act, the senator presents an overview of the Fulbright scholarship program. He discusses the program's purpose, his reasons for sponsoring the legislation, the strategy that he employed in Congress to secure passage, additional legislation to strengthen and consolidate the program, costs, and the role of the Board of Foreign Scholarships and the binational commissions.

56 "The Eighty-fifth Congress and the Arkansas Economy." *The Arkansas Economist* 1 (Fall 1958): 3-8.

Fulbright discusses new legislation designed to further the economic development of Arkansas: disaster and community facility loans, the Small Business Investment Act, the area development bill, emergency housing legislation, river development appropriations, highway construction and unemployment compensation, farm legislation, and the reciprocal trade extension bill. Fulbright is featured on the cover.

57 "Eleven Voices on the Third Great Revolution . . . Our Lost Educational Preeminence." *The Intercollegian* 76, No. 1 (1958): 5.

This is a short statement in which the senator stresses the importance of education in the conflict with the Soviet Union.

58 Fulbright, J. William, with Pierre Mendès-France, Joseph S. Clark, and Viscount Hailsham. *The Elite and the Electorate: Is Government by the People Possible?* Santa Barbara, Calif.: Center for the Study of Democratic Institutions, 1963. (The senator's paper is also published in *Challenges to Democracy: The Next Ten Years,* edited by Edward Reed, 75-127. New York: Frederick A. Praeger, Publisher, 1963; excerpts in *The Center Magazine* 1 [November 1968]: 61-68, under the title "Second Edition: Elite and Electorate"; and *Democracy, Liberalism, and Revolution: Reflections upon the Issues That Divide America and the Institutions Which Confront Those Issues,* edited by Karl A. Lamb, 15-34. Palo Alto, Calif.: James E. Freel and Associates, 1971.)

This is an abridgement of an address before a convocation sponsored by the Fund for the Republic in New York in January 1963 on "Challenges to Democracy in the Next Decade." Fulbright examines the political philosophy of a democracy in a scholarly treatise in which he states that "government by the people is possible but highly improbable." In concluding remarks, the senator returns to ideas expressed in a 1946 speech about the role of the legislator, specifically his responsibilities to his constituents, his nation, and his conscience. Commentators on the paper are theologian John Courtney Murray and philosopher Charles Frankel.

59 "End Military Aid." *The Progressive* 37 (August 1973): 13.

In a statement calling for an end to military aid programs, the senator argues that they belong to another era and have little bearing on the present world.

60 "Energy and the Middle East: Interests and Illusions." *Vital Speeches of the Day,* 15 March 1975, 331-35.

The senator discusses the impact of the energy crisis on the domestic front and its connection with the Arab-Israeli conflict, asserting that policy makers deny the connection in order to give Israeli policy top priority. His concluding remarks concern the requirements for a negotiated settlement of the Middle East crisis, with the assistance of the Russians and the Palestinians in working out an agreement. The article is drawn from the senator's Alfred M. Landon Lecture on February 13, 1975, at Kansas State University in Manhattan.

61 "Exchange Students." *Epworth Notes* 2 (September 1958): 2-4.

This is a Fulbright statement concerning the uniqueness of the exchange experience in terms of the benefits received and the services rendered by the participants. *Epworth Notes* is a publication of the General Board of Education of the Methodist Church.

62 "Exchange Teachers Are American Ambassadors." *The Instructor* 65 (November 1955): 12.

This guest editorial honors exchange teachers for their contributions to their host countries and the United States.

63 "The Fatal Obsession in U.S. Foreign Policy." *The Progressive* 22 (September 1958): 14-17. (Excerpts published in *U.S. News and World Report,* 15 August 1958, 86, under the title "Fulbright: 'Mistaken Policies' Behind U.S. Troubles in World.")

The article is an adaptation of remarks before the Senate in which Fulbright calls for a complete reexamination and reorientation of U.S. foreign policy. In an assessment of the position of the United States in the world, he warns against using Soviet communism as justification for inadequate policies and ineffective leadership. He further discusses the implications of that obsession for our relations with revolutionary movements.

64 "The First Fifteen Years of the Fulbright Program." *The Annals of The American Academy of Political and Social Science* 335 (May 1961): 21-27.

In a review of the Fulbright program, the senator discusses the provisions for study opportunities, the support of the public and private sectors, the administrative apparatus, and the binational foundations. He also suggests steps to strengthen the program.

65 "For a Concert of Free Nations." *Foreign Affairs* 40 (October 1961): 1-18. (Slightly condensed version printed in *U.S. News and World Report,* 2 October 1961, 80-85, under the title "From Senator Fulbright: 'U.N. Has Fallen Short; We Must Look Elsewhere.'")

Asserting that the "United Nations . . . has fallen far short of the hopes which attended its creation," the senator recommends organizing an international community of free nations, initially North Atlantic nations, and spells out the requirements for the creation of such a community. His proposal calls for broadening and implementing existing instrumentalities, particularly NATO and the Organization for Economic Cooperation and Development. He incorporates a review of models from nineteenth century European history as well as a consideration of the League of Nations and the United Nations.

66 "For a New Order of Priorities at Home and Abroad." *Playboy* 15 (July 1968): 110-12, 116, 152-53, 155-57.

In an article expressing views on a variety of issues, the senator calls for a reassessment of our national priorities for new agendas in both domestic and foreign affairs. Initially, he examines the reasons for the lack of support of much of the world in the Vietnam War effort. He turns next to a discussion of the military-industrial-academic complex as a political force in U.S. society and the destructive effects of the affiliation of the university on teaching and learning. Another issue that he addresses is the crisis created by poverty in the United States. Concluding remarks regard the importance of the U.S. example in the world and how the loss of our understanding of that concept has impacted on Vietnam. Some of the ideas expressed in this article originated in the senator's book, *The Arrogance of Power,* and other thoughts concerning the military-industrial-academic complex are found in the entry titled "Crisis—Academic and National" in this chapter.

67 "Foreign Aid? Yes, But with a New Approach." *The New York Times Magazine,* 21 March 1965, 27, 102, 104-6.

Fulbright discusses the problems associated with the foreign aid program and suggests basic reforms in the bilateral approach. His proposal concerns the economic component and includes three main points: authorization of funds for the long term; separation of economic aid from the military and political components; and internationalization of development aid.

68 "Foreign Policy Forum: Does U.S. Foreign Policy Meet Today's Problems? Views of John Foster Dulles and J.W. Fulbright." *Foreign Policy Bulletin,* 15 September 1958, 4-6.

In a critique of the Eisenhower-Dulles foreign policy, the senator argues that more flexible and responsible policies are needed to meet the challenges of the Soviet Union. His concluding remarks concern the ancillary role of Congress in the development and implementation of foreign policy. The article is excerpted from a speech in the Senate on June 20, 1958.

69 "Foreign Policy Forum: Should U.S. Aid Program Be Changed?" *Foreign Policy Bulletin,* 15 June 1959, 148-51.

The article includes excerpts from Fulbright's remarks explaining his five amendments to the proposed Mutual Security Act of 1959. His objections to the Eisenhower strategy of basing the program primarily on military considerations are addressed in the amendments.

70 "Foreign Policy: Old Myths and New Realities." In *Representative American Speeches: 1963-1964,* edited by Lester Thonssen, 91-114. The Reference Shelf. Vol. 36, No. 4. New York: H.W. Wilson Company, 1964. (Excerpts published in *Newsweek,* 6 April 1964, 18, under the title "Fulbright's 'Unthinkable Thoughts'"; condensed versions in *Vital Speeches of the Day,* 15 April 1964, 388-94; *Concern,* 15 April 1964, 2-4, 10-11, under the title "Old Myths and New Realities"; and *The Progressive* 28 [May 1964]: 27-31; highlights in *Current,* No. 49 [1964]: 6-8, under the title "The Uses of U.S. Power: Are We Ready for Unthinkable Thoughts?" Comments by Walter Lippmann, David Lawrence, Arthur Krock, and Eric Sevareid follow. Abbreviated versions in *Ideas and Diplomacy: Readings in the Intellectual Tradition of American Foreign Policy,* edited by Norman A. Graebner, 861-69. New York: Oxford University Press, 1964, under the title "Senator Fulbright's Address Before the Senate, March 1964"; and *America's Foreign Policy.* Rev. ed., edited by Harold Karan Jacobson, 343-48. New York: Random House, 1965; full text in *The Puritan Ethic in United States Foreign Policy,* edited by David L. Larson, 145-66. New Perspectives in Political Science Series, edited by Franklin L. Burdette and William G. Andrews. Princeton, N.J.: D. Van Nostrand Company, 1966, under the title "Old Myths and New Realities"; abridged version in *The Annals of America.* Vol. 18, *The Burdens of World Power, 1961-1968,* 225-31. Chicago: Encyclopaedia Britannica, 1968, under the title "Old Myths and New Realities"; two excerpts in *Security in a World of Change: Readings and Notes on International Relations,* edited by Lee W. Farnsworth and Richard B. Gray, 54-56, 89-94. Wadsworth Series in World Politics, edited by Fred Greene. Belmont, Calif.: Wadsworth Publishing Company, 1969, under the titles "Panama and American National Interests" and "Foreign Policy: Old Myths and New Realities"; slightly abbreviated version in *Basic Issues in American Public Policy,* edited by George S. Masannat, 480-97. Boston: Holbrook Press, 1970, under the title "Old Myths and New Realities"; full text in *A Treasury of Great American Speeches,* selected by Charles Hurd, 374-93. New ed., revised and edited by Andrew Bauer. New York: Hawthorn Books, 1970, under the title "We are Clinging to Old Myths in the Face of New Realities"; abridged version in *The Challenge of Politics: Ideas and Issues.* 3d ed., edited by Alvin Z. Rubinstein and Garold W. Thumm, 375-78. Englewood Cliffs, N.J.: Prentice-Hall, 1970, under the title "Myth and Illusion in American Foreign Policy"; and extract in *The Dynamics of World Power: A Documentary History of United States Foreign Policy, 1945-1973*, edited by Arthur M. Schlesinger, Jr. Vol. 4, *The Far East*. Edited by Russell Buhite, 275-76. New York: Chelsea House Publishers in association with McGraw-Hill Book Company, 1973.)

This is the senator's landmark speech in which he challenges long-standing American myths in foreign affairs and calls for a reassessment of U.S. policies toward the Soviet Union, Panama, Cuba, Latin America, China, and Vietnam. Additional thoughts concern changes in the character of the cold war and in the monolithic nature of the communist bloc. These remarks in the Senate on March 25, 1964, were the senator's contribution to the southern filibuster against the civil rights bill. For a revised and expanded version, see chapter 1 of Fulbright's *Old Myths and New Realities and Other Commentaries.*

71 "Foreign Service Needs Young People: Create Political Leadership for World." *Vital Speeches of the Day,* 1 November 1944, 41-43. (Slightly condensed version published in *Industrial News Review,* December 1944, 17-21, under the title "Foreign Service Needs Young People.")

In an address before the *New York Herald-Tribune* Forum in New York City on October 17, 1944, the senator emphasizes the importance of the human element in the creation of a collective security system. He maintains that our ability to provide political leadership in the postwar world turns on the election of capable legislative officials at all levels and the attraction of competent people to other areas of government service.

72 "Foreign Trade and the Poultry Industry." In *1962 Year Book of the Arkansas Poultry Improvement Association,* 6, 8, 10. Fayetteville, Ark.: [Arkansas Poultry Improvement Association] in cooperation with the Arkansas Livestock Sanitary Board and the University of Arkansas College of Agriculture, [1962].

The article concerns the importance of poultry export problems for Arkansas, primarily those associated with the development of the European Economic Community.

73 Foreword to *A Two-Way Street,* by Norman Dawes. New York: Asia Publishing House, 1962.

The senator praises the Indo-American Fulbright program in its first decade, 1950-1960, and discusses some of the results of the program in India.

74 Foreword to *Chapultepec: Road to San Francisco,* by Herbert Elliston. Booklet.

In the foreword to a reprint of Herbert Elliston's editorials and news dispatches written for the *Washington Post* concerning the conference in Mexico City, Fulbright praises Elliston's reporting of the Inter-American Conference on the Problems of War and Peace, February 23-March 8, 1945, and encourages other newspapers to follow suit in covering the San Francisco conference.

75 Foreword to *Common Sense in U.S.-Soviet Relations,* edited by Carl Marcy. Washington, D.C.: American Committee on East-West Accord, 1978.

The senator expresses concern about the future of U.S.-Soviet relations and the importance of developing policies to bring the arms race under control.

76 Foreword to *Diversity and Interdependence Through International Education,* edited by Allan A. Michie. Report on a symposium marking the twentieth anniversary of the International Educational Exchange (Fulbright) Program. New York: Education and World Affairs for the Board of Foreign Scholarships, 1967.

In a wise and perceptive essay, Fulbright discusses the aims of education in international relations. He examines the new concepts necessary to develop new methods and new attitudes for changing relations between nations. For an expanded version of these remarks, see the Fulbright entry titled "Education for a New Kind of International Relations" in this chapter.

77 Foreword to *Educating Students from Other Nations,* by Hugh M. Jenkins and Associates. San Francisco: Jossey-Bass Publishers, 1983.

In the foreword to a book sponsored by the National Association for Foreign Student Affairs, the senator asserts that educational exchange is the most effective force for humanizing international relations, with the result that reason, not violence, will be the arbiter of international conflicts.

78 Foreword to *J. William Fulbright and America's Lost Crusade: Fulbright's Opposition to the Vietnam War,* by Lee Riley Powell. Little Rock, Ark.: Rose Publishing Company, 1984.

The senator views the author's study as a useful guide for senators responsible for voting on issues related to foreign affairs and also for those interested in a reexamination of the U.S. constitutional system. Fulbright suggests a consideration of the parliamentary system.

79 Foreword to *New Horizons in Education: The Benefits of Study Abroad: Pan American's Guide to the Principal Universities of the World,* edited by George Gardner and Stanley Washburn, Jr. N.p., Pan American Airways, 1961.

The senator emphasizes the importance of the exchange experience, particularly for students.

80 Foreword to *Old Myths and New Realities in United States-Soviet Relations,* edited by Donald R. Kelley and Hoyt Purvis. New York: Praeger, 1990.

The senator stresses the importance of resolving our differences with the Soviet Union and expresses optimism for an improvement in relations between the two nations. He mentions the significance of educational exchange in promoting international understanding, noting that Alexander Yakovlev, close associate of former President Mikhail Gorbachev, had a Fulbright scholarship to study at Columbia University in 1958. The book of readings grew out of a symposium sponsored by the Fulbright Institute of International Relations at the University of Arkansas, Fayetteville, in 1989 on U.S.-Soviet relations. Established in 1982, the Fulbright Institute is an interdisciplinary unit concerned with historical research and contemporary foreign policy analysis at the university.

81 Foreword to *Retrospective for a Critic: Duncan Phillips,* by Bess Hormats. College Park: University of Maryland, 1969.

This is a tribute by the senator to Duncan Phillips, art critic, collector, and public benefactor.

82 Foreword to *The Fourth Dimension of Foreign Policy: Educational and Cultural Affairs,* by Philip H. Coombs. New York: Harper and Row, 1964.

Fulbright discusses the importance of international educational and cultural exchange in foreign policy.

83 Foreword to *The Fulbright Experience, 1946-1986: Encounters and Transformations,* edited by Arthur Power Dudden and Russell R. Dynes. New Brunswick, N.J.: Transaction Books, 1987.

Drawing on the thoughts of Albert Einstein, the senator emphasizes the importance of the international educational experience in bringing about mutual understanding, particularly between the United States and the Soviet Union.

84 Foreword to *The Fulbright Program: A History,* by Walter Johnson and Francis J. Colligan. Chicago: University of Chicago Press, 1965.

In an introduction to the definitive history of the Fulbright exchange program, Fulbright uses Webster's definition of civilization to explain educational exchange programs. He also discusses the objectives of the program.

85 Foreword to *The People vs. Presidential War,* compiled and edited by John M. Wells with Maria Wilhelm. New York: Dunellen Company, 1970.

The senator praises the effort by the Massachusetts legislature, in the form of the Shea-Wells bill, to challenge the constitutionality of U.S. involvement in Vietnam.

86 Foreword to *The Price of Defense: A New Strategy for Military Spending,* by The Boston Study Group. New York: Times Books, 1979.

Praising their research methods, analysis, and conclusions, the senator recommends the authors' book on ways to reduce the military budget.

87 Foreword to *The Razorbacks: A Story of Arkansas Football.* 3d ed., rev. and enl., by Orville Henry and Jim Bailey. Huntsville, Ala.: Strode Publishers, 1980.

The senator contrasts the game of his playing days in the twenties with the game of today. He also discusses the importance of the Razorbacks as a unifying force in the state.

88 Foreword to *The United States in the Middle East: Interests and Obstacles,* by Seth P. Tillman. Bloomington: Indiana University Press, 1982.

Fulbright suggests that Dr. Tillman's analysis of our interests in the Middle East be used as the basis for a congressional investigation of U.S. policy in the region.

89 Fulbright, J. William, et al. Foreword to *The University and World Affairs,* by Harold Boeschenstein, Harvie Branscomb, Arthur S. Flemming, J.W. Fulbright, John W. Gardner, J.L. Morrill, Franklin D. Murphy, Philip D. Reed, and Dean Rusk. Report of the Committee on the University and World Affairs, December 1960.

The foreword is primarily a statement of the purpose of the study and an acknowledgment of persons who assisted the committee.

90 Foreword to "Trade with the People's Republic of China" in *Law and Policy in International Business* 5, No. 3 (1973): 737-42.

In an issue concerning trade with the People's Republic of China, the senator discusses the concept of an international security community envisioned in the United Nations Charter and the importance of education in shaping that community.

91 "The Foundations of National Security." In *Great Issues of International Politics: The International System and National Policy.* 1st and 2d eds., edited by Morton A. Kaplan, 237-47, 255-65. Chicago: Aldine Publishing Company, 1970, 1974. (Abbreviated version published in *Readings in American Foreign Policy.* 2d ed., edited by Robert

A. Goldwin and revised by Harry M. Clor, 380-89. New York: Oxford University Press, 1971, under the title "Toward a Relaxation of Tensions.")

The senator discusses the advantages of a limited détente for both the Soviet Union and the West. Included is an outline of his concept of security in the nuclear age. His concluding remarks concern the importance of "the alteration of attitudes" in our efforts to modify and eventually end the cold war. The article consists of excerpts from a chapter titled "The Foundations of National Security" in Fulbright's *Old Myths and New Realities and Other Commentaries.*

92   "Four Fronts for Peace: III. The Peace Treaty Front." *The Living Church,* 3 March 1946, 23.

This is the third in a series of articles sponsored by the Commission on a Just and Durable Peace and concerned with a general strategy for achieving peace in the postwar world. Fulbright's article pertains to postwar peace making, particularly the nature of the peace process, and stresses the importance of U.S. leadership in the effort. The set of articles appeared in a publication of the Episcopal Church.

93   "The FPC Gas Producer Exemption Is in the Consumer's Interest." *Public Utilities Fortnightly,* 5 January 1956, 13-24.

In a defense of his bill proposing deregulation of independent natural gas producers, the senator refutes his opponents' argument that the producer's interest takes precedence over the consumer's. He cites Senator Paul Douglas's article in the October 13, 1955, issue of *Public Utilities Fortnightly,* in which Douglas takes a pro-regulation position. For additional information regarding the Fulbright article, see the section titled "Pages with the Editors" on pages 6 and 8 of this issue.

94   "France and the Western Alliance: Actual Cooperation Is Needed." *Vital Speeches of the Day,* 15 November 1963, 75-78. (Quotations included in *U.S. News and World Report,* 11 November 1963, 26, under the title "Fulbright Target: De Gaulle.")

Responding to remarks expressed by President Charles de Gaulle in a press conference on July 29, Fulbright warns that French antagonism toward U.S. policy in Europe endangers the Western Alliance. He answers de Gaulle on three issues: economic and trade relations between Europe and the United States, the U.S. commitment to defend Europe, and de Gaulle's position on the nuclear test ban treaty.

95   "From Broilers to Brussels: European Common Market Puts High Tariff on U.S. Poultry—Pattern for Other Farm Exports?" *Rural Arkansas Magazine* 17 (July 1963): 5, 10.

The senator examines the difficulties involved in efforts to reverse the protectionist trade policies of the European Economic Community, particularly regarding poultry products. Stressing the importance of Europe looking beyond its own borders, he advocates a partnership of cooperation and community between the United States and Europe.

96   "Fulbright: Courts Should Recognize 'Southern Mind.'" *U.S. News and World Report,* 5 September 1958, 97.

Asserting that the relationship between the races in the South has a special history, the senator urges the Supreme Court to consider the particular situation of the South when it looks at the race issue. The remarks are from a brief filed by the senator with the Supreme Court and are part of an article titled "Pro and Con on Little Rock—Record of Week of Controversy—On Mixed Schools: The Key Speeches, the

Court Arguments," which begins on page 94 of this issue. The brief is reproduced in chapter 5 of Karl E. Meyer's book, *Fulbright of Arkansas: The Public Positions of a Private Thinker.*

97 "Fulbright Exchanges Enhance Our National Security." *The Chronicle of Higher Education,* 10 December 1986, 104.

On the fortieth anniversary of the Fulbright program, the senator discusses the importance of the exchange activity in the nuclear age, particularly the program with the Soviet Union.

98 "Fulbright, Ford Agree: Education Prime Factor." *Education Newsmagazine* 1 (July 1963): 6.

The article is a reprint of Fulbright's Senate newsletter regarding his bill pertaining to federal aid for education and supported by Arch Ford, Arkansas's commissioner of education.

99 "Fulbright on the Press." *Columbia Journalism Review* 14 (November- December 1975): 39-45. (Slightly condensed version published in *Foreign Service Journal* 53 [February 1976]: 4, 6, 15-18.)

The senator lectures on the excesses of the press since Vietnam and Watergate and reminds journalists of their responsibility to exercise self-restraint in the practice of their profession. He also addresses the media's treatment of the so-called "paradoxes" in his personality and career. Other remarks concern the failure of the press to be objective in its coverage of his criticism of the Israeli lobby. He charges the media with a "shifting of attention from the event to its author, from statement to motive, from song to singer." Fulbright is featured on the cover. For other Fulbright remarks on the press, see the entry titled "The Neglect of the Song" in this chapter.

100 "The Fulbright Resolution." In *Plans for Winning the Peace.* Addresses Made at the "Post-War Clarification" Meeting, Sponsored by The New York Times, Times Hall, Sept. 24, 1943. Booklet.

Congressman Fulbright talks about his resolution calling for U.S. participation in a postwar collective security system and includes a discussion of his concept of sovereignty. He made the speech at a clarification meeting in New York City called to consider a variety of proposals for postwar global planning. The booklet consists of the texts of the participants' addresses and an open forum discussion.

101 "Fulbright Speaks on Campaign Issues—An Editorial." *The Journal of Arkansas Education* 37 (October 1964): 14-15.

Fulbright discusses the positions of presidential candidates Barry M. Goldwater and Lyndon B. Johnson on issues in both domestic and foreign affairs.

102 "Fulbright Urges a Larger Program." *The New York Times Magazine,* 13 August 1961, 10, 92-93.

In a reappraisal of the academic exchange bearing his name, Fulbright advocates a larger program for Asia, Africa, and Latin America, without cutting the European side of the operation.

103 "Fulbright's Solution: 'Honorable Compromise.'" *U.S. News and World Report,* 5 February 1968, 31.

This is a position statement on Vietnam prepared for *U.S. News and World Report.*

104   "The Future of Exchanges." *Institute of International Education News Bulletin* 30 (February 1955): 2-4.

The senator reports on the Fulbright program since its beginning in 1948, noting both the successes of the academic exchange and the threats to its continuation.

105   Fulbright, J. William, et al. *The Future of the United Nations*. Washington, D.C.: American Enterprise Institute for Public Policy Research, 1977.

In a forum on the future of the United Nations, panel members, including Fulbright, discuss the importance of supporting the UN, the reasons for hostility in the organization toward the United States, the challenge of the Third World, the role of peace-keeping, the lack of UN action on arms control negotiations, and the role of the UN in the Middle East. Other participants were Leonard Garment, Congressman Larry P. McDonald, Joseph J. Sisco, and moderator John Charles Daly.

106   "Getting Along with the Russians: U.S. Forces in Europe." *Vital Speeches of the Day,* 15 September 1973, 706-10.

In a speech before the American Bankers Association on July 11, 1973, Fulbright discusses ways of improving relations between the United States and the Soviet Union, focusing primarily on arms control and trade. He warns against the dangers of the Jackson amendment to the trade bill, noting that "the purpose it is meant to serve exceeds the interests and responsibilities of the United States." He also advocates reduction of U.S. forces in Europe.

107   "The Governance of the Pentagon." *Saturday Review,* 7 November 1970, 22-25, 57-58. (Also published in *The Texas Observer,* 25 December 1970, 10-13.)

The article is adapted from Fulbright's book, *The Pentagon Propaganda Machine,* and warns against the dangers of militarism in a democratic society. It includes a program for civilian defense against the military.

108   "The High Cost of Secrecy." *The Progressive* 35 (September 1971): 16-21.

The senator criticizes the operation of the foreign policy apparatus centered around the National Security Council, including presidential advisors and assistants, specifically their exercise of executive privilege. He asserts that the practice destroys the congressional oversight function, adding that "secrecy and subterfuge are themselves more dangerous to democracy than the practices they conceal."

109   "Higher Education and the Crisis in Asia." In *1966 Current Issues in Higher Education: Higher Education Reflects—On Itself and on the Larger Society: The Proceedings of the Twenty-first Annual National Conference on Higher Education, March 13-16, 1966,* edited by G. Kerry Smith, 24-30. Washington, D.C.: Association for Higher Education, 1966.

Starting with a discussion of the "highest purpose of higher education," the senator maintains that the university can play an important role in the inquiry into the Asian side of foreign affairs, particularly regarding China. His remarks include a discussion of ways in which scholars can help in the search for peace. The senator concludes with an assessment of the Foreign Relations Committee hearings on Vietnam.

110   "Higher Education and the Maintenance of American Freedom." In *Current Issues in Higher Education, 1955: Proceedings of the Tenth Annual National Conference on Higher Education, Chicago, Illinois, February 28-March 2, 1955,* edited by G. Kerry Smith, 25-30. Washington, D.C.: Association for Higher Education, 1955.

In a paper read before the Tenth Annual National Conference on Higher Education in Chicago, the senator discusses his theory of education and the importance of reestablishing the humanities as the foundation of an educational system for a democratic society.

111 "The Higher Patriotism." In *Contemporary Political Speaking,* edited by L. Patrick Devlin, 18-39. Belmont, Calif.: Wadsworth Publishing Company, 1971. (Abridged versions published in *The New York Times Magazine,* 15 May 1966, 28-29, 103-5, under the title "The Fatal Arrogance of Power"; *The Progressive* 30 [July 1966]: 10-13; *Teach-Ins: U.S.A.: Reports, Opinions, Documents,* edited by Louis Menashe and Ronald Radosh, 212-19. New York: Frederick A. Praeger, Publishers, 1967; and *The Annals of America.* Vol. 18, *The Burdens of World Power, 1961-1968,* 362-67. Chicago: Encyclopaedia Britannica, 1968, under the title "The Arrogance of Power.")

In an eloquent defense of dissent, Fulbright examines the function of criticism in a democracy, calling it "an act of patriotism, a higher form of patriotism . . . than the familiar rituals of national adulation." He discusses the significance of debate and discussion in the formulation of foreign policy and offers advice to student protesters, encouraging them to communicate through conventional channels. His concluding remarks concern the role of the Senate and the senator in the foreign policy realm. This article was adapted from the first of the Christian A. Herter Lectures given by the senator at the School for Advanced International Studies at Johns Hopkins University on April 21, 1966, on the "arrogance of power."

112 "Historical Overview." In *China, Vietnam, and the United States: Highlights of the Hearings of the Senate Foreign Relations Committee,* 3-14. Washington, D.C.: Public Affairs Press, 1966. (Also published in *The Viet-Nam Reader: Articles and Documents on American Foreign Policy and the Viet-Nam Crisis.* Rev. ed., edited by Marcus G. Raskin and Bernard B. Fall, 444-56. New York: Random House, Vintage Books, 1967, under the title "On the Arrogance of Power.")

The senator reviews the history of China's relations with the West in the nineteenth century and the United States's subsequent Open Door policy in the twentieth century. Included is an examination of the effects of Western imperialism. Stressing the importance of trying to understand China's hostility toward the United States, the senator discusses the steps required to alter "the fatal expectancy of war" between the two nations.

113 Fulbright, J. William, with Eric Johnston, Charles P. Brannan, and Carlos P. Romulo. "How Can the World's Free Peoples Share Peace and Well-Being?" *The Rotarian* 75 (August 1949): 17-19, 57-59.

The article consists of the opening statements of participants in a symposium broadcast on radio and television on June 14, 1949. The senator analyzes the Point Four program, which he calls "a vast educational program."

114 Fulbright, J. William, et al. "How Can We Correct World Misconceptions About America?" *The University of Chicago Round Table,* 6 May 1951, 1-11.

Fulbright, Walter Johnson, and Perry Miller discuss the Fulbright program.

115 "How to Get Better Men Elected." *Ladies Home Journal* 68 (November 1951): 52, 218-19.

The senator points out that the public's low opinion of its elected officials perpetuates the selection of mediocre people because it deters more capable persons from running for office. Concluding remarks include a prescription for reversing the situation.

116 "How We Make Foreign Policy." *The American Oxonian* 46 (July 1959): 130-35.

The new Foreign Relations Committee chairman discusses the reasons for the country's inadequate foreign policy and the importance of defining the national interests. He also talks about the significance of public discussion and debate in a nonpartisan approach to the formulation of foreign policy. The remarks were made before the American Society of Newspaper Editors in Washington on April 16, 1959.

117 "If Congress Is Bad, Then So Is the Voter." *The New York Times Magazine,* 3 November 1946, 7, 65-66.

Asserting that the legislature is a reflection of the voters who elect it, Fulbright examines the role of the legislator in a democratic society. He notes some of the difficulties confronting the elected representative, particularly the problem of acting in behalf of the national interests without offending the beliefs and prejudices of the constituents.

118 "In the Name of Humanity." *United Palestine Appeal Yearbook, 1945,* 28, 142-43.

This is a statement in which Fulbright urges prompt response to President Truman's request for the immigration of one hundred thousand European Jews to Palestine. He quotes from the Balfour Declaration of November 2, 1917, proposing the creation of a Jewish homeland in Palestine, and reviews the history of Britain's League of Nations mandate over Palestine.

119 "International Co-operation for Peace." In *Proceedings: American Pharmaceutical Manufacturers' Association,* 145-53. New York City, December 10-11, 1945.

The freshman senator discusses the importance of establishing international law within the framework of the United Nations for the purpose of controlling atomic energy. His argument also includes an explanation of his concept of sovereignty.

120 "International Education: Focus for Corporate Support." *Harvard Business Review* 55 (May-June 1977): 137-41.

In an argument for greater involvement by U.S. corporations in international education, the senator discusses the kinds of public service programs beneficial to both corporations and host countries. His concluding remarks concern the larger purpose of international education and its importance in a world that is becoming increasingly interdependent.

121 Introduction to *Arkansas Men at War,* by James Guy Tucker, Jr. Little Rock, Ark.: Pioneer Press, 1968.

Written on Christmas Day in 1967, this piece expresses the hope that the author's account of the Vietnam War in all its brutality will help people to understand the men who are fighting the war and the people who are trying to end it.

122 Introduction to *Liberia: Black Africa in Microcosm,* by Charles Morrow Wilson. New York: Harper and Row, 1971.

In an introduction to a book by his old friend, Charles Morrow Wilson, the senator offers interesting background information about the oldest African republic.

123 Introduction to *Strategy for the 60s,* edited by Jay H. Cerf and Walter Pozen. New York: Frederick A. Praeger, Publisher, 1961.

The senator acknowledges the Foreign Policy Clearing House for its preparation of summaries and analyses of thirteen studies completed for use by the Senate Foreign Relations Committee and concerned with U.S. foreign and defense policies, particularly challenges of the sixties and strategies for meeting them.

124 Introduction to *The Soviet Viewpoint,* by Georgi A. Arbatov and Willem Oltmans. New York: Dodd, Mead and Company, 1983.

Fulbright recommends Professor Arbatov's analysis of U.S.-Soviet relations and emphasizes the importance of the two great powers understanding the psychology of the other.

125 "'Irrigation's Greatest Future Is in the South.'" *Dairy News* 12, No. 1 (1954): 3.

Fulbright discusses his bill, cosponsored by Senators James O. Eastland and Edward J. Thye, to extend the benefits of the Water Facilities Act of 1937 to the rest of the country.

126 "Is a Constitutional Amendment to Provide for Cases of Presidential Disability Needed?" *Congressional Digest* 37 (January 1958): 12, 14.

Fulbright's comments concern Senate Joint Resolution 100, a proposed amendment that he introduced regarding presidential succession in case of presidential disability. The senator outlines the provisions in the amendment and points out its merits vis-à-vis President Truman's proposal.

127 "Is the Dixon-Yates Contract in the Public Interest?" *Congressional Digest* 34 (January 1955): 20, 22, 24.

This is an excerpt from the senator's testimony before the Joint Committee on Atomic Energy on November 12, 1954, concerning the Dixon-Yates contract. Arguing for the development of private power, he defends his support of the Dixon-Yates proposal.

128 "Is the Project Apollo Program to Land Astronauts on the Moon by 1970 a Sound National Objective?" *Congressional Digest* 44 (February 1965): 47, 49, 51, 53.

Fulbright argues that space exploration, particularly the lunar program, does not deserve priority over important national programs, particularly education and antipoverty, among others.

129 "The Johnson Presidency and Vietnam." In *Portraits of American Presidents.* Vol. 5, *The Johnson Presidency: Twenty Intimate Perspectives of Lyndon B. Johnson.* Edited by Kenneth W. Thompson, 237-48. Lanham, Md.: University Press of America, 1986.

The senator discusses his relationship with Lyndon Johnson during Johnson's years as majority leader, vice-president, and president. He also reviews Vietnam's history from 1945, focusing on the beginnings of U.S. involvement.

130 "Julian S. Waterman—A Memorial." *Arkansas Law Review and Bar Association Journal* 8, No. 1 (1953-1954): 64-66.

In these remarks at the dedication of Waterman Hall at the University of Arkansas School of Law, Fulbright honors Julian S. Waterman, his former teacher and colleague. The senator was a student at the university in the early twenties and a member of the law faculty from 1936 until 1939 when he became president of the university.

131 "Law: The Basis of World Peace." *The Journal of the National Education Association* 35 (February 1946): 61-62.

In an NBC radio address on November 23, 1945, Fulbright appeals to the people of the United States to press their government to support the United Nations.

132   "The Legislator." In *The Works of the Mind,* edited by Robert B. Heywood, 119-34. Chicago: University of Chicago Press, 1947. (Also published in *Vital Speeches of the Day,* 15 May 1946, 468-72, under the title "The Legislator: Duties, Functions and Hardships of Public Officials"; and *The Madison Quarterly* 6 [May 1946]: 99-112; condensed version in *Think* 12 [August 1946]: 9-10, 40, under the title "On Being a Legislator.")

Calling the legislator "an indispensable guardian of our freedom," Fulbright, in a landmark speech at the University of Chicago on February 19, 1946, presents some of his initial impressions of politics and the role of the legislator. His remarks focus on the election process, the legislator-constituent relationship, and proposed congressional reforms.

133   "The Legislator as Educator." *Foreign Affairs* 57 (Spring 1979): 719-32.

Citing Edmund Burke and Thomas Jefferson, Fulbright declares that the primary responsibility of the legislator in a democracy is "to lead and to educate." The senator's thesis is that the modern legislator is more interested in serving the constituency and special interests than in educating the public. He examines the reasons for the change, focusing on the influence of the media, the public relations industry, and modern methods of campaigning. Included also is a consideration of the executive-legislative relationship in the foreign policy realm. The article is drawn from Fulbright's Elihu Root Lecture on January 23, 1979, before the Council on Foreign Relations.

134   "The Legislator: Congress and the War." *Vital Speeches of the Day,* 1 March 1971, 290-94.

In remarks at South Florida University, Tampa, on February 4, 1971, Fulbright returns to ideas expressed in a 1946 speech about the role of Congress as protector of the people's liberties. He discusses the loss of power by Congress and the usurpation by the executive in the foreign policy realm, particularly the power to declare war. His remarks include an examination of the role of Congress in the repeal of the Tonkin Gulf resolution, approval of a supplemental aid authorization for Cambodia, and passage of the Cooper-Church amendment. For a summary of the earlier speech, see the Fulbright entry titled "The Legislator" in this chapter.

135   "Let the Navy Serve Margarine!" *The Cotton Gin and Oil Mill Press,* 31 October 1959, 5, 29.

The senator explains the background and strategy associated with his bill amending the Navy ration statute to include margarine.

136   "Let's Convert Hill Brush into Profits." *The Ozarks Mountaineer* 7 (September 1959): 2.

This article concerns the senator's views on the benefits of clearing scrub timber from farms in the Ozarks area.

137   "Looking Forward in Government." *Farm Equipment Retailing,* December 1946, 24, 84.

The article consists of excerpts from Fulbright's address before the National Retail Farm Equipment Association convention in Chicago on October 31, 1946. His remarks concern industrial-labor relations and U.S. involvement in postwar international relations, particularly with the Soviet Union. For comments about the senator's remarks and additional quotations, see page 20 of this issue.

138   "Madness on the Grand Scale." *The New Republic,* 18 April 1970, 19.

This is a statement by Fulbright on the Senate floor on April 2, 1970, related to his argument for a negotiated political settlement in Vietnam.

139 *The Marfleet Lectures: The New World Looks at the Old World.* [Toronto]: University of Toronto Press, 1948. (Lectures were adapted for *Maclean's Magazine,* 1 March 1948, 7-8, 50-51, under the title "Our Stake in a Federated Europe.")

The senator calls for the creation of a United States of Europe, arguing that an economically and politically unified Europe would be in the interest of the United States, Western Europe, and the Soviet Union. He outlines the obstacles to federation, concluding that they are manageable, and cites examples of unity and cooperation from the Americas. His concluding remarks regard the importance of Britain's membership. The senator delivered the lectures at the University of Toronto in December 1947.

140 "Medicine—The Universal Language." *The Journal of the Arkansas Medical Society* 57, No. 2 (1960): 54-58.

The article concerns the role of medical aid in foreign policy. Fulbright discusses a number of international health projects undertaken by persons, foundations, private companies, universities, and government and their impact on peoples and nations. Included is a statement by Dr. Tom Dooley on his work in Southeast Asia.

141 "Members of Congress Realize Ideals by Serving the Public." *The George Washington University Federalist* 7 (Fall 1959): 6-8.

The senator discusses the Fulbright exchange program.

142 "Message to Social Studies Teachers." *Bulletin of the Arkansas Council for the Social Studies* 15 (Fall 1959): 5-6.

The senator emphasizes the importance of the social studies teacher in educating young people about their government and their nation's role in the world.

143 "Militarism: Impact of the Military upon American Democracy." In *The Owens-Corning Lectures, 1968-69,* 19-39. Granville, Ohio: Denison University, 1969. (Also published in *Vital Speeches of the Day,* 15 May 1969, 455-60, under the title "Militarism and American Democracy: The Complex.")

The senator discusses geopolitics in the nuclear age, focusing on the case for the ABM; the military-industrial complex and the affiliation of the university; and militarism in the United States. He made the remarks in an address at Denison University, Granville, Ohio, on April 18, 1969.

144 "Military Men and Partisan Politics." *Army, Navy, Air Force Register,* 7 October 1961, 25.

Fulbright explains and defends his memorandum alerting the president and the secretary of defense to the military's educational and political activities.

145 Fulbright, J. William, et al. "Missiles and Anti-Missiles . . . Six Views." *Bulletin of the Atomic Scientists* 25 (June 1969): 20-28, 43.

Inspired by the Senate debate on the Nuclear Non-Proliferation Treaty, Fulbright expresses his concern for what the deployment of an ABM system would mean for both U.S. domestic and foreign policies, particularly with the Soviet Union. The senator's analysis is one of six positions presented in the article.

146 "Moral Standards of Governmental Conduct: Materialism a Greater Danger Than Any Enemy Guns." *Vital Speeches of the Day,* 15 April 1951, 386-87. (Excerpts published in *Time,* 9 April 1951, 21, under the title "'Morality Has Become Legality'"; *Life,* 9 April 1951, 42, under the title "Something to Paste in Your Hat"; and *The New Republic,* 9 April 1951, 8, under the title "Where the Law Stops Short"; also published in *The Reader's Digest* 58 [June 1951]: 1-4, under the title "The Moral Threat to America"; *Representative American Speeches: 1951-1952,* edited by A. Craig Baird, 60-65. The Reference Shelf. Vol. 24, No. 3. New York: H.W. Wilson Company, 1952, under the title "Moral Revival in Government"; and *Maturity in Reading: Its Nature and Appraisal,* by William S. Gray and Bernice Rogers, 257-58. Chicago: University of Chicago Press, 1956, under the title "The Moral Threat to America"; quotations from the speech appear on the cover of *The Arkansas Banker* 37 [August 1953], under the title "The Moral Threat to America.")

In a Senate speech inspired by the investigation of the activities of the Reconstruction Finance Corporation, Fulbright discusses his opinions about the current standards of moral and ethical conduct and the implications for the United States in its foreign relations. Reflecting on the reduction of ethical conduct to a concern for upholding the letter of the law but not the spirit, he proposes a commission of prominent Americans to study the problem and make recommendations.

147 "The Most Powerful Country; The Most Populous Country." *Vital Speeches of the Day,* 15 February 1969, 258-62.

In a speech about U.S.-Chinese "relations," the senator questions the soundness of the original assumptions underlining postwar policies toward China. His comments include a discussion of steps to improve relations and encourage China to join the world community. The senator delivered this address before the Japanese-American Parliamentary Group in Santa Barbara, California, in January 1969.

148 "The Most Significant and Important Activity I Have Been Privileged to Engage in During My Years in the Senate." *The Annals of The American Academy of Political and Social Science* 424 (March 1976): 1-5.

The senator discusses the legislation creating the Fulbright scholarships, the influence of Fulbright alumni, and the importance of educational and cultural exchange. He also notes Secretary of State Henry Kissinger's support of the program.

149 "National Goals and National Consensus." In *Education: An Instrument of National Goals: Papers Presented at 1961 Cubberley Conference, School of Education, Stanford University,* edited by Paul R. Hanna, 175-91. New York: McGraw-Hill Book Company, 1962. (Condensed version adapted for *Arkansas Alumnus,* n.s. 15 [October 1961]: 12-14, under the title "An Alumnus Speaks . . . Our National Goal: The Individual.")

In a discussion of the philosophy of national goals, the senator focuses on the special problem involved in defining the national purpose in a democratic society with a value system based on the individual. The second part of his paper concerns the shaping of national consensus and includes a discussion of the role of the president and the university in achieving it. The critical question for the senator is whether the United States can develop new kinds of strategies to meet the challenges of the day while still holding to basic democratic principles and values. The paper was prepared for the 1961 Cubberley Conference at Stanford University.

150 "The Neglect of the Song." In *Representative American Speeches: 1974-1975,* edited by Waldo W. Braden, 109-16. The Reference Shelf. Vol. 47, No. 4. New York: H.W. Wilson Company, 1975. (Slightly condensed version published in *Lithopinion* 10, No. 1, Issue 37 [1975]: 17-19, under the title "'Our Ultimate Defense Against Tyranny.'")

This is a critique of investigative reporting in which the senator expresses concern for the excesses of the press since Vietnam and Watergate. He made the remarks in an address to the National Press Club in Washington on December 18, 1974. For other Fulbright remarks on the media, see the entry titled "Fulbright on the Press" in this chapter.

151 "A New Channel of Communication." *International Educational and Cultural Exchange* 1 (Summer 1965): 3-5.

Fulbright stresses the importance of international education in international relations, particularly its role in bringing about an order based on the concept of community. He made the remarks in Belgrade at the signing of the U.S.-Yugoslav educational exchange agreement in November 1964. For further thoughts on his trip, see his report to the Foreign Relations Committee titled *Yugoslavia, 1964.*

152 "New Debate over Aswan: The Dam That Wasn't Built—What Really Blocked It?" *U.S. News and World Report,* 30 August 1957, 50-51.

The article includes remarks by Fulbright in the Senate on August 14, 1957, regarding the controversy surrounding the State Department's withdrawal of its offer to help Egypt with its Aswan Dam project. Fulbright asserts that the move was a mistake. President Eisenhower and Senator William F. Knowland take issue with his conclusion.

153 "A New Look at an Old Problem: The Two Americas." In *Representative American Speeches: 1965-1966,* edited by Lester Thonssen, 115-41. The Reference Shelf. Vol. 38, No. 4. New York: H.W. Wilson Company, 1966. (Excerpt published in *The Progressive* 30 [June 1966]: 6, under the title "A Kind of Madness"; condensed version in *News Front* 10 [August 1966]: 60-61, under the title "The Two Americas." *News Front* is management's news magazine with a limited circulation to select executives in industry, finance, government, education, and opinion formation. The University of Connecticut at Storrs also published the speech in 1966 under the title "The Two Americas.")

The senator prefaces his remarks about U.S. involvement in Asia and Latin America with a discussion of the conflicting sides of the national character, one finding its expression in democratic humanism, the other in crusading moralism. Asserting that this contradiction accounts for the instability in our foreign relations, he proceeds to examine the ambivalence in our policies toward Vietnam, China, and Latin America and to make suggestions for new directions for policy makers. The senator delivered the remarks at the Ninth Brien McMahon Lecture at the University of Connecticut at Storrs on March 22, 1966.

154 "Now We Are Six." *The Reporter,* 21 April 1955, 7-8.

In a letter to the editor, Fulbright praises the *Reporter* on its sixth anniversary.

155 *Old Myths and New Realities and Other Commentaries.* New York: Random House, 1964.

This is a book of commentaries based primarily on Fulbright addresses from 1964. It is organized around a revised and expanded version of the senator's "Old Myths and New Realities" speech of March 25, 1964 (see Fulbright entry titled "Foreign Policy: Old Myths and New Realities"). The stated purpose of the book is to encourage public examination of long-standing foreign policy beliefs. Other comments concern Fulbright's concept of national security in the nuclear age, a limited détente with the Soviet Union, the Atlantic design for cooperation and community, the impact of the cold war on the domestic front, and nationalism.

156　"Old Myths and New Realities—II: The Middle East." In *The Arab-Israeli Conflict.* Vol. 2, *Readings.* Edited by John Norton Moore, 1038-64. Princeton, N.J.: Princeton University Press in association with the American Society of International Law, 1974. (An abstract of the senator's speech appears in *U.S. News and World Report,* 7 September 1970, 43, under the title "The Fulbright Proposal for Peace in the Mideast"; excerpts in *The New Republic,* 10 October 1970, 20-23, under the title "An Arab-Israeli Settlement: Fulbright's Proposal, and His Colloquy with Senator Ribicoff"; *War/Peace Report* 10 [October 1970]: 14-19, under the title "The Middle East: Old Myths and New Realities; Ribicoff Probes Fulbright's Proposals"; and *The Annals of America.* Vol. 19, *Détente and Domestic Crisis, 1969-1973,* 159-66. Chicago: Encyclopaedia Britannica, 1974, under the title "Old Myths and New Realities in the Middle East.")

In a Senate speech on August 24, 1970, Fulbright examines the mythology underpinning the conflict in the Middle East as well as the perspectives of the major parties: the Israelis, the Arabs, the Russians, and the Americans. His concluding remarks concern an agenda for a negotiated settlement in the Middle East, with the United Nations playing an important role in guaranteeing the peace. He also proposes an additional guarantee to Israel in the form of a bilateral treaty with the United States. The abbreviated versions of the speech in the *New Republic* and *War/Peace Report* conclude with questions by Senator Abraham Ribicoff.

157　Fulbright, J. William, with Paul-Henri Spaak, N.N. Inozemtsev, George F. Kennan, Carlo Schmid, Adam Schaff, Robert Buron, Arnold J. Toynbee, Yevgenyi Zhukov, and Abba Eban. *On Coexistence: An Occasional Paper Resulting from an International Convocation on the Requirements of Peace.* Santa Barbara, Calif.: Center for the Study of Democratic Institutions, [1965]. (The senator's statement is also published in *Peace on Earth: Pacem in Terris,* edited by Edward Reed, 201-4. New York: Pocket Books, 1965.)

Fulbright examines ideologies as a major hindrance to coexistence. The senator made the remarks in February 1965 in New York City, where he participated in the International Convocation on the Requirements of Peace, sponsored by the Center for the Study of Democratic Institutions.

158　"On 'Eisenhower Doctrine'—Fulbright: Dulles Should Tell What Really Went on in Mideast." *U.S. News and World Report,* 1 February 1957, 56-57.

Fulbright calls for a white paper from Secretary of State John Foster Dulles regarding his conduct of U.S. foreign policy in the Middle East. He also urges the Senate to defer consideration of Dulles's Middle East resolution until the policy questions are resolved. The article includes the secretary's response to the Fulbright proposal.

159　"Open Doors, Not Iron Curtains." *The New York Times Magazine,* 5 August 1951, 18, 26.

Fulbright discusses the importance of the Fulbright program in its first five years and notes its effectiveness as a tool in the cold war with the Soviet Union.

160　"Opposing Views by Congressmen on the Question . . . Should the U.S. Reduce Radio Programs to Communist Countries?" *The American Legion Magazine* 93 (September 1972): 32-33.

Fulbright takes the affirmative side of the question, and Congressman Edward J. Derwinski takes the opposing position.

161　"Origins and Aims of the Fulbright Scholarships: A Fortieth Anniversary Retrospect." *The American Oxonian* 73 (Fall 1986), 147-50.

The senator recalls the origins and the aims of the Fulbright educational exchange program in its fortieth year. In a review of the program, he cites the importance of the "multiplier effect" in international education and its possibility of affecting the conduct of international affairs.

162 "Our Foreign Policy." In *Academy Papers: Addresses on the Evangeline Wilbour Blashfield Foundation of the American Academy of Arts and Letters.* Vol. 2, 204-14. New York: American Academy of Arts and Letters, 1951.

Fulbright's remarks concern the Soviet Union in the postwar transitional period, particularly its aggressive policies, and the importance of formulating strategies for restraining the Soviets without alienating them. The paper was presented before the American Academy of Arts and Letters in 1946.

163 "Our Responsibilities in World Affairs: The Role of the Senate." *Vital Speeches of the Day,* 15 June 1959, 527-32.

Fulbright discusses foreign policy issues confronting the United States, focusing on the significance of three forces affecting U.S. policy: nationalism, the technology revolution, and the demand for economic advancement. He argues that more flexible and responsible policies are required to meet those challenges as well as the economic competition from the Soviet Union. His concluding remarks concern the role of the Senate in the development of policy. Fulbright delivered the remarks at the sixth annual Gabriel Silver Lecture at Columbia University on May 7, 1959.

164 "The Outlook for Peace: Sovereignty Must Give Way to Law." *Vital Speeches of the Day,* 1 April 1946, 358-60.

The senator discusses his objections to the establishment of the United Nations Organization on the principle of national sovereignty. He argues, instead, that the organization should be founded on the principle of law. His argument is supported by a critique of passages from Secretary of State James F. Byrnes's speech on the United Nations. He made the remarks before the Canadian Club, Ottawa, on March 5, 1946.

165 "Partners with a Future." *NATO Letter* 11 (February 1963): 7-13.

The senator emphasizes the importance of a partnership between the United States and a united Europe. He discusses the different levels of partnership—economic, political, and military—and advocates the use of existing institutions, particularly NATO, in the development of Western unity. The article is taken from a speech before the Italian Society for International Organization.

166 *The Patriotic and Intelligent Thoughts of Chairman Fulbright, Complete and Unabridged.*

This is a blank booklet presented by the senator to the University of Arkansas Library.

167 "The Patriotism of Dissent." *Redbook Magazine* 128 (November 1966): 44, 47, 49.

Fulbright expands his "patriotism of dissent" theme to include a discussion of the effects of the Vietnam War on domestic life in the United States.

168 "The Peace We Want—A Continuing Peace." *The New York Times Magazine,* 22 July 1945, 5, 28-30. (Also published in *American Foreign Policy Since 1945,* edited by Robert A. Divine, 23-29. Chicago: Quadrangle Books, 1969.)

In an argument for U.S. leadership in the postwar world, the senator discusses the problems associated with the exercise of leadership and the need to develop nonpartisan policies promoting international peace and cooperation. Included is a treatment of the nature of the peace process.

169 "Penrose Memorial Lecture: In Need of a Consensus." *Proceedings of the American Philosophical Society,* 105, No. 4 (1961): 349-53.

In a paper read on April 20, 1961, before the American Philosophical Society, Fulbright examines the elements that make up a national consensus, including a consideration of the concepts of national style and national interest. He also examines the reasons for the failure to achieve a consensus. His remarks conclude with a pessimistic assessment of U.S. society and include an outline of steps required to develop a scale of social and cultural values that harmonize with the issues facing the nation, particularly in foreign affairs. The thesis of the paper is based on a quotation from Erasmus's work, *The Praise of Folly.*

170 *The Pentagon Propaganda Machine.* New York: Liveright, 1970.

This book is an exposé of the public relations apparatus of the Department of Defense and includes an examination of the programs of the Navy; the Army, including its promotion of the ABM; and the Air Force. The senator includes a treatment of the role of the Defense Department in assisting filmmakers, particularly its association with John Wayne's movie, *The Green Berets.* Concluding remarks warn of the dangers of militarism. The book is an expanded version of a series of Fulbright speeches in the Senate in December 1969.

171 "A Plea for Freedom of Expression." *Arkansas Alumnus,* n.s. 8 (March 1955): 8-10. (Condensed versions also published in *Saturday Review,* 12 February 1955, 22, 48, under the title "The Mummification of Opinion"; and *The American Oxonian* 42 [April 1955]: 64-68, under the title "Courage or Conformity?")

Drawing on Alexis de Tocqueville's observations of nineteenth century America, the senator discusses the restraints on freedom of expression and the implications for politicians and for society. He concludes with suggestions for politicians and writers on how to resist the pressures to conform. The remarks were delivered at the National Book Awards dinner in New York on January 25.

172 "A Point of View." *Science* 158, No. 3808 (1967): 1555.

The article is an abridgement of a speech by Fulbright to the Senate on December 13, 1967. He discusses the relationship between the universities and the military-industrial complex and reviews the harmful effects of the affiliation of the university.

173 "The Political Structure of Effective World Organization." In *Organizing for Peace,* 41-51. Washington, D.C.: Graduate School, U.S. Department of Agriculture, 1945.

In a lecture sponsored by the Graduate School of the U.S. Department of Agriculture, the senator discusses the problems associated with organizing and maintaining world peace. He focuses on features of the Dumbarton Oaks plan, including the principle of sovereignty, voting procedures in the Security Council, and the creation of regional and subsidiary organizations.

174 "Position of the United States in the Berlin Crisis: Urgent That Entire World Understand Our Intentions." *Vital Speeches of the Day,* 1 April 1959, 362-63.

In a brief statement in the Senate on March 16, 1959, Fulbright outlines the intentions of the United States regarding its commitment to Berlin and West Germany.

175 "Poultry Industry and the Common Market." *Broiler Industry* 25 (March 1962): 21-22.

The senator discusses the significance of poultry export problems for the industry, primarily those associated with the emerging European Economic Community. He suggests the appointment of an industry representative to advise U.S. government officials during agricultural trade negotiations in Brussels.

176 "Poultry Issue: 'For Good or Evil, A Landmark in Future U.S.-ECC [*sic*] Relations.'" *Broiler Industry* 26 (September 1963): 23-24.

The senator discusses the importance of U.S. poultry export problems with the European Economic Community.

177 Preface to *Sanity and Survival: Psychological Aspects of War and Peace,* by Jerome D. Frank. New York: Random House, 1967.

Fulbright recommends that the principle of community be used as the basis for a new global peace-keeping system in the nuclear age.

178 Preface to "The Fulbright Experience and Academic Exchanges" in *The Annals of The American Academy of Political and Social Science* 491 (May 1987): 10.

In an issue devoted to the Fulbright program, the senator stresses the importance of intercultural education in the nuclear age.

179 "Present-Day American Life: Its Order of Values, and Its Sense of Direction." In *Representative American Speeches: 1958-1959,* edited by A. Craig Baird, 127-32. The Reference Shelf. Vol. 31, No. 3. New York: H.W. Wilson Company, 1959. (Adapted for *The New York Times Magazine*, 14 September 1958, 24, 30-31, under the title "Challenge to Our Complacency.")

In a Senate speech on August 21, 1958, Fulbright presents an analysis of American society in the fifties, identifying its primary characteristic as "its weakness for the easy way." He stresses the importance of educating the public and developing a base of social and cultural values that harmonize with the issues and decisions facing the United States, particularly in foreign affairs.

180 "President Describes the University's Role." *Arkansas Alumnus* 17 (January 1940): 4-6.

Describing the university's role, Fulbright asserts that an important duty is the education of the people about their government, particularly through the social sciences, for leadership and citizenship. The remarks were made at the University of Tulsa on January 12, 1940, when he was president of the University of Arkansas.

181 "President's Statement." *University of Arkansas Bulletin* 34, No. 15 (1940): 1-6. (Excerpts published in *Arkansas Alumnus* 18 [January 1941]: 5-6, under the title "University News: University Needs.")

In a statement from his first report for the governor and for the University of Arkansas Board of Trustees, Fulbright describes the university's progress and outlines its most pressing needs in the areas of faculty maintenance and development, agricultural research, research funds for the College of Business Administration, and construction of dormitories.

182 "Press and Politicians." In *Public Speaking as Dialogue: Readings and Essays,* comp. by Jon L. Ericson and Robert F. Forston, 159-60. Dubuque, Iowa: Kendall/Hunt Publishing Company, 1970.

Responding to press coverage of his "arrogance of power" speeches, the senator claims that reporters misinterpreted him and disregarded his themes in favor of secondary remarks. He made the remarks to the National Press Club in Washington on May 17, 1966.

183 "The Price of Empire." *The North American Review,* n.s. 4, No. 6 (1967): 12-18. (First published in *The New York Times Magazine,* 20 August 1967, 30-31, 88, 90, 92-93, 95-96, under the title "Says Senator Fulbright, The Great Society Is a Sick Society"; excerpts in *U.S. News and World Report,* 21 August 1967, 16, under the title "Is the 'Great Society' Now a 'Sick Society'?"; full text in *Vital Speeches of the Day,* 1 September 1967, 678-82, under the title "The Price of Empire: Traditional Values"; excerpts in *Current,* No. 88 [1967]: 39-43, under the title "The Uses of U.S. Power: What Are the Priorities?"; full text in *Man Against Poverty: World War III: A Reader on the World's Most Crucial Issue,* edited by Arthur I. Blaustein and Roger R. Woock, 4-15. New York: Random House, 1968; abbreviated version in *America in the Cold War: Twenty Years of Revolutions and Response, 1947-1967,* edited by Walter LaFeber, 10-15. Problems in American History, edited by Loren Baritz. New York: John Wiley and Sons, 1969, under the title "The Great Society Is a Sick Society [August 8, 1967]"; full text in *War: An Anthology,* edited by Edward and Elizabeth Huberman, 80-91. New York: Washington Square Press, 1969.)

Asserting that the United States is waging two wars, one in Vietnam and the other in the streets of U.S. cities, the senator explains the connection between the two in terms of their impact on traditional democratic values and on U.S. society. Included also is an examination of the philosophy underlying the dissent from the war. He concludes with an expression of faith in the spirit of the younger generation and their message that "the price of empire is America's soul, and that price is too high." The remarks were made before the American Bar Association in Honolulu on August 8, 1967.

184 Fulbright, J. William, with Seth P. Tillman. *The Price of Empire.* New York: Pantheon Books, 1989.

The senator collaborated with long-time aide Seth P. Tillman on this collection of critical essays regarding the role of the United States in the postwar world. Topics of analysis include U.S.-Soviet relations, the U.S. constitutional and electoral systems, the escalation of the Vietnam War and Fulbright's break with Johnson, the role of the Israeli lobby in Middle East policy, the effects of the military on the economy, and U.S. postwar interventionism. They conclude with a consideration of two interests from the early years: the United Nations and the educational exchange program. Dr. Tillman, former member of the professional staff of the Senate Foreign Relations Committee, is research professor of diplomacy at Georgetown University. For an article inspired by *The Price of Empire,* see Gaddis Smith's "Reflections of a Conservative Optimist" in the February 19, 1989, issue of the *New York Times Book Review.*

185 "The Price of Peace Is the Loss of Prejudices." *Vogue,* 1 July 1945, 80-81. (Adapted for *Arkansas Baptist,* 27 September 1945, 7, under the title "Prejudices Must Go . . . Prerequisites for Peace"; and *The Chaplain* 2, No. 11 [1945]: 2-4, under the title "Prejudices and the Peace"; abbreviated version reprinted in *Assignments in Exposition,* edited by Louise E. Rorabacher, 194-203. New York: Harper and Brothers, Publishers, 1946.)

The senator advocates a foreign policy based on collective security. He discusses the adjustments required for the United States to assume a constructive postwar international role and includes arguments for overcoming fears and prejudices, specifically those regarding the Russians and the British. The article is drawn primarily from Fulbright's maiden speech in the Senate on March 28, 1945.

186 Fulbright, J. William, et al. "Prospects for Peace." *Newsweek,* 11 September 1978, 41-43.

Five Middle Eastern observers evaluate the prospects for a peace settlement. Fulbright advocates guarantees by the United Nations Security Council of an Arab-Israeli peace agreement and an additional guarantee to Israel in the form of a bilateral treaty insuring its territorial integrity.

187 Fulbright, J. William, et al. *Prospects for Peace in the Middle East.* Washington, D.C.: American Enterprise Institute for Public Policy Research, 1977.

In a forum on the outlook for a negotiated settlement of the Arab-Israeli conflict, the senator urges the United States to take advantage of the moment and press for a peace conference. His primary focus is on U.S. policy objectives in the Middle East and the impact of the crisis on our national interests. Other participants were George Ball, Rita Hauser, Jacob Javits, and moderator Joseph J. Sisco.

188 *Prospects for the West.* Cambridge, Mass.: Harvard University Press, 1963.

The essays in this book are based primarily on the senator's William L. Clayton Lectures at the Fletcher School of Law and Diplomacy, Tufts University, Medford, Massachusetts, in the spring of 1963. His principal focus is on ways in which the United States and the West can strengthen their societies and their ties with each other. Topics of analysis include the challenge posed by the Soviet Union; the concept of an Atlantic partnership; and the problems confronting U.S. society, particularly those associated with unemployment, education, race relations, cities, and foreign policy. For annotations of the three Fulbright lectures, see the entries titled "Russia and the West," "A Concert of Free Nations," and "The American Agenda."

189 "The Prospectus: A Community of Nations, Not a Superstate." *The New York Times Book Review,* 17 June 1962, 3.

The senator reviews Joseph Kraft's *Grand Design: From Common Market to Atlantic Partnership,* a book that explores the possibilities of closer economic, political, and military cooperation between the United States and Europe. Kraft's ideas harmonize with those of the senator, a long-standing advocate of European unity and Atlantic partnership.

190 "Public Policy and Military Responsibility." *Social Action* 28, No. 6 (1962): 17-21. (Excerpts published in *U.S. News and World Report,* 4 September 1961, 80-82, under the title "Military's Role in Fighting Communism—A Growing Debate.")

This is a speech at the opening session of the National War College and the Industrial College of the Armed Forces on August 21, 1961, in which Fulbright talks about the problems associated with separating military issues from political issues in the development of national policies. The main topic is his memorandum to the president and the secretary of defense concerning the military's role in public education programs on issues related to the cold war. He concludes with some considerations of military and political life which require the subordination of the military to civilian control.

191 "A Quarter-Century of Educational Exchange: Values and Future Perspectives." *School and Society* 100 (Summer 1972): 298-300.

In an article commemorating the twenty-fifth anniversary of the Fulbright Act, the senator looks back at the predecessors of the program bearing his name—the visit of Cuban teachers to Harvard in 1900, the Boxer indemnity, and the beginnings of a cultural exchange program with Latin America in 1938—and reflects on the "almost accidental character" of international exchanges in the United States. He discusses the Fulbright program, including the legislation underpinning the program; its special features, particularly the Board of Foreign Scholarships and the binational commissions; and the difficulty of evaluating the program in statistical terms.

192 "The Question of Encouraging Expansion of Trade with the Red-Bloc Nations at the Present Time." *Congressional Digest* 43 (February 1964): 50, 52.

This is an excerpt from the senator's testimony before the Senate Banking and Currency Committee on November 21, 1963, on S. 2310, a bill banning the U.S. government from guaranteeing the credit of communist countries. Fulbright argues that trade is one way that the United States can improve relations with the Soviet Union.

193 "Reflections: In Thrall to Fear." *The New Yorker,* 8 January 1972, 41-46, 48-62. (Abbreviated version published in *Détente and Defense: A Reader,* edited by Robert J. Pranger, 18-40. Washington, D.C.: American Enterprise Institute for Public Policy Research, 1976, under the title "In Thrall to Fear.")

In an examination of the Truman Doctrine, the senator discusses its origin and the influence of its philosophy in shaping postwar policy. He questions its subsequent application in our relations with the communist world, stressing the long-term impact on U.S. policies, particularly in Vietnam. He also examines how and why the United Nations succumbed to the cold warfare of the postwar period. Seeing Vietnam as a "watershed" in our history, he calls for a return to the original principles of the United Nations Charter and its brand of internationalism. The article is excerpted from Fulbright's book, *The Crippled Giant: American Foreign Policy and Its Domestic Consequences.*

194 "Region's Leaders Call for Construction of Beaver Dam." *The Ozarks Mountaineer* 3 (February 1955): 2.

This article includes a statement by the senator in which he makes a case for Beaver Dam and pledges his efforts to secure appropriations for its construction.

195 "A Report on Aspects of the London Conference." *Education for Victory,* 3 June 1944, 3-4, 16.

In an address broadcast over CBS, the senator reports on the Allied Ministers of Education Conference in London, specifically issues related to educational reconstruction of war-torn countries. He also discusses the importance of creating a postwar international organization for keeping the peace. Fulbright was chairman of the American delegation sent to London in the spring of 1944 by Secretary of State Cordell Hull to devise plans for the postwar educational and cultural restoration of Europe.

196 "Research Backlash." *Aviation Week and Space Technology,* 30 August 1965, 17.

This is an editorial in which the senator uses Project Camelot, an Army study of revolutionary movements in Chile, as a springboard to question the entire program of government research.

197 "Revolution in Latin America." In *Readings in American Foreign Policy.* 2d ed., edited by Robert A. Goldwin and revised by Harry M. Clor, 238-43. New York: Oxford University Press, 1971.

The senator examines the reluctance of the United States to support the forces of political and social reform in Latin America and the manifestations of its anti-revolutionary bias in the intervention in the Dominican Republic in 1965. The remarks are excerpted from his book, *The Arrogance of Power.*

198   Fulbright, J. William, and John C. Stennis. *The Role of Congress in Foreign Policy*. Rational Debate Seminars. Washington, D.C.: American Enterprise Institute for Public Policy Research, 1971.

Fulbright discusses the constitutional imbalance between the legislative and executive branches and the importance of restoring congressional prerogatives in the foreign affairs realm, particularly those regarding war and treaty powers. His remarks are part of the record of an American Enterprise Institute's Rational Debate Seminar on the question of the effectiveness of congressional participation in the foreign policy process. Senator John C. Stennis argues that Congress has an important policy role.

199   "The Role of the Peace Pact." In *Toward a Permanent Peace: A Symposium by J. William Fulbright*, et al., 9-11. [New York]: American Nobel Center, [1945].

This is a compilation of addresses and comments by participants in a symposium marking the forty-eighth anniversary of Alfred Nobel's death and includes Fulbright remarks promoting a postwar international peace-keeping organization.

200   "Russia and the West." Parts 1, 2. *Foreign Service Journal* 40 (October, November 1963): 23-25, 28-29.

In an examination of the practice of communism under Stalin and Khrushchev, the senator discusses the nature of the challenge posed by the Soviet Union and the development of policies designed to strengthen Western societies. Stressing the changes on the Soviet foreign and domestic fronts, Fulbright asserts that the "operating strategy" of the communists, not their "theoretical objectives," should be the concern of U.S. policy makers. His concluding remarks regard a course of action in which the United States and its allies can promote Soviet moderation. The article is an excerpt from the first of the senator's three William L. Clayton Lectures on April 29 at the Fletcher School of Law and Diplomacy, Tufts University. Harvard University Press published the lectures in 1963 in a book titled *Prospects for the West*.

201   Fulbright, J. William, Henry M. Jackson, and Alan Cranston. "SALT Accords Debate." In *Détente and Defense: A Reader*, edited by Robert J. Pranger, 363-76. Washington, D.C.: American Enterprise Institute for Public Policy Research, 1976.

In Senate debate on August 14 and September 7, 1972, Senator Henry M. Jackson defends his proposed formula for achieving balance between the United States and the Soviet Union in the realm of intercontinental strategic forces. Fulbright disagrees with Jackson's concept of nuclear parity, arguing that his formula does not take into account "forward bases" outside the United States.

202   "The Search for National Purpose: The Assault on Private Luxury." *Current*, No. 1 (1960): 7.

This is a short statement from the *Congressional Record* of March 5, 1960, in which the senator calls for strengthening the public sector of the economy in order to effectively compete with the Soviet Union.

203   "The Senate and the Peace." *The New Republic*, 6 March 1944, 322-23.

In a review of Kenneth Colegrove's *American Senate and World Peace*, Fulbright agrees with the author's proposal for changing the Constitution from a two-thirds to a simple majority requirement for congressional approval of treaties.

204   "Senate Bill Proposes Revamping U.S. Military Aid Program." *Defense Management Journal* 9 (October 1973): 35-37, 62.

Blaming overextension abroad for financial trouble at home, the senator explains the provisions of Senate Bill 1443 to revise the Foreign Military Aid and Sales Program. He notes the objective of returning arms sales transactions to the private sector. The article is adapted from Fulbright's introductory remarks in the Senate on April 3, 1973.

205   "Senator Fulbright Addresses Bankers." *The Arkansas Banker* 57 (June 1973): 24, 56.

In an address to the eighty-third annual convention of the Arkansas Bankers Association, Fulbright talks about a number of topics, including the national budget, Israel and the energy crisis, dollar devaluation, and trade relations with China and the Soviet Union.

206   "Senator Fulbright Discusses Middle-East Crisis." *The Ozarks Mountaineer* 6 (August 1958): 15.

This is a critique of the Eisenhower administration's foreign policy in the Middle East, particularly the strategy of basing policies primarily on military considerations.

207   "Senator Fulbright on Federal Aid." *The Journalette of Arkansas Education* 4, No. 7 (1948): [1-2].

Fulbright predicts that the measure concerning federal aid for education will pass the Congress.

208   "Senator Fulbright on Senator Goldwater." *War/Peace Report* 4 (September 1964): 7-9. (Adapted version also published in *Saturday Review,* 24 October 1964, 24-25, 71, under the title "Dangerous Delusions: A Note on Senator Goldwater.")

Fulbright analyzes Barry Goldwater's foreign policy views in a Senate speech on September 8, 1964. Calling the leaders of the Republican party "angry dissenters against the present," he warns of the dangers in the Republicans' proposed radical change in U.S. foreign policy. Fulbright compares Goldwater Republicanism with Russian Stalinism, noting the devotion of each to its ideology: the Goldwaterites to their singular concept of freedom and the Stalinists to communism. In an insert on page 9, Goldwater takes considerable exception to Fulbright's remarks.

209   "Senator Fulbright—One of Our Best Salesmen Because . . . Arkansas Does Big Business Overseas." *The Arkansas Union Farmer* 39 (July 1962): 6.

Fulbright argues for trade legislation which will benefit the farmer, especially in Arkansas, and pledges to support efforts to expand foreign markets.

210   "Senator Fulbright Presents Merits of Beaver Dam." *The Ozarks Mountaineer* 7 (February 1959): 2.

The senator discusses the benefits which will accrue to the Ozarks region from the completion of Beaver Dam.

211   "Senator Fulbright Speaks Before the Subcommittee on Education of the Senate Committee on Labor and Public Welfare." *The Journal of Arkansas Education* 33 (April 1961): 8-9, 25.

This is a statement in which the senator discusses his views on education in a democracy and his support of legislation providing for federal assistance.

212   "Senator J.W. Fulbright Calls for a New Approach to the Latin American Policy of the United States, May 9, 1961." In *What Happened in Cuba? A Documentary History,* edited by Robert F. Smith, 335-37. New York: Twayne Publishers, 1963.

During debate on the Inter-American Social and Economic Cooperation Program, the senator challenges the United States to put its relationship with Latin America on a new level by beginning a program of assistance that will encourage social and economic development for the people.

213 "Senator J. William Fulbright Remembers Edward Durell Stone." *Dimensions* 5, No. 2 (1969): 9.

The senator recalls the story of Stone's winning first prize in a birdhouse competition sponsored by the Fulbright family's newspaper, the *Fayetteville Democrat. Dimensions* is a publication of the Arkansas Chapter of the American Institute of Architects.

214 "Senator J. William Fulbright's Remarks on the Concept of Total Victory, July 24, 1961." In *Ideas and Diplomacy: Readings in the Intellectual Tradition of American Foreign Policy,* edited by Norman A. Graebner, 849-52. New York: Oxford University Press, 1964. (Abridged version in *Dialogue* 2 [November 1961]: 7, under the title "Another View . . . Our Means and Our Ends.")

Fulbright prefaces his response to Barry Goldwater's July 13 speech with a series of questions about the nature and consequences of a "total victory" in the struggle between the United States and the Soviet Union. He further challenges Goldwater's argument with a discussion of his position on intervention and his concept of a clearly defined foreign policy operating on other levels besides the military.

215 "Senator James W. Fulbright Responds to an Introduction." In *The Toastmaster's Handbook,* by Herbert V. Prochnow, 122. New York: Prentice-Hall, 1949.

The senator responds to a generous introduction with an Arkansas farmer story.

216 "The Session in Retrospect." *Inter-Parliamentary Bulletin* 37, No. 4 (1957): 149-51.

In order to increase understanding and participation, Fulbright suggests changes in the conference format for sessions associated with major world issues.

217 "Should Congress Give Authority to the War Labor Board to Enforce Its Own Decisions?" *The United States News,* 16 February 1945, 30, 32.

Fulbright replies that the War Labor Board should have the power to enforce its orders as long as an appeal process is available.

218 "Should Congress Re-enact the Vetoed Douglas Bill for New Federal Aid to Depressed Areas?" *Congressional Digest* 38 (February 1959): 49, 51, 53.

Speaking in the Senate on May 13, 1958, on the proposed Area Redevelopment Act, Fulbright objects to provisions of the bill concerning criteria for development assistance. The bill was reported out of Fulbright's Banking and Currency Committee without his concurrence.

219 "Should Congress Remove All Major Restrictions on Margarine?" *Congressional Digest* 28 (May 1949): 142, 144.

In a Senate speech on January 5, 1949, Fulbright calls for the repeal of license fees and taxes on margarine.

220 "Should Hawaii and Alaska Be Given a Commonwealth Status Now?" *Congressional Digest* 33 (June-July 1954): 191.

Participating in a debate in the Senate on March 29, 1954, the senator states his opposition to statehood for Hawaii. He was cosponsor of an amendment to grant commonwealth status to the islands.

221 "Should Present Military Assistance Programs of U.S. Foreign Aid Be Substantially Curtailed?" *Congressional Digest* 52 (March 1973): 76, 78, 80.

Fulbright's comments during the Senate floor debate of September 25, 1972, concern the House-passed version of the foreign aid program for Fiscal 1973. The senator declares his opposition to the Scott amendment proposing an increase in the military assistance component of the aid bill.

222 "Should Present Senate Rules to Limit Debate Be Retained?" *Congressional Digest* 36 (February 1957): 54, 56.

This is an excerpt from the floor debate in the Senate on January 4, 1957, in which Fulbright argues that changing the rules of the Senate, particularly Rule 22, would destroy its power and effectiveness.

223 "Should State Poll Tax Laws as Applied to Federal Elections Be Uniformly Abolished?" *Congressional Digest* 41 (May 1962): 141, 143, 145, 147.

Fulbright's remarks in the Senate on March 22, 1962, pertain to the proposed constitutional amendment to abolish the poll tax. Citing Section 2, Article I of the Constitution regarding the establishment of voter qualifications by the states, he defends the poll tax in Arkansas and four New England states.

224 "Should the Administration's Foreign Aid Proposal for Fiscal Year 1967 Be Substantially Curtailed?" *Congressional Digest* 45 (August-September 1966): 204, 206, 208.

The senator discusses the foreign aid program, focusing on the efforts of the Foreign Relations Committee to effect changes in the economic assistance component. He also explains his reasons for continuing to authorize the program on an annual basis.

225 "Should the $500 Million Authorization for Latin American Economic Aid Be Appropriated?" *Congressional Digest* 40 (February 1961): 50, 52.

Fulbright's comments in the Senate on August 19, 1960, during the debate on S. 3839 concern the authorization of funds for social development programs in Latin America. Emphasizing the importance of planning by the United States and the Latin American countries, he outlines the guidelines for preparation of the aid program.

226 "Should the Reconstruction Finance Corporation Be Abolished?" *Congressional Digest* 32 (April 1953): 107, 109, 111, 113.

In an address given during debate in the Senate on the fate of the Reconstruction Finance Corporation, the senator expresses opposition to the Byrd bill, a measure proposing the abolition of certain functions of the RFC and the assignment of the remaining production and lending functions to another agency. Fulbright argues that the new legislation does not provide an organizational apparatus that would promote efficient operation of the remaining functions.

227 "Should the State Electoral Vote Be Cast in Ratio to Its Popular Vote?" *Congressional Digest* 32 (August-September 1953): 210, 212.

In an address in the Senate on January 31, 1950, the senator expresses support for Senate Joint Resolution 2, a measure that would reduce the power exercised by minority parties on elections.

228 "Should the Treaty Authority of the U.S. Senate Be Curtailed?" *Congressional Digest* 22 (October 1943): 242.

The freshman congressman speaks in behalf of his proposal, House Concurrent Resolution 25, calling for U.S. participation in a postwar international peace-keeping organization. He made the remarks on September 20, 1943, one day before the House passed the resolution by a vote of 360-29.

229 "Should U.S. Aid for Mutual Security Be Curtailed?" *Congressional Digest* 39 (June-July 1960): 179, 181, 183.

Reviewing some of the arguments surrounding the mutual security bill, the senator calls for support of the program despite its shortcomings.

230 "The Significance of SALT." In *In Search of Peace,* edited by Waris Shere, 6-22. Hauppauge, N.Y.: Exposition Press, 1980. (First published in *AEI Defense Review* 2, No. 4 [1978]: 2-14.)

The senator examines the reasons for misperceptions underlying U.S. attitudes toward the Soviet Union in a discussion of the cold war and the détente schools of thought regarding the Russians. In an argument for the détente approach, he asserts that the prospects for improved relations with the Soviet Union, including ratification of SALT II, turn on changing preconceptions on both sides. His remarks include an assessment of the practice of "linkage" in U.S. foreign policy, in both its negative and positive approaches.

231 "The Situation in the Dominican Republic: Compliance with the Law." *Vital Speeches of the Day,* 1 October 1965, 747-55. (Condensed versions published in *Concern,* 1 November 1965, 4-6, 14, under the title "Dominican Republic: Ambiguous Action"; *Congressional Digest* 44 [November 1965]: 269, 271, 273, 275, 277, under the title "Debate over the Soundness of the U.S. Action in the Dominican Republic"; and *Current,* No. 65 [1965]: 37-42, under the title "Making Foreign Policy: The Role of Advice and Dissent"; an interview with Fulbright by Chalmers M. Roberts and remarks by Marquis Childs follow the senator's speech. Abridged version in *America in the Cold War: Twenty Years of Revolutions and Response, 1947-1967,* edited by Walter LaFeber, 165-70. Problems in American History, edited by Loren Baritz. New York: John Wiley and Sons, 1969, under the title "Intervention in Santo Domingo: We Are Much Closer to Being the Most Unrevolutionary Nation on Earth [September 15, 1965]"; full text in *The Dynamics of World Power: A Documentary History of United States Foreign Policy, 1945-1973,* edited by Arthur M. Schlesinger, Jr. Vol. 3, *Latin America.* Edited by Robert Burr, 658-74. New York: Chelsea House Publishers in association with McGraw-Hill Book Company, 1973, under the title "Critique by Senator William J. [*sic*] Fullbright [*sic*], Before the Senate, on United States Policy in the Dominican Republic.")

In a critique of U.S. intervention in the Dominican Republic, Fulbright outlines his conclusions, based on Foreign Relations Committee hearings, concerning the April 1965 crisis in Santo Domingo. He also examines the reluctance of the United States to support the forces of social and political reform in Latin America and the implications for future relations. Contrary to popularly held notions about the United States being a revolutionary nation, we are, he notes, "much closer to being the most unrevolutionary nation on earth." These remarks in the Senate on September 15, 1965, precipitated his break with President Johnson.

232 "The Social Sciences and the Law." *New York University Law Review* 27, No. 1 (1952): 101-4.

The senator stresses the importance of an education in the social sciences and the law in the preparation of people for careers in politics. His remarks relate to his experiences in Congress and include a discussion of ways in which social scientists can contribute to the preparation of the United States for its international leadership role. Fulbright made the remarks as a participant in a panel discussion during a symposium at New York University on "The Relation Between General Education and Law School Training in the Preparation of a Lawyer."

233 "Some Official Proposals." *A Center Occasional Paper* 1 (June 1968): 28-35.

This paper of the Center for the Study of Democratic Institutions consists of a selection of statements on the resolution of the Vietnam War, including Fulbright's eight-point peace proposal for Vietnam.

234 "The South: The Nation's New Economic Frontier." *Arkansas Alumnus,* n.s. 9 (July 1956): 26-29.

Fulbright discusses the reasons for the growth of the southern economy, citing the preliminary findings of a study by the Senate Banking and Currency Committee. He made the remarks in the Senate on April 19, 1956, when he was chairman of the committee.

235 "Sovereignty and the Charter." *The New Republic,* 6 August 1945, 158-59.

Fulbright discusses his reservations about the principle of national sovereignty in Article Two of the United Nations Charter.

236 "Space and National Priorities: Space Exploration or Elevation." *Vital Speeches of the Day,* 1 November 1963, 41-44. (Also published in *The Progressive* 27 [December 1963]: 12-15, under the title "A Time to Choose.")

In a Senate speech on October 17, 1963, Fulbright refutes the arguments supporting Project Apollo and presents his case for curtailing the program. He charges Congress with the responsibility of ordering their priorities regarding important domestic programs, particularly education and employment.

237 "Speaking Out: Let's Talk Sense About Cuba." *The Saturday Evening Post,* 16 May 1964, 8, 10.

Fulbright answers criticisms of his speech in the Senate on March 25, 1964, examining the "myths" that support U.S. foreign policy. In a cogent defense, he further discusses his ideas about Cuba and examines the issues associated with the Western Alliance, including an assessment of Charles de Gaulle's ideas regarding organization of the European community.

238 "Speaking Out: We Must Negotiate Peace in Vietnam." *The Saturday Evening Post,* 9 April 1966, 10, 12, 14.

Fulbright outlines the steps for a compromise settlement in Vietnam. He also addresses the issue of China and recommends measures to encourage its return to the world community.

239 Statement in *Fulbright Alumni Association Directory 1989.* White Plains, N.Y.: Bernard C. Harris Publishing Company, 1989.

In selected remarks from his commencement address at Johns Hopkins University on May 26, 1988, Fulbright discusses the importance of educational exchange. He cites the importance of the "multiplier effect" in international education and its possibility of affecting the conduct of nations.

240 Statement in *Fulbright Painters.* N.p., n.d.

This is a catalogue of a traveling exhibition organized by the Smithsonian Institution, with the assistance of the Institute of International Education, commemorating the tenth anniversary of the Fulbright program in 1958. The senator acknowledges the universality of the artist's language as an important means of promoting mutual understanding. He sponsored the exhibition.

241 "'The Synthesis of Both Liberty and Unity': Some Aspects of Our Foreign Policy." *Vital Speeches of the Day,* 1 October 1960, 739-42.

Declaring that our foreign policy is "the summation of all our policy," the senator notes the problems facing the United States and the free world and discusses the requirements for winning the cold war. Recognizing the problems associated with achieving unity among the Western allies, he concludes with a quotation from Salvador de Madariaga. The remarks were made before a School of Banking seminar at the University of Wisconsin in Madison on August 23, 1960.

242 "Testimony of Senator J. William Fulbright (Ark.), Chairman of Committee." In *The Dynamics of World Power: A Documentary History of United States Foreign Policy, 1945-1973,* edited by Arthur M. Schlesinger, Jr. Vol. 4, *The Far East.* Edited by Russell Buhite, 524-26. New York: Chelsea House Publishers in association with McGraw-Hill Book Company, 1973.

This is an extract from the testimony of Fulbright on March 11, 1968, regarding the Vietnam War during hearings before the Senate Foreign Relations Committee on the Foreign Assistance Act of 1968.

243 "To Enlarge and Strengthen Exchanges." In *The Arts and Exchange of Persons,* 21-23. Report of a Conference on the Arts and Exchange of Persons at the Institute of International Education, New York City, October 1956.

Fulbright maintains that the exchange of persons in education and the arts can affect the course of international relations.

244 "Toward a More Creative Foreign Policy." *The Progressive* 23 (November 1959): 20-23. (Overbrook Press, Stamford, Connecticut, reprinted the speech in pamphlet form in December 1959.)

Asserting that "diplomatic style is necessarily a reflection of national style," the senator proceeds to discuss the requirements of an effective foreign policy, beginning with a well informed, educated electorate. Other issues examined by the senator include the national security program and the economic federation of the United States and its allies.

245 "Toward a World Community." *War/Peace Report* 5 (May 1965): 3-7.

The senator discusses the problems associated with building an international community, focusing on the psychological aspect rather than the organizational. He outlines a program promoting "practical cooperation," particularly with the communist world, and includes such projects as multilateralism in foreign aid, expansion of international trade, joint business undertakings, settlement of financial claims, and educational and cultural exchange.

246 "Transportation: A National Problem." *TAB* 37 (October 1968): 5.

In an article in the monthly publication of the Arkansas Bus and Truck Association, the senator expresses concern for the deteriorating transportation problems in the cities and the lack of adequate roads to rural areas.

247 "Tribute to Robert A. Leflar." *Arkansas Law Review* 25, Nos. 1 and 2, Part 1 (1971): 70.

Fulbright honors University of Arkansas Professor Robert A. Leflar for his contributions to the state as educator and jurist.

248 "Twenty-five Years Old." *Action* 1 (March 1945): 4.

This is a congratulatory message from Fulbright on the silver anniversary of the National League of Women Voters.

249 "2,000 U.S. Bases Overseas—Another Target in Congress." *U.S. News and World Report,* 21 June 1971, 35.

In this excerpt from Fulbright's Senate speech of May 18, 1971, he cites statistics related to the size and cost of the U.S. military bureaucracy overseas. The remarks are an insert in an article entitled "The Real Problem—How to Cut Defense Billions: Inflation vs. Military Security," which begins on page 30.

250 "The United States and Responsibilities of Power." *Journal of Historical Studies* 1, No. 3 (1968): 240-42.

Fulbright takes issue with the views of the political "realists" that the primary function of large nations is to engage in power politics. Rejecting their doctrine of determinism, he argues that the country does have choices and should be concerned with the force of the U.S. example in the world.

251 "United States Foreign Policy: Recent Events and Continuing Problems." *Vital Speeches of the Day,* 1 August 1961, 616-19. (Also published in *Concern,* 15 August 1961, 8-10, 13, under the title "Recent Events, Continuing Problems"; condensed version in *Foreign Service Journal* 38 [August 1961]: 26, 34, 52, under the title "Reflections on Recent Events.")

Fulbright discusses the importance of policy and national style in our relations with other nations, particularly in the conflict with the communist countries, stressing the importance of not succumbing to their methods. He assesses our policy in Laos, our role in Vietnam, and the situation in Cuba and includes an outline of measures to strengthen U.S.-Latin American relations.

252 "A United States of Europe?" *The Annals of The American Academy of Political and Social Science* 257 (May 1948): 151-56.

Drawing on thoughts expressed in his Marfleet Lectures as the University of Toronto, Fulbright advocates the federation of Europe and suggests that the United States incorporate political unification as an integral part of the European Recovery Program. He argues that the obstacles to a united Europe are manageable and cites examples of unification and cooperation, along with attendant difficulties, from early U.S. history.

253 "United States Senators Speak Out for Religious Liberty." *Liberty* 56 (July-August 1961): 9-10.

Five senators, including Fulbright, make statements supporting religious freedom. The other senators are Kenneth B. Keating, Francis Case, Strom Thurmond, and Frank Church.

254 "The University and American Foreign Policy." *VISTA* 2, No. 5 (1967): 2-9, 51-54. (First published in *Center Diary: 12,* May-June 1966, 1-9; reprinted in *The Center Magazine* 5 [November-December 1972]: 34-38, under the title "Second Edition: University and Foreign Policy.")

Stressing that "the highest function of higher education is the 'teaching of things in perspective,'" the senator outlines the responsibilities of the university. His focus is on ways in which scholars can contribute constructively in the consideration of policy problems and in the search for peace. He also examines the harmful effects of a close government-university affiliation on teaching and learning. The senator made the remarks on May 10, 1966, in Los Angeles before a convocation of the Center for the Study of Democratic Institutions on "The University in America."

255 Untitled. *American Vocational Journal* 28 (February 1953): 4.

In a guest editorial, Fulbright discusses the need for additional vocational training to meet the demands of industry.

256 Untitled. *The Coupon,* No. 71 (1945): 2-12.

In a foreign policy address before the Bond Club of New York on December 11, 1944, Fulbright argues that prospects for postwar international security lie in pursuing a policy of collective action.

257 Untitled. In *The United States and International Educational Exchanges: Eighth Annual Conference of the National Association of Foreign Student Advisers,* 16-20. New York: National Association of Foreign Student Advisers, New York University, [1956].

Fulbright discusses the purpose of the educational exchange program and offers suggestions for funding it.

258 "The U.S. Is Not Out of This World." *Brandon's Shipper and Forwarder,* 14 November 1960, 9, 30.

Fulbright examines the reluctance of the United States to take up the role of leadership in the world, focusing on the pressure of special interest groups on national policy, particularly on international trade. He also expresses concern about the reemergence of protectionist trade policies in Europe, mainly regarding poultry products, and the role of special interests on both sides of the Atlantic in the trend. The senator wrote the article for the weekly journal of the United Forwarding Industry.

259 "The Uses of Flexibility." *Saturday Review,* 8 May 1965, 19-21, 75. (Selections from the lecture also published in *Concern,* 15 June 1965, 9-11, 14, under the title "Ideology and Foreign Policy"; and *Current,* No. 61 [1965]: 15-18, under the title "A New U.S. Foreign Policy? Can It Be Less Ideological?")

Asserting that Americans are not entirely free of "doctrine and dogma," the senator examines the presence of Puritanism as a force in our national character and history. He also examines ideology as a hindrance to an effective foreign policy and recommends policies of "cautious accommodation" in the areas of trade, educational and cultural exchange, and cooperative projects, among others. The article is adapted from a lecture at Johns Hopkins University on March 12, 1965.

260 "Vietnam: A Holding Action." *Vital Speeches of the Day,* 1 July 1965, 546-48.

In a speech on June 15, 1965, Fulbright calls for a negotiated settlement of the Vietnam War. He also comments on nationalism as a force in Southeast Asia and the emerging nations and the nature of its relationship to communism.

261 "Vietnam Debate: Dirksen vs. Fulbright." *The New Leader,* 23 October 1967, 9-19.

This is an adaptation of a confrontation between Senators Fulbright and Everett

McKinley Dirksen in the Senate on October 3, 1967, regarding U.S. military involvement in Vietnam. Major points of disagreement include whether U.S. security is an issue and whether our Vietnam policy is in the national interest. Other points of contention are the objective of the war, the role of the United Nations in effecting a settlement, criticism of administration policy during wartime, and treaty commitments to South Vietnam.

262 *The Vietnam Hearings with an Introduction by J. William Fulbright.* New York: Random House, Vintage Books, 1966.

Fulbright introduces a collection of statements and excerpts from the testimony of Dean Rusk, James M. Gavin, George F. Kennan, and Maxwell D. Taylor before the Senate Foreign Relations Committee hearings on the Vietnam War in January and February of 1966. His remarks note the significance of the hearings for the nation.

263 "Vietnam Policy—Debate on the Floor of the Senate." *Congressional Digest* 45 (April 1966): 119-21.

Fulbright's remarks in the Senate on March 1, 1966, are part of a debate over supplemental military appropriations for the war in Southeast Asia. Calling for a policy of accommodation, the senator outlines a program for resolving the conflict between China and the United States by means of a neutralization agreement for the region.

264 "Vietnam: The Crucial Issue." *The Progressive* 34 (February 1970): 16-18.

Fulbright responds to President Nixon's November 3, 1969, address on the Vietnam War. He critiques the Nixon strategy in Vietnam, particularly the role of the Thieu-Ky government in the U.S. policy process.

265 "Vietnam: Where Do We Go From Here?" *The Saturday Evening Post,* 8 February 1969, 24-25, 49.

The senator outlines a foreign policy for the United States following the end of the Vietnam War, stressing the importance of domestic over foreign commitments. He also outlines a program for strengthening the United Nations.

266 "The War in Viet-Nam." In *The Viet-Nam Reader: Articles and Documents on American Foreign Policy and the Viet-Nam Crisis.* Rev. ed., edited by Marcus G. Raskin and Bernard B. Fall, 205-10. New York: Random House, Vintage Books, 1967. (Article first appeared in the 1965 edition, published by Random House.)

In an early statement cautioning against an expansion of the war, the senator advocates a negotiated settlement based on the Geneva Accords of 1954. He also comments on the power of nationalism as a force in Southeast Asia and its association with the communist movement.

267 "The Wars in Your Future: A Warning by Senator J. William Fulbright." *Look,* 2 December 1969, 82, 84-85, 88.

The senator warns against the dangers of overcommitment abroad, particularly military commitments resulting from executive agreements, using Thailand and Spain as cases in point. His comments include an outline of steps for reversing the trend. He also takes issue with the U.S. commitment in Vietnam.

268 "We Can Do What We Want to Do." *The Journal of Arkansas Education* 32 (January 1960): 28.

Fulbright calls for spending at the level necessary to meet pressing needs in education and national defense.

269 "We Must Not Fight Fire with Fire." *The New York Times Magazine,* 23 April 1967, 27, 122, 124, 126-29.

Asserting that "conflict is a great leveler," the senator expresses concern that the United States, in its struggle with the communists, is subverting democratic values by using some of their tactics. Included is a discussion of the Central Intelligence Agency apparatus, particularly its affiliation with the National Student Association. Fulbright also expresses concern for the expansion of presidential power and concludes with suggestions for restoring balance between the executive and legislative branches.

270 "We're Tongue-tied." *Newsweek,* 30 July 1979, 15.

Fulbright discusses the importance of language and international studies in U.S. high schools and colleges, stressing that cultural understanding affects the conduct of both foreign policy and business abroad.

271 "The West Faces the Challenge of Totalitarianism." *Cotton Trade Journal.* 15th International Ed., 1947, 37-38.

The senator discusses the importance of cotton in international trade and the problems associated with developing a strong cotton export program.

272 "What Is the National Interest? The Term Raises More Questions Than It Answers." *The Center Magazine* 7 (January-February 1974): 40-43, 45-48. (Excerpts published in *The Progressive* 37 [November 1973]: 4-5, under the title "'Tragedy Brings Opportunity'"; and *U.S. Catholic,* February 1974, 27-33, under the title "All They Were Saying . . . Has Peace a Chance?"; the senator's paper is also published in *Pacem in Terris III.* Vol. 1, *The Nixon-Kissinger Foreign Policy: Opportunities and Contradictions,* edited by Fred Warner Neal and Mary Kersey Harvey, 18-39. Santa Barbara, Calif.: Center for the Study of Democratic Institutions, 1974, under the title "Basic Aspects of the National Interest.")

The senator interweaves an evaluation of the Nixon-Kissinger foreign policy into a discussion of three issues associated with his concept of the national interest: strengthening détente with the Soviet Union, rebuilding the national economy, and reviving the United Nations. Included is a treatment of the Jackson amendment. He made the remarks before a foreign policy convocation sponsored by the Center for the Study of Democratic Institutions in Washington in October 1973.

273 "What Kind of a Country Do You Want America to Be?" In *Issues 1968,* edited by William W. Boyer, 13-27. Lawrence: University Press of Kansas, 1968.

The senator prefaces his remarks with a consideration of the administration's defensive posture regarding its Vietnam policy and its inflexibility regarding alternatives. Reflecting on the broader issues of U.S. responsibility and commitment, he discusses his concern for the trend of the United States toward the imperial role of arbiter of the world's conflicts. He concludes with his own vignette of the America he would like to see. Fulbright prepared the remarks for the Alfred M. Landon Lecture Series at Kansas State University, Manhattan, in May 1967.

274 "What Makes U.S. Foreign Policy?" *The Reporter,* 14 May 1959, 18-21.

Quoting Alexis de Tocqueville on democracies, the senator discusses the difficulties that democratic nations encounter in the formulation and implementation of foreign policy. He also questions the wisdom of bipartisanship in foreign policy and calls for U.S. support of a federation of European democracies. Fulbright made the remarks at the tenth anniversary banquet of the *Reporter* on April 16, 1959.

275 "What Students Can Do for Peace." *The Progressive* 34 (June 1970): 15-17.

Asserting that dissent reaffirms democracy, the senator advises war protesters to operate within the constitutional system and outlines strategies for influencing U.S. policies in Vietnam. He also critiques key elements in the New Left's concept of social reform. The article was written following the deaths of four students at Kent State University and two students in Jackson, Mississippi.

276 "When the World's Peoples Talked Peace: Highlights of the *Pacem in Terris* Convocation." *Saturday Review,* 1 May 1965, 22-26, 65-69.

The article consists of excerpts from addresses, panel discussions, and evaluation sessions associated with the *Pacem in Terris I* convocation in New York in February 1965. It includes Fulbright's thoughts on coexistence and the importance of the United Nations. *Pacem in Terris I,* an international convocation called by the Center for the Study of Democratic Institutions, was inspired by the 1963 Easter encyclical of Pope John XXIII.

277 "Whither Are We Tending?" *The Officer* 34, No. 3 (1958): inside front cover.

In this excerpt from Fulbright's address before the National Council of the Reserve Officers Association in Washington on February 8, 1958, the senator asserts that education is the key to strengthening our position in the struggle with the Soviet Union.

278 "The Word That Blocks Lasting Peace." *The New York Times Magazine,* 6 January 1946, 8, 40.

Asserting that the word sovereignty is used as a strategy to confuse, the senator argues that the principle of law should take precedence in the effort to maintain international peace. He emphasizes the importance of delegating necessary power to the United Nations to enforce the rule of law against its members. His remarks include an explanation of his concept of sovereignty.

279 "Your Role in America's Future." *Southwestern Bulletin,* n.s. 35 (July 1948): 1-10.

In a commencement address at Southwestern at Memphis, the senator discusses the United Nations, particularly steps to make it a viable organization. He also considers other measures to promote international peace: the Fulbright program and the federation of Europe.

280 *Yugoslavia, 1964.* Report to the Committee on Foreign Relations, United States Senate. 89th Cong., 1st sess., July 1965. Committee Print.

Fulbright discusses problem issues regarding U.S.-Yugoslav relations and the importance of establishing a normal relationship between the two countries. The report includes a review of the country's history, its government, its leadership, and its special position between East and West. The senator traveled to Yugoslavia in November 1964 to attend the signing of the U.S.-Yugoslav Educational Exchange Agreement.

3

Biographical and Other Scholarly Works

281 Anderson, Joel E., Jr. "The Fulbright Strategy: A Critique." Master's thesis, American University, 1966.

The author reviews and analyzes Fulbright's foreign policy ideas from 1943 until 1965, focusing on the following: the Fulbright resolution of 1943 regarding postwar peace planning; the resolution of 1947 concerning the political unification of Western Europe; and the proposal of 1961 calling for an international community of free nations. He continues his critique with an examination of Fulbright's cold war thought, concentrating on U.S. relations with the Soviet Union and the importance of that relationship for Eastern Europe. The cold war critique resumes with a treatment of U.S. policy toward underdeveloped countries in Latin America, the Middle East, Africa, and the Far East. His concluding remarks concern Fulbright's assessment of the domestic consequences of the cold war and the shortcomings of the U.S. constitutional system in the foreign policy realm.

282 Bailey, Richard E. "Fulbright's Universe of Discourse." *The Southern Speech Journal* 36, No. 1 (1970): 33-42.

Stressing the importance of the senator's rhetorical goals, the writer examines Fulbright's universe in terms of his development of a rhetorical structure and the primary components in his perspective of a nation. He concludes with a discussion of how an acceptance or a rejection of the senator's view would influence U.S. foreign and domestic policies. For another analysis of Fulbright's discourse, see Bailey's dissertation, "A Rhetorical Analysis of James William Fulbright's Speaking on 'The Arrogance of Power,'" Ohio State University, 1968.

283 ———. "James William Fulbright." In *American Orators of the Twentieth Century: Critical Studies and Sources,* edited by Bernard K. Duffy and Halford R. Ryan, 159-66. Westport, Conn.: Greenwood Press, 1987.

In a rhetorical assessment of the senator's political speaking, the author incorporates a discussion of Fulbright's philosophic discourse, including the primary ideas in his universe, with an evaluation of his persuasive discourse. He incorrectly cites the Ozarks Regional Library, Fayetteville, as the repository with the most comprehensive collection of Fulbright source materials. The largest collection of Fulbright materials, including the senator's official papers, is housed in the Special Collections Division of the University of Arkansas Libraries, Fayetteville.

284 Baker, Russell. "An Ozark 'Professor' Studies Wall Street." *The New York Times Magazine,* 6 March 1955, 17, 36, 38, 42.

In a profile inspired by the senator's stock market inquiry, the author examines the influence of Fulbright's family background and Oxford education on his political career. He concludes that Oxford and Europe shaped his thinking in international affairs but maintains that Arkansas molded his thinking on domestic issues.

285 Brower, Brock. "The Roots of the Arkansas Questioner." *Life,* 13 May 1966, 92-94, 96, 98, 100, 102, 106-8, 110, 113-15.

In an article stressing the significance of Arkansas and Oxford in molding Fulbright's philosophy, the author treats important events in the senator's career, including his confrontation with Senator Joseph R. McCarthy, the Little Rock integration crisis, the Vietnam War, and his break with President Johnson. He concludes with a consideration of the question of Fulbright's taking up the role of opposition leader.

286 Brown, Donald Eugene. "Fulbright and the Premises of American Foreign Policy." Ph.D. diss., State University of New York at Binghamton, 1982.

In this assessment of Fulbright's public career, the author examines the philosophical and operational premises underlying the senator's ideas regarding international relations and concludes that his foreign policy dissent was basically conservative. He argues that Fulbright was a critic of means who held mainstream opinions about the nation's interests in international affairs.

287 ———. *J. William Fulbright: Advice and Dissent.* Iowa City: University of Iowa Press, 1985.

This is the published version of the author's doctoral thesis. See the preceding entry.

288 Carter, Philip. "Our Neighbor, Senator Fulbright." *The Texas Observer,* 15 April 1966, 6-8.

The author refutes the argument that Fulbright's freedom to dissent on Vietnam resulted from his compromises on domestic issues, saying that the thesis rests on uncertain assumptions. Acknowledging that Oxford may have shaped his international view, Carter maintains that the Ozarks molded his domestic view.

289 Coffin, Tristram. "Senator Fulbright." *Holiday* 36 (September 1964): 34-37, 90, 92-94.

Using the senator's "Old Myths and New Realities" speech as a base, the author profiles Fulbright as a thinker and a critic.

290 ———. *Senator Fulbright: Portrait of a Public Philosopher.* New York: E.P. Dutton and Company, 1966.

This uncritical account of the senator's life and career focuses on Fulbright's legislative accomplishments; his congressional encounters, including Joseph R. McCarthy; and his dissent from Johnson administration policies in the Dominican Republic and Vietnam. The author quotes extensively from the senator's speeches and conversations and includes key speeches in the appendix. For a full-scale review of this first Fulbright biography, including an account of those parts left out of the Fulbright chronicle, see I.F. Stone's critique in the December 29, 1966, and the January 12, 1967, issues of the *New York Review of Books.*

291 ———. "World Affairs Prophet." *VISTA* 1 (May-June 1966): 2-14.

In a profile of the senator, the author outlines Fulbright's ideas regarding foreign affairs, including the risks of modern warfare; nationalism in Asia, Africa, and Latin America; imperialism; communism as a monolithic force; modification of the cold war; accommodation with China; the influence of the military on foreign policy; and the impact of the cold war on U.S. society. Reviewing his role as foreign policy critic, the author describes Fulbright as a man with the ability to incorporate the past, present, and future in his thinking about foreign relations.

292 Crabb, Cecil V., Jr. *Policy-Makers and Critics: Conflicting Theories of American Foreign Policy.* New York: Praeger Publishers, 1976, 128, 134, 171, 176-77, 179, 181, 197, 200, 203-4, 263-66, 273-75, 278, 281, 284-85.

The author examines seven schools of thought regarding the role of the United States in the postwar world. He identifies Fulbright as an advocate of the liberal neoisolationist approach to foreign policy, noting the status his ideas have attained among some members of the group.

293 Davenport, Walter. "Just a Boy from the Ozarks." *Collier's,* 10 February 1945, 14, 48, 50, 52.

The author looks at Fulbright's family background, especially his father, for this account of the senator's life.

294 Downs, Calvin Wharton. "A Thematic Analysis of Speeches on Foreign Policy of Senator J.W. Fulbright." Ph.D. diss., Michigan State University, 1963.

Using quantitative content analysis, the author examines selected Fulbright speeches to determine the senator's fundamental foreign policy ideas, specifically the development of his political ideology regarding international relations. The analytic results of the study are related to his emergence as an internationalist. Finally, the author ties the senator's biographical profile in with his ideological profile, stressing the importance of family, educational, and professional background in his development. The study is based on the identification and analysis of forty themes found in twenty-four speeches delivered between February 1959 and April 1962.

295 Ferguson, John L. *Arkansas Lives: The Opportunity Land Who's Who.* Hopkinsville, Ky.: Historical Record Association, 1965, 171.

This is a reference edition of short biographical sketches of contemporary leaders in Arkansas and includes Fulbright.

296 "Fulbright Starred as Razorback." *TAB* 37 (October 1968): 5, 7.

This is a biographical sketch of the senator in the monthly publication of the Arkansas Bus and Truck Association. The issue also includes an article by Fulbright, "Transportation: A National Problem," on page 5.

297 Haskell, Deborah Peek. "A Rhetorical Analysis of J. William Fulbright's Speeches on the American Character." Ph.D. diss., New York University, 1971.

Basing her study on the Thonssen and Baird, Bryant and Wallace, and Wayne Minnick interpretations of the Aristotelian model of rhetorical analysis, the author undertakes an investigation of four rhetorical categories: invention (content), disposition (arrangement), style, and delivery. Chapter 4 includes a comparison of the senator's style with those of William Jennings Bryan, Winston Churchill, Franklin Roosevelt, Theodore Roosevelt, and Woodrow Wilson. A set of twenty-eight Fulbright speeches concerning the American character from the period 1951 through 1967 make up the text for this analysis.

298 Herlick, Gary. *J.W. Fulbright: Democratic Senator from Arkansas.* Ralph Nader Congress Project: Citizens Look at Congress. Washington, D.C.: Grossman Publishers, 1972.

This is a biographical and congressional profile of Fulbright and focuses on his campaigns, constituency, accomplishments, and voting record. The profile opens with a sketch of his early years, from 1905 until 1942, and closes with a note about his concern for increasing presidential power and decreasing congressional power.

299 Herndon, Dallas T., ed. *Annals of Arkansas, 1947.* Vol. 4. Hopkinsville, Ky.: Historical Record Association, n.d., 1746-47, 1974-75.

The volume includes profiles of the senator and his father.

300 Herzog, Arthur. *The War-Peace Establishment.* New York: Harper and Row, 1965, 16, 24, 88, 91-92, 94-96, 98-99, 119-20.

The author examines the thoughts of the foreign policy realists and notes Fulbright's position within the school.

301 Howe, Neil, and Gary Bullert. "Fulbright: Thirty Years of Sagacity." *Alternative* 8 (January 1975): 8-10.

In a review of Fulbright's thirty-year senatorial career, the writers examine his foreign policy ideas as internationalist, cold warrior, and dissenter. They focus on the affinities and differences between Fulbright and Woodrow Wilson in their foreign policy thinking and on the reversal of the senator's belief that the president should have more control over foreign policy than Congress.

302 Johnson, Haynes, and Bernard M. Gwertzman. *Fulbright: The Dissenter.* Garden City, N.Y.: Doubleday and Company, 1968.

This biography of the senator, the best of the genre to date, is a perceptive portrait of Fulbright as student, congressman, senator, and critic. The book is based on extensive research in the Fulbright Papers and a number of interviews with the senator and others. It includes landmark Fulbright speeches and bibliographical notes. Although two men worked on the project, the writing was done by Haynes Johnson.

303 Kelly, Lera Rowlette. "The Speaking of J. William Fulbright." *The Southern Speech Journal* 27 (Spring 1962): 232-38.

In an article based on the examination of twenty-five Fulbright addresses delivered during the period 1955 to 1960, the author considers the senator's speech making in terms of his educational background, his method of preparation, his organization, his use of ethical and motive appeals, his style, and his delivery. The article is illustrated with numerous quotations from Fulbright speeches.

304 Lynn, Naomi B. "Senator J. William Fulbright's Views on Presidential Power in Foreign Policy." Ph.D. diss., University of Kansas, 1970.

The author examines the change in the senator's position on presidential power in foreign policy, from a staunch supporter of a strong presidency to one of its most important critics. She also examines Fulbright's positions on related policy issues, including the role of public opinion in a democratic society, the role of the United States in the world, communism, right-wing extremism, foreign aid, alliances, and the military. All of these views are analyzed within the context of the senator's philosophy of pragmatism and his personal and professional background, particularly his tenure as Foreign Relations Committee chairman.

305 Lynn, Naomi B., and Arthur F. McClure. *The Fulbright Premise: Senator J. William Fulbright's Views on Presidential Power*. Lewisburg, Pa.: Bucknell University Press, 1973.

The authors examine the transition in the senator's thinking concerning presidential power in foreign policy, from an advocate of a strong executive to an important voice for restraining the president. They also examine his positions on related policy issues (see preceding annotation). Special attention is given to his posture as Foreign Relations Committee chairman, particularly his efforts to strengthen the role of the Senate in the foreign policy process. See also Professor Lynn's dissertation, "Senator J. William Fulbright's Views on Presidential Power in Foreign Policy," University of Kansas, 1970.

306 Manske, Robert Fred. "The Fulbright Foreign Policy Thought, 1964-1971: A Co-organic Critique." Ph.D. diss., American University, 1973.

Using William Y. Elliott's construct for conceptualizing international politics, the author discusses and assesses Fulbright's political philosophy and his suggested policies regarding U.S. relations with other nations. He introduces the study with a description of the dimensions of Elliott's co-organic theory and proceeds to examine the senator's foreign policy views and philosophy for the years 1964-1971 from the perspective of its organic and purposive requirements. His focus is on three issue areas: power politics, security, and nuclear warfare. He continues with a study of selected features of Fulbright's political philosophy and concludes with an evaluation of his view of the global role of the United States.

307 Meyer, Karl E. "Fulbright of Arkansas." *The Progressive* 26 (September 1962): 26-31.

In a penetrating profile of the senator as a skillful parliamentarian and independent thinker, the writer discusses some of the ideas underpinning Fulbright's political philosophy. The author concludes with a discussion of the Little Rock integration crisis, placing the senator's position on the race issue within the context of his view of the legislator's role in a democracy.

308 ———, ed. *Fulbright of Arkansas: The Public Positions of a Private Thinker*. Washington, D.C.: Robert B. Luce, 1963.

The editor incorporates a perceptive commentary with significant Fulbright speeches, memoranda, and other writings to document the development of the senator's ideas regarding national and international affairs. This book is the first major work to be published about Fulbright and marks his twentieth year in Congress. The preface is by Walter Lippmann.

309 Paris, Carol Ann. "Senator J.W. Fulbright and American Foreign Policy, 1943-1949." Master's thesis, Southern Methodist University, 1970.

In a review of U.S. foreign policy for the period 1943-1949, the author traces Fulbright's role, focusing on the ideas expressed in his resolution of 1943 regarding postwar international cooperation and his resolution of 1947 concerning European unification.

310 Perry, Bruce. "Senator J. William Fulbright on European and Atlantic Unity." Ph.D. diss., University of Pennsylvania, 1968.

The author examines Fulbright's long-time advocacy of European and North Atlantic unity and evaluates his views within the context of the real political world in which he worked. The focus of the study is on issues related to economic, military, scientific, and technological cooperation among the nations of the North Atlantic area. Special attention is given to issues associated with the Western Alliance, including Charles de Gaulle's position, and Fulbright's proposals regarding the alliance. The author also examines issues related to the Common Market and the Arkansas economy, particularly the poultry industry.

311 Scott, Frank H. "Major Contributions and Opinions of J. William Fulbright in the Field of American Foreign Policy, 1943 to 1964." Master's thesis, Kansas State College of Pittsburgh, 1964.

The study focuses on the senator's major contributions and speeches regarding foreign policy for the period 1943-1964. Special attention is given to the Fulbright resolution of 1943, the Fulbright Act of 1946, the senator's views on Russia's intentions in 1946 and the Berlin situation in 1959, his opposition to the Bricker amendment, his criticism of John Foster Dulles, the U-2 crisis, the invasion of Cuba at the Bay of Pigs, Fulbright-Goldwater foreign policy differences, Atlantic unity, and the "Old Myths and New Realities" speech.

312 "Senator J. William Fulbright." *The Arkansas Lawyer* 7 (September 1973): 209-40.

This is a photo essay reviewing the senator's political career and contributions to Arkansas and the nation. It includes biographical information, excerpts from his books, and salutes from his colleagues in the Senate. The senator's picture is on the cover. The article continues on the end pages.

313 Shill, Harold B., III. "Senate Activism and Security Commitments: The Troops-to-Europe and National Commitments Resolutions." Ph.D. diss., University of North Carolina at Chapel Hill, 1973, 7, 26n, 57n, 158, 173n, 203-4, 235n, 237, 247, 259n, 270, 271n, 275, 279n, 284-85, 296, 326-27, 330-32, 334, 336-40, 342-46, 348-50, 351n, 352, 356, 358-60, 363-69, 370n, 371, 373, 374n, 375n, 377n, 378-79, 383, 387-88, 391-92, 394-402, 403n, 404n, 405-10, 412-15, 419n, 420, 424-26, 429-35, 437, 439-54, 456, 461-62, 467, 483, 504, 516, 520, 528, 564-65, 588, 590, 594, 596.

This is an analysis of the Senate's participation in the military commitments policy process and focuses on the troops-to-Europe resolution of 1951 and the national commitments resolution of 1969. The author outlines Fulbright's strategy associated with the introduction and eventual passage of the 1969 resolution, along with its two-year legislative history. He used the analytic case study approach and the Guttman scale analysis of roll-call data in the study.

314 Smith, Gaddis. "Reflections of a Conservative Optimist." *The New York Times Book Review,* 19 February 1989, 7.

The senator's book, *The Price of Empire,* inspired this article in which the author reviews the collection of essays and assesses Fulbright's significance as a historical figure. Focusing on one essay in the book, "Our Constitutional and Political Impasse," he discusses the pros and cons of the senator's argument that a parliamentary system would serve the nation better than the present constitutional system based on the distribution of powers between Congress and the president.

315 Stone, I.F. "Fulbright of Arkansas: I." *The New York Review of Books,* 29 December 1966, 5-6. (Reprinted in Stone's *In a Time of Torment.* New York: Random House, 1967, 328-37.)

In a review of Tristram Coffin's *Senator Fulbright: Portrait of a Public Philosopher,* the writer criticizes Coffin for the parts of the Fulbright chronicle that are left out of this first biography of the senator. He proceeds to flesh out the account regarding Fulbright's voting record on civil liberties during the McCarthy period; his record on domestic issues, particularly race and labor; and the reversal of his belief that the president should have more control over foreign policy than Congress. Coffin's comparison of Fulbright with Prometheus inspires Stone to discuss the senator's preferred style of operating within private channels to effect policy changes. The review continues in the January 12, 1967, issue under the title "Fulbright: From Hawk to Dove (Part 2)" and in the January 26, 1967, issue under the title "Fulbright: The Timid Opposition." For annotations of the two articles, see chapter 5 on the Vietnam War.

316 ——. *In a Time of Torment.* New York: Random House, 1967, 35, 45, 105-6, 125, 199-200, 226, 232, 234, 328-54. (The three Fulbright selections in this collection of Stone writings first appeared in *The New York Review of Books,* 29 December 1966, 5-6, under the title "Fulbright of Arkansas: I"; 12 January 1967, 8, 10, 12, under the title "Fulbright: From Hawk to Dove [Part 2]"; and 26 January 1967, 10, 12-13, under the title "Fulbright: The Timid Opposition.")

This collection of Stone writings from the period 1961-1967 has both incidental and substantive references to Fulbright, including a reprint of the author's three-part review of Tristram Coffin's *Senator Fulbright: Portrait of a Public Philosopher* in the *New York Review of Books.* For annotations of the three Stone articles, see the preceding entry and chapter 5 on the Vietnam War.

317 Stuart, Roger Winship. *Meet the Senators.* New York: MacFadden-Bartell Corporation, 1963, 34-36.

This volume of biographical sketches of the senators includes information about Fulbright.

318 Tobler, Judith Ann. "The Education of a Legislator: The Evolution of J. William Fulbright's Attitudes Toward the Soviet Union." Master's thesis, University of Arkansas, 1983.

The author examines the development of Fulbright's position regarding the Soviet Union in the postwar period, from cold warrior to strong supporter of détente. She focuses her study on the influence of three men in the shaping of the senator's thinking regarding U.S.-Soviet relations: Walter Lippmann, George F. Kennan, and Seth P. Tillman.

319 Trask, David F. "The Congress as Classroom: J. William Fulbright and the Crisis of American Power." In *Makers of American Diplomacy from Benjamin Franklin to Henry Kissinger,* edited by Frank J. Merli and Theodore A. Wilson, 649-75. New York: Charles Scribner's Sons, 1974.

The writer traces the evolution of the senator's foreign policy ideas for the thirty-year period from 1942, incorporating themes articulated in his books, *Old Myths and New Realities and Other Commentaries* and *The Arrogance of Power.* In an assessment of his political and social philosophy, he stresses the importance of Fulbright's contributions as an educator on issues related to international relations.

320 Truslow, Marion A., Jr. "A Discussion and Analysis of J. William Fulbright's Political Thought." Master's thesis, Vanderbilt University, 1969.

The writer organizes his study of Fulbright's political thought around five themes found in the senator's speaking and writing. The first part of the paper is a discussion of Fulbright's ideas regarding domestic issues and involves an examination of three of the themes: the role of the legislator, education in a democracy, and shortcomings in the U.S. system of government. The second part of the paper concerns two motifs regarding U.S. foreign policy: Fulbright's efforts to advance new ways of looking at old problems and his hopes for international peace. The author focuses on the senator's foreign policy ideas during the second Eisenhower administration, with a discussion of the Hungarian revolution and the Middle East crisis of 1956, Sputnik, the Berlin crisis of 1959, and the U-2 incident. He also examines Fulbright's concept of a unified Europe and includes a discussion of the senator's books, *Prospects for the West* and *Old Myths and New Realities and Other Commentaries*, to further explain Fulbright's thinking on foreign policy.

321   Tweraser, Kurt Karl. "The Advice and Dissent of Senator Fulbright: A Longitudinal Analysis of His Images of International Politics and His Political Role Conceptions." Ph.D. diss., American University, 1971.

This two-volume study is one of the most comprehensive treatments of the senator's changing conceptions of the U.S. role in international politics. The author treats the changes in Fulbright's foreign policy positions within the context of internationalism, identifying three phases: reformer, 1943-1945; cold warrior, 1946-1965; and revisionist, 1966-1967. He examines the senator's conceptual and behavioral responses to selected issues and events, focusing on postwar international organization, the cold war, and the Vietnam War and its domestic consequences. Significant motifs and topics include the United Nations, the Fulbright resolution, European unity, free trade, foreign aid, Fulbright's views on development of the Third World, and his views on presidential powers in the conduct of foreign policy. The study concludes with an interpretation of Fulbright's legislative role conceptions and his operational code.

322   ———. *Changing Patterns of Political Beliefs: The Foreign Policy Operational Codes of J. William Fulbright, 1943-1967.* Sage Professional Papers in American Politics, edited by Randall B. Ripley, Series No. 04-016, Vol. 2. Beverly Hills: Sage Publications, 1974.

In a study of Fulbright's belief system, the author bases his investigation on five philosophical questions and five instrumental, or policy, questions posed by Alexander George's construct for the study of political beliefs. The purpose of the monograph is to articulate two sets of beliefs underpinning the senator's work in the foreign policy realm from 1943 until 1967. He concludes that political beliefs may be the most restraining of all the forces acting upon a legislator.

323   ———. "J. William Fulbright—Belief Systems, Models of Representation and Re-election Strategies, 1942-1962." *Arkansas Political Science Journal* 6, No. 1 (1985): 55-70.

The author presents an analysis of Fulbright's political behavior, focusing on the relationship between certain aspects of his belief system and his conceptions of representation for the period 1942-1962. He identifies the models of representation of constituent interests adopted by the senator in three policy areas: foreign policy, race, and public welfare. Describing the senator's political behavior in terms of these constructs, the author argues, removes the description of Fulbright's ideology from the arena of moral reflection.

324   Williams, Fay. "Straight Through the Line." In Williams's *Arkansans of the Years.* Vol. 1. Little Rock, Ark.: C.C. Allard and Associates, 1951, 145-51.

The book consists of personality sketches which appeared in the Sunday magazine section of the *Arkansas Democrat* during 1950 and 1951 and includes a profile of the senator.

325 Wise, David. "The J. William Fulbright We Know and . . . Is But One of Several." *The Washingtonian,* May 1968, 39-41, 64, 66-69.

The author profiles the senator as Oxford scholar, businessman, educator, guardian of Arkansas poultry and farming interests, southerner, dissenter, and Vietnam War critic. He also examines Fulbright's association with presidents, particularly his relationship with Lyndon Johnson, and the senator's connection with his constituency.

326 Yergin, Daniel. "Fulbright's Circle: Conversation with the Senator from Arkansas." *Worldview* 16, No. 2 (1973): 7-13.

This is an account of a conversation with the senator in which he discusses the evolution of his ideas regarding postwar U.S. foreign policy, particularly his break in the mid-sixties with the cold war consensus. The account includes a summary of Fulbright's proposals for a sound foreign policy. The writer concludes with an acknowledgment of Fulbright's influence as Foreign Relations Committee chairman and his contributions as dissenter and teacher in suggesting new directions for policy makers.

4

The Early Years, 1905-1942

327 "Addresses and Occupations of Rhodes Scholars and Other Oxonians." *The American Oxonian* 47 (October 1960): 22, 132.

This issue is a directory of information about Rhodes scholars and other Oxonians and includes Fulbright, who attended Oxford from 1925 until 1928. The directory is part 2 of issue number 4. The magazine is the official publication of the Association of American Rhodes Scholars.

328 "Arkansas Razorbacks." *University of Arkansas Bulletin* 17, No. 19 (1924): 12.

The publication includes a picture of the Arkansas Razorback football team of 1923. Fulbright was a member of the team.

329 "As Rhodes Dreamed It." *Newsweek,* 16 December 1946, 100.

Fulbright is listed as an alumnus in a story about Cecil John Rhodes and his scholarship program at Oxford.

330 Aydelotte, Frank. *The American Rhodes Scholarships: A Review of the First Forty Years.* Princeton, N.J.: Princeton University Press, 1946, 84, 99, 126, 156.

The book includes an American Rhodes scholar list that provides information about Fulbright's tenure. The author, Frank Aydelotte, served as long-time American secretary of the Rhodes Trustees.

331 Bradley, Matt, ed. *The Hogs: Moments Remembered.* Little Rock, Ark.: Bradley Publishing, 1981, 16.

This pictorial history of the University of Arkansas Razorbacks includes Fulbright as a football player in 1924.

332 "Class Notes—1925." *Arkansas Alumnus* 10 (September 1932): 14.

This entry in the "Class Notes" column announces Fulbright's marriage to Elizabeth Williams of Philadelphia on June 15, 1932. They were married for fifty-three years until her death in October 1985.

333 *The First Fifty Years of the Rhodes Trust and the Rhodes Scholarships, 1903-1953.* Oxford: Basil Blackwell, 1955, photograph facing page 176, 212, 227-28, 249.

The volume includes records and statistics associated with Rhodes scholars.

334 "Fulbright Named President U of A." *The Arkansas Publisher* 10 (October 1939): 1.

The article announces Fulbright's appointment to the office of president of the University of Arkansas. He served from 1939 until 1941.

335 "The Fulbright Papers." *Arkansas Alumnus,* n.s. 25 (April 1972): 6-7.

The article announces the senator's donation of his public papers to the University of Arkansas in April 1972. It also reviews his close association with the university, as a student on the campus from 1910 until 1925, as a lecturer in law from 1936 until 1939, and as president of the institution from 1939 until 1941.

336 "Fulbright to Oxford." *Arkansas Alumnus* 3 (October 1925): 4.

This is a news item announcing Fulbright's departure for Oxford in September 1925 to begin a three-year course in modern history.

337 Gunn, Herb. "The Continuing Friendship of James William Fulbright and Ronald Buchanan McCallum." *The South Atlantic Quarterly* 83 (Autumn 1984): 416-33.

The author examines the friendship between Fulbright and Ronald Buchanan McCallum, his Oxford tutor, and the merging of the roles of student and tutor during their forty-eight-year friendship. The two men exchanged over one hundred letters between 1945 and 1970. The letters are housed with the senator's papers in the Special Collections Division of the University of Arkansas Libraries, Fayetteville.

338 Hale, Harrison. *University of Arkansas, 1871-1948.* Fayetteville, Ark.: University of Arkansas Alumni Association, 1948, 22, 125-29, 222, 257.

The volume includes a short summary of Fulbright's administration as president of the University of Arkansas from 1939 until 1941.

339 "J.W. Fulbright Honored in Graduation Exercises of Oxford University." *Arkansas Alumnus* 6 (September 1928): 7.

The article reporting Fulbright's graduation from Oxford in 1928 includes a sketch of his activities while he was a student at the University of Arkansas.

340 Leflar, Robert A. *The First 100 Years: Centennial History of the University of Arkansas.* Fayetteville, Ark.: University of Arkansas Foundation, 1972, 136, 143, 153, 173-82, 191, 231, 243, 264, 267, 271, 361.

The book includes information concerning Fulbright's two-year administration as president of the University of Arkansas and the controversy surrounding his dismissal in 1941.

341 ———. "Legal Education in Arkansas: A Brief History of the Law School." *The Arkansas Historical Quarterly* 21 (Summer 1962): 99-131.

The writer mentions Fulbright's association with the University of Arkansas Law School as a student and teacher. He was a part-time member of the first class in 1924 and a part-time lecturer from 1936 until 1939.

342 "Letters from the Class Secretaries: The Class of 1925 Letter." *The American Oxonian* 41 (January 1954): 34-35.

The column mentions Fulbright's honorary Doctor of Civil Laws degree from Oxford University in 1953.

343 "A Picture Portfolio of Campus Memories from the University of Arkansas." *Flashback* 15 (November 1965): 17-24.

The portfolio includes photographs of the senator, his mother Roberta, and his sister Helen. The previous issue of *Flashback* (October 1965, facing page 46) includes a picture of Fulbright with the University of Arkansas Glee Club. *Flashback* is published by the Washington County Historical Society of Fayetteville, Arkansas.

344 "Razorbacks of 1924." *Arkansas Alumnus* 2 (December 1924): 2.

The publication includes a group picture of the 1924 University of Arkansas Razorback football team. Fulbright was a member of the team.

345 *Register of Rhodes Scholars, 1903-1945.* New York: Oxford University Press, Geoffrey Cumberlege, 1950, 199-200.

The volume includes information associated with the senator's tenure as a Rhodes scholar at Oxford University.

346 "'Return Journey to Oxford.'" *The American Oxonian* 40 (October 1953): 195-202.

In a reprint of a broadcast by the BBC of impressions and remarks associated with the Rhodes Scholars' Jubilee Reunion, Fulbright comments on the continuity at Oxford and the hope it imparts for the future.

347 *Rhodes Scholarships: Record of Past Scholars Elected Between the Years 1903 and 1927 Inclusive.* Oxford, 1931, 359.

The volume includes brief biographical information about the senator and his tenure at Oxford University.

348 "Roster of Rhodes Scholars Attending the Reunion." *The American Oxonian* 40 (October 1953): 203-12.

The issue includes a Rhodes scholar list that provides information about those participating in the reunion.

349 Sagmaster, Joseph. "The Jubilee Reunion." *The American Oxonian* 40 (October 1953): 163-75.

In an article in part 1 of the "Oxford Reunion Number," the writer notes the conferring of an honorary Doctor of Civil Laws degree on the senator during graduation exercises in July.

350 Stone, Edward Durell. *The Evolution of an Architect.* New York: Horizon Press, 1962, 19-20, 85, 97, 99, 102-3, 150-51.

The author includes remarks regarding his friendship and association with Fulbright. The two grew up together in Fayetteville, Arkansas.

351 "Summer Commencement." *Sooner Magazine* 13 (September 1940): 6-7.

The article concerns Fulbright's commencement address at the University of Oklahoma and includes quotations on the importance to the United States of a British victory over Germany. He made the remarks when he was president of the University of Arkansas.

352 "University News: New President." *Arkansas Alumnus* 18 (June 1941): 5-6.

This article is an introduction to Dr. A.M. Harding, the new president of the

University of Arkansas and Fulbright's successor. Fulbright was dismissed from the office in June 1941.

353 "University of Arkansas Senior Wins Rhodes Scholarship." *Arkansas Alumnus* 2 (January 1925): 15.

This article announcing the appointment of Fulbright as a Rhodes scholar includes a biographical sketch of his years at the University of Arkansas. He was nineteen years old when he learned that he had been chosen for a scholarship to Oxford.

354 Untitled. *Arkansas Alumnus* 3 (March 1926): 5.

The article announces Fulbright's forthcoming trip to the United States in the spring of 1926 as a member of the Oxford University lacrosse team.

355 "We Present—New President: J.W. Fulbright '25 Named to Succeed Late Dr. Futrall." *Arkansas Alumnus* 17 (October 1939): 4-5, 9, 16.

This article presents a portrait of the new president of the University of Arkansas and includes a biographical sketch of his activities as a student and a professor before his appointment to the office of president in September 1939.

5

The Congressional Years, 1942-1944

356 "Analysis of House Votes." *The New Republic,* 8 May 1944, 651-52.

The article examines a number of House votes, including the passage of the Fulbright resolution, a proposal calling for U.S. participation in a postwar international peace-keeping apparatus.

357 "The Awakening." *Time,* 11 October 1943, 17.

The article focuses on Senator Tom Connally's announcement that the Foreign Relations Committee would report out a completely new postwar resolution, separate from the Fulbright resolution, following pressure from Senator Joseph Ball, newspapers, and constituents.

358 Briggs, Philip J. "Congress and Collective Security: The Resolutions of 1943." *World Affairs* 132 (March 1970): 332-44.

The author examines the passage of the Fulbright resolution in the House and the Connally resolution in the Senate. He focuses on the role of bipartisanship in the endeavor, the cooperative relations between Congress and the president, and the principals responsible for creating a climate which permitted ratification of the collective security concept. The article is drawn from chapter 2 of Briggs's dissertation (see following entry) and adapted for *World Affairs.*

359 ——. "Executive-Congressional Relations in the Formulation of American Post-World War II Collective Security Agreements." Ph.D. diss., Syracuse University, 1969, 1, 3, 11-14, 26-31, 37, 39-40, 48, 51, 77, 79, 149, 175, 178, 180, 182-83, 186, 197, 200, 202-4.

Using the case study approach, the author examines five postwar collective security policies, including the Fulbright resolution of 1943 (see preceding entry). Other policies featured in the study are the counterpart of the Fulbright resolution in the Senate, the Connally resolution; the Vandenberg resolution; the Pact of Madrid; the Formosa resolution and the Mutual Defense Treaty with the Republic of China; and the Eisenhower Doctrine.

360 "Building a Postwar Policy: Issues of 1919 Reappear." *The United States News,* 1 October 1943, 20.

In an article about the Fulbright resolution calling for a postwar international peace-keeping organization, the author notes the significance of the proposal for

President Roosevelt's upcoming diplomatic undertakings and reviews the parallels between the congressional debate and the earlier struggle over the League of Nations. Congressman Fulbright's picture is on the cover.

361   Carlisle, Irene. "J.W. Fulbright, 'Minister from Arkansas.'" *Flashback* 16 (May 1966): 1-11.

The article is a previously unpublished manuscript written soon after Fulbright's election to Congress in 1942 and published by the Washington County Historical Society in 1966. It concentrates on the young congressman's early years and includes some of his objections to the article, in the form of footnotes. Fulbright's picture is on the cover.

362   Carr, William G. "Education in American Foreign Policy." *The Journal of the National Education Association* 33 (May 1944): 115-16.

The article includes information about the U.S. delegation appointed by the State Department to attend the Allied Ministers of Education Conference in London in April 1944. Congressman Fulbright was chairman of that delegation.

363   "Charting Our Postwar Course." *The United States News,* 5 November 1943, 19.

The author mentions Congressman Fulbright's resolution in an article concerned primarily with the Connally resolution in the Senate.

364   "Conference of Allied Ministers of Education in London." *The Department of State Bulletin,* 6 May 1944, 413-15.

This press release pertains to the Allied Ministers of Education Conference in London in April 1944 and includes a report of its work on plans for a postwar educational and cultural reconstruction agency. Congressman Fulbright was chairman of the U.S. delegation and chairman of the sessions concerned with drafting a constitution for the proposed organization.

365   "Congress Reconvenes." *The Nation,* 18 September 1943, 312-13.

The editorial mentions the passage of the Fulbright resolution in the House in September 1943.

366   "Default." *Time,* 4 October 1943, 22.

The article focuses on the failure of Senator Tom Connally, chairman of the Foreign Relations Committee, to bring the Fulbright resolution up for floor debate. The resolution, a one-sentence statement calling for U.S. participation in a postwar international peace-keeping organization, had passed the House by an overwhelming vote in September.

367   Divine, Robert A. *Second Chance: The Triumph of Internationalism in America During World War II.* New York: Atheneum, 1967, 87, 90, 110-13, 127, 129, 141-45, 149, 233, 241, 250, 260-61, 312.

The book includes an account of the passage of the Fulbright resolution in the House in September 1943.

368   Ferrell, Robert H., ed. *America in a Divided World, 1945-1972.* Documentary History of the United States, edited by Richard B. Morris. New York: Harper and Row, Harper Torchbooks, 1975, 1-2.

The volume includes the text of the Fulbright resolution.

369   "Free Flow." *Time,* 25 September 1944, 82.

The article mentions the resolution introduced by Fulbright in the House on international freedom of the press.

370   "Fulbright Idea." *Newsweek,* 28 June 1943, 38, 40.

The item concerns freshman Congressman Fulbright's resolution calling for U.S. participation in a postwar international peace-keeping organization.

371   "Fulbright Pledge on Peace Policy: Views of Press." *The United States News,* 1 October 1943, 36.

The article consists of quotations from major newspapers concerning Congressman Fulbright's resolution proposing U.S. membership in a postwar international peace-keeping organization.

372   "The Fulbright Resolution." *The Nation,* 2 October 1943, 368.

The article concerns the significance of the House vote in favor of the Fulbright resolution. It also compares the congressman's resolution with the one introduced in the Senate.

373   "The Fulbright Resolution for Post-war Collaboration." *The Magazine of Sigma Chi,* February-March 1944, 55-57.

Two articles, one reprinted from the *Washington Star* and the other from *Time,* focus on Congressman Fulbright's resolution calling for participation by the United States in a postwar international peace-keeping organization. Fulbright was a member of Sigma Chi when he was a student at the University of Arkansas in Fayetteville.

374   "Fulbright's Resolution: A Young Congressman Offers a Foreign Policy Plank That Both Parties Can Accept." *Life,* 28 June 1943, 28.

The editorial concerns the Fulbright resolution, particularly its effect on the concept of bipartisanship in foreign policy.

375   "Guidance for Capitol Hill: Programs on Food, Man Power and Taxes Outlined by Executive." *The United States News,* 24 September 1943, 40.

The article mentions the Fulbright resolution coming up in the House for floor consideration and its future in the Senate.

376   Hachey, Thomas E., ed. "American Profiles on Capitol Hill: A Confidential Study for the British Foreign Office in 1943." *Wisconsin Magazine of History* 57 (Winter 1973-1974): 141-53.

This study by Sir Isaiah Berlin for the British Foreign Office in the spring of 1943 focuses on congressional committees, specifically the Foreign Relations Committee and the House Foreign Affairs Committee. He profiles committee members, including Fulbright, whom he describes as a promising internationalist. Sir Isaiah, author, diplomat, and lecturer, was president of Wolfson College, Oxford, when this article was published.

377   Hall, Max. "J. William Fulbright: Hell-Bent on His Objective." In *Public Men In and Out of Office,* edited by J.T. Salter, 181-95. Chapel Hill: University of North Carolina Press, 1946.

In a profile of the young congressman, the author outlines the strategy that Fulbright employed to get House approval of his resolution calling for U.S. participation in a postwar international peace-keeping organization.

378 "House Internationalist Gesture Faces Tougher Senate Sledding." *Newsweek,* 4 October 1943, 42, 44.

The article examines the significance of the vote on the Fulbright resolution in the House and includes a profile of the young congressman.

379 Hull, Cordell. *The Memoirs of Cordell Hull.* Vol. 2. New York: Macmillan Company, 1948, 1258-63, 1314, 1649.

The secretary of state discusses the passage of the Fulbright resolution in September 1943 in the House of Representatives.

380 Kotschnig, Walter M. "Realism in Educational Reconstruction." *The Annals of The American Academy of Political and Social Science* 235 (September 1944): 17-24.

The author mentions tentative plans made at the Allied Ministers of Education Conference in London in April 1944 for a postwar educational and cultural reconstruction instrumentality. Fulbright was chairman of the sessions concerned with that effort.

381 Lemke, W.J. "Lore . . . Sen. Fulbright as a Country Squire." *The Ozarks Mountaineer* 14 (July 1966): 6.

In his column "Lore," the author previews Irene Carlisle's article, "J.W. Fulbright, 'Minister from Arkansas,'" in the May 1966 issue of *Flashback,* published by the Washington County Historical Society of Fayetteville. The article concerned the young congressman's early years.

382 Lindley, Ernest K. "Why Our Allies Keep Their Fingers Crossed." *Newsweek,* 25 October 1943, 50.

Columnist Lindley compares Congressman Fulbright's resolution calling for participation by the United States in a postwar international peace-keeping organization with the resolution adopted by a subcommittee of the Senate Foreign Relations Committee. He also examines the reasons that the Senate subcommittee set aside the Fulbright resolution.

383 "More Nonsense from the Colonel." *The New Republic,* 18 October 1943, 505.

The editorial defends former Rhodes scholars from an attack by Robert R. McCormick. Fulbright spent three years at Oxford, from 1925 until 1928, on a Rhodes scholarship.

384 "Passage of the Fulbright Resolution by the House of Representatives." *The Department of State Bulletin,* 25 September 1943, 207-8.

This is a press release pertaining to the passage of the Fulbright resolution in the House of Representatives and includes the secretary of state's comments.

385 "People of the Week." *The United States News,* 2 July 1943, 64-65.

This is a biographical profile featuring the young congressman as author of the Fulbright resolution.

386 "Postwar Catalyst." *Time,* 28 June 1943, 15.

The article concerns the one-sentence resolution written and introduced by Fulbright, a statement calling for U.S. participation in a postwar organization to maintain international peace. It was passed unanimously by the House Foreign Affairs Committee on June 15.

387 "Private Bogey." *Time,* 25 October 1943, 61-62.

The article concerns the *Chicago Tribune's* Anglophobic view of Rhodes scholarships and its attack on former scholars in public life, including Fulbright. The rejoinder is by Frank Aydelotte, American secretary of the Rhodes Trustees.

388 Robinson, James A. *Congress and Foreign Policy Making: A Study in Legislative Influence and Initiative.* The Dorsey Series in Political Science, edited by Norton E. Long. Homewood, Ill.: Dorsey Press, 1962, 10, 13, 33-36, 63, 65-66, 72, 78-80, 84, 87-89, 96, 134, 136, 193, 211-14.

The author includes an account of Congressman Fulbright's efforts in 1943 to secure passage of the Fulbright resolution, noting his work in Congress and with the executive branch to gain support for the proposal. He also discusses Fulbright's concept of his role as Foreign Relations Committee head and its implications for the congressional role in the foreign policy-making process.

389 Schlesinger, Arthur M., Jr., ed. *The Dynamics of World Power: A Documentary History of United States Foreign Policy, 1945-1973.* Vol. 5, *The United Nations—Subsaharan Africa.* Edited by Richard C. Hottelet and Jean Herskovits. New York: Chelsea House Publishers in association with McGraw-Hill Book Company, 1973, 12.

The volume includes the text of the Fulbright resolution of 1943.

390 "The Shape of Things." *The Nation,* 26 June 1943, 878.

The item includes an examination of the passage of the Fulbright resolution by the House Foreign Affairs Committee.

391 "The Shape of Things." *The Nation,* 9 October 1943, 393-94.

This item concerns the Senate Foreign Relations Committee's decision to set aside the Fulbright resolution for one of its own on postwar international peace-keeping.

392 "Should the Treaty Authority of the U.S. Senate Be Curtailed?" *Congressional Digest* 22 (October 1943): 243-45.

Congressmen Albert Gore and Estes Kefauver and columnist Ernest Lindley urge support of the Fulbright resolution and present opinions regarding the role of the House of Representatives in the foreign policy process.

393 Stone, I.F. "Straw Vote on the Future." *The Nation,* 2 October 1943, 370-71.

The article concerns the Fulbright resolution and the debate in the House preceding its passage.

394 T.R.B. "Varied Matters." *The New Republic,* 4 October 1943, 456.

T.R.B. notes the passage of the Fulbright resolution in the House. Richard Lee Strout wrote the column "T.R.B. from Washington" for the *New Republic* for forty years, beginning in 1943.

395 Vorys, John M. "Party Responsibility for Foreign Policy." *The Annals of The American Academy of Political and Social Science* 289 (September 1953): 165-71.

The author notes the passage of the freshman congressman's famous Fulbright resolution supporting the organization of a postwar international peace-keeping apparatus.

396 "We Salute." *The School Executive* 63 (July 1944): 17.

The article is an acknowledgment of Fulbright's leadership in foreign affairs. It cites the Fulbright resolution proposing U.S. membership in a postwar international peace-keeping organization and the congressman's efforts in behalf of an international agency to promote postwar educational and cultural reconstruction.

397 "We Tested Our Leaders: These Are the Ten . . . Rated Topmost by a Panel of Authorities." *Newsweek,* 6 December 1943, 30-32.

Fulbright receives an honorable mention in the *Newsweek* leadership survey.

398 "We'll Cooperate with World, But Question Now Is, How?" *Newsweek,* 25 October 1943, 42, 45.

The writer mentions Fulbright's resolution in an article concerned primarily with the adoption by the Foreign Relations Committee of Senate Resolution 192 on postwar international peace-keeping policy.

399 Westerfield, H. Bradford. *Foreign Policy and Party Politics: Pearl Harbor to Korea.* New Haven: Yale University Press, 1955, 115, 148-51, 153, 155-59, 181, 326-27.

The book includes an account of the passage of the Fulbright resolution in the House.

400 "What Is the Senate Waiting For?" *The New Republic,* 11 October 1943, 472.

The editorial examines the Senate's reaction to the passage of the Fulbright resolution in the House.

6
The Senatorial Years, 1944-1974

GENERAL

401 Abell, Tyler, ed. *Drew Pearson Diaries, 1949-1959.* New York: Holt, Rinehart and Winston, 1974, 33, 161-63, 231, 237, 245-46, 302, 328, 346, 383-84, 388, 430, 480, 519-20, 534, 542-43.

The author mentions several anecdotes concerning his encounters with Fulbright.

402 "The Accent of Greatness." *The Nation,* 20 February 1954, 142-43.

This editorial praises Fulbright's speech denouncing the Bricker amendment and mentions him as a possible presidential nominee.

403 "After the Deluge." *Newsweek,* 9 January 1956, 19-20.

An article concerning the floods in California includes a note about Fulbright's intention to consider a federal disaster insurance program for flood victims.

404 "Aid and EDC." *Time,* 26 July 1954, 9-10.

The story concerns two amendments, one introduced in the House by James P. Richards and the other introduced in the Senate by William Knowland, making military assistance to France and Italy contingent upon their ratification of the European Defense Community treaty. Fulbright urges the Foreign Relations Committee to substitute Richards's amendment to the foreign aid bill for Senator Knowland's.

405 "Ambassadorial Anguish." *Newsweek,* 12 August 1957, 27-28.

The article includes excerpts from Maxwell H. Gluck's testimony before the Senate Foreign Relations Committee on his nomination as ambassador to Ceylon.

406 "Amiable Confusion." *Time,* 3 February 1958, 13.

Using the issue of federal education assistance, Fulbright speaks out against the Eisenhower administration. He recommends reform of the U.S. educational system as a way of solving many of the problems confronting the country. The writer interweaves the senator's silence on the Little Rock desegregation crisis throughout the story.

407 Andrew, Jean Douglas. "The Effect of Senate Foreign Relations Committee Membership in Terms of Support of Foreign Policy, 1946-1966." Ph.D. diss., University of Connecticut, 1968, 24, 28, 35-36, 39, 41, 56, 63, 65, 67, 69, 72, 74-76, 79, 82, 85, 88-91, 98-99, 107, 125, 127-28, 130-31, 133, 135-36, 162-71, 178, 180, 192, 200, 203-8, 213-25, 227.

The author examines Fulbright's opposition to bipartisanship in the second Eisenhower administration, focusing on his role as critic of the Middle East Doctrine. She recalls his public criticism of both Secretary of State John Foster Dulles and Majority Leader Lyndon Johnson on points of policy and credibility regarding the Middle East situation. Seeing a pattern beginning in the Dulles era, the writer maintains that the senator's 1965 break with President Johnson was the result of a long-standing point of view. See Kenneth W. Grundy's article, "The Apprenticeship of J. William Fulbright," in the summer 1967 issue of the *Virginia Quarterly Review* for a similar view.

408 "The Art of Selection." *The Nation,* 24 December 1960, 493.

This is an editorial praising President Kennedy for his selection of key State Department staff and expressing understanding of the reasons for not appointing Fulbright secretary of state.

409 Ascoli, Max. "Central High and Quemoy." *The Reporter,* 18 September 1958, 12.

In an editorial regarding the aftermath of the Little Rock school integration crisis, the writer discusses the predicament of southern senators like Fulbright and the importance of regional interests, particularly the race issue, in preventing them from achieving higher office.

410 Ashmore, Harry S. "Presents J. William Fulbright." In *I Am Happy to Present: A Book of Introductions.* 2d ed., compiled by Guy R. Lyle and Kevin Guinagh, 205-6. New York: H.W. Wilson Company, 1968.

In a book of introductions, journalist Harry S. Ashmore presents Fulbright to a convocation of the Center for the Study of Democratic Institutions on May 10, 1966.

411 "At the House on N Street—Kennedy's New Team Begins to Take Shape." *U.S. News and World Report,* 12 December 1960, 55-57.

The article mentions Fulbright for the office of secretary of state in the Kennedy administration.

412 "Atlantic Assembly." *Freedom and Union* 19 (January 1964): 19.

This is a reprint of an editorial in the *New York Times* which cites a proposal by Congressman John Lindsay and Fulbright for an Atlantic Parliamentary Assembly to bring European and American legislators together for consultation.

413 "Atlantic Convention 'Desirable'—Gruenther." *Freedom and Union* 11 (July-August 1956): 4-5.

This is a transcript of question-and-answer testimony of General Alfred M. Gruenther, SHAPE commander-in-chief, and members of the Senate Foreign Relations Committee on the importance of Atlantic unity.

414 "AU Resolution Sponsor List Grows." *Freedom and Union* 4 (October 1949): 18-19.

The article focuses on the growing number of congressional supporters of the Atlantic Union resolution and includes pictures of five additional senators: John Sparkman, Harry P. Cain, Robert C. Hendrickson, J. William Fulbright, and Harley M. Kilgore. As early as March 1947, Fulbright introduced a resolution, along with Senator Elbert Thomas, that would have secured congressional approval of the political unification of Europe. The Senate, however, failed to adopt the resolution.

415   Becnel, Thomas A. "Fulbright of Arkansas v. Ellender of Louisiana: The Politics of Sugar and Rice, 1937-1974." *The Arkansas Historical Quarterly* 43 (Winter 1984): 289-303.

After a review of the affinities between Fulbright and Allen Ellender, the author proceeds to explain the long-standing conflict between the two in terms of economic and political accommodation of their respective regions.

416   Bess, Demaree. "How Our Allies Tricked Us." *The Saturday Evening Post,* 20 April 1957, 23, 77-78, 80-82.

In an article about the Middle East, the author examines the events leading up to the announcement of the Eisenhower Doctrine, including the attack by Great Britain and France on Egypt. The author includes an account of his talk with Fulbright regarding the Eisenhower Doctrine.

417   "Bid for 15 Million." *Newsweek,* 19 December 1955, 24.

Although the article concerns Adlai Stevenson's bid for the labor vote in the presidential race in 1956, it includes a picture of Stevenson with Fulbright while the two were on a duck hunting trip.

418   "Bipartisan Policy Requires G.O.P. Changes." *Time,* 20 December 1954, 30.

Fulbright discusses President Eisenhower's desire for bipartisanship in foreign policy and the prerequisites that must be met by the administration.

419   "Britain's Financial Trouble and Her Plan to Combat It; Determination to Avoid Loans, Despite Gestures of U.S. Bankers." *The United States News,* 13 July 1945, 50, 52, 54, 56.

The article notes Fulbright's support of postwar aid for Great Britain.

420   "Business Footnotes." *Newsweek,* 26 July 1948, 12.

The item includes a note regarding Fulbright's plans to press for repeal of taxes on oleomargarine.

421   "Busy Man." *Time,* 8 October 1951, 26-27.

In an article about Joseph R. McCarthy, Fulbright challenges the senator's charges against Philip C. Jessup. The encounter occurred during hearings before the Foreign Relations Committee to confirm Jessup as a U.S. delegate to the United Nations General Assembly.

422   "A Cabinet Post of Health, Education and Security." *American Journal of Public Health* 37 (April 1947): 453-55.

The article concerns the bill introduced by Senators Fulbright and Robert Taft proposing a new executive department for the areas of health, education, and social security. It also includes criticism of the bill.

423   "Case for the South." *Newsweek,* 19 March 1956, 33-34.

The article mentions Fulbright as a signer of the Southern Manifesto.

424   "Change v. Rigidity." *Time,* 18 November 1946, 22.

The article centers on the controversy created by Fulbright's suggestion that President Truman appoint a Republican secretary of state and resign from office when the Republicans gained control of both houses of Congress in the midterm elections.

425 "Chinks in Fulbright's Armor." *The Christian Century,* 22 April 1964, 509.

This editorial challenges Fulbright to substitute reality for myth in his approach to racial problems in the United States.

426 Coffin, Tristram. "The Past Recaptured." *The Nation,* 16 November 1946, 546-47.

The article concerns the Republican victory in the 1946 midterm congressional elections and mentions Fulbright's proposal of a Truman resignation in favor of a Republican.

427 "Colleagues Eulogize Kefauver in Senate Memorial Session." *Freedom and Union* 18 (December 1963): 10-12.

The article consists of excerpts from more than a dozen senatorial tributes eulogizing Senator Estes Kefauver, including Fulbright's, which praises Kefauver's work for Atlantic unity.

428 "Comments on Bricker-George Issue Editorial." *Freedom and Union* 9 (June 1954): 24.

This is a collection of excerpted letters from U.S. senators regarding *Freedom and Union's* editorial in the April issue explaining questions involved in the proposed Bricker and George amendments to the U.S. Constitution. Letters include one from Fulbright expressing support for the editorial position of the magazine.

429 "Congress: The Needs." *Newsweek,* 31 December 1956, 16-17.

The article mentions Fulbright's criticism of John Foster Dulles.

430 "Congressional Leadership for UNESCO." *The Journal of the National Education Association* 35 (April 1946): 167.

The article is an acknowledgment of the leaders in Congress working for the establishment of the United Nations Educational, Scientific and Cultural Organization. It includes recognition of Fulbright's sponsorship of Senate Resolution 122 regarding the organization. The Senate adopted the resolution in May 1945.

431 "Congressmen, Former Diplomats Urge Atlantic Union." *Freedom and Union* 5 (September 1950): 5.

The item concerns the visit of a congressional delegation, including Fulbright, to the State Department to press for Atlantic unity.

432 "Controlling McCarthy: The President Has Declined—Will Congress Take on the Job?" *The New Republic,* 15 March 1954, 6-12.

The article includes a statement by the senator on the importance and the necessity of the congressional power to conduct investigations.

433 Cook, Fred J. *The Nightmare Decade: The Life and Times of Senator Joe McCarthy.* New York: Random House, 1971, 203-4, 423-24, 462, 523-24, 528, 534, 571n.

The author discusses some of Fulbright's clashes with Joseph R. McCarthy, including the ones associated with the Philip C. Jessup nomination and the student exchange program. The author also mentions Fulbright's lone vote against appropriations for McCarthy's investigating subcommittee and his role in the censure of the Wisconsin senator.

434 "Correcting an Oversight." *Newsweek,* 18 August 1958, 31-32.

The article regards Democratic senators' criticism of President Eisenhower's foreign policy and includes remarks by Fulbright.

435 Dear, Ann, and Joseph Dear. "Foreign Policy Makers." *Freedom and Union* 4 (April 1949): 10-12.

The authors include a short profile of Fulbright as a newly appointed member of the Senate Foreign Relations Committee.

436 "Dear Congressman." *Freedom and Union* 21 (September 1966): 19-20.

The "Dear Congressman" column includes a letter to Fulbright calling for the senator's leadership in promoting two resolutions: Senate Concurrent Resolution 64 and Senate Resolution 128, both concerning Atlantic unity.

437 Drew, Elizabeth. "What's Good for the Gander." *Newsweek,* 11 June 1973, 13.

In a column on the uses and purposes of governmental power, Drew mentions Fulbright's argument for a strong presidency in the foreign policy realm.

438 Du Boff, Richard. "Nixon's Secret Plan: The Budget." *The Commonweal,* 5 March 1971, 543-45.

Professor Du Boff introduces his article with a thoughtful Fulbright quotation concerning the budget.

439 "The Economy: What's the Word? Humphrey Talks Taxes vs. 'Dip.'" *Newsweek,* 15 February 1954, 69.

The article includes a Fulbright quotation on tax cuts.

440 "The Egghead Again." *Newsweek,* 26 September 1955, 32.

The article includes Fulbright's remarks on the scarcity of intellectuals in the Republican party.

441 "Excerpts from Hearings by the Senate Public Works Subcommittee on Transportation, February 8, 1973." *Limestone* 10, No. 35 (1973): 34-35, 68-74.

This is a presentation by Clark McClinton before the Senate Public Works Subcommittee on Transportation on highway funding. Fulbright introduced his fellow Arkansan to the committee.

442 "Explanation." *Newsweek,* 22 November 1948, 43.

The item concerns Fulbright's explanation of his suggestion that Harry Truman resign from the presidency after the Republicans won control of Congress in the 1946 midterm elections.

443 Farnsworth, David N. *The Senate Committee on Foreign Relations.* Illinois Studies in the Social Sciences, Vol. 49. Urbana: University of Illinois Press, 1961, 8, 22, 25-27, 42, 45-47, 52, 115, 140, 142, 148, 153-54.

The author analyzes the role played by the Senate Foreign Relations Committee during the period 1947-1956 and includes several Fulbright references. He mentions the Fulbright resolution of 1943, the senator's assignment to the Foreign Relations Committee, and his exchange with Joseph R. McCarthy during the Philip C. Jessup hearings.

444 ———. "The Senate Committee on Foreign Relations: A Study of the Decision-Making Process." Ph.D. diss., University of Illinois, Urbana, 1959, 27, 43, 51, 56-57, 59, 85, 92, 94-95, 105, 223, 248, 252.

In a study of the Foreign Relations Committee's role in the development of policy, the author examines the position of the committee in relation to Congress and other congressional committees, the executive branch, and organized groups. His primary focus is on organized groups and their efforts to influence committee decisions. See the preceding entry for a listing of Fulbright references.

445 "The Firestone Case." *Newsweek,* 9 August 1965, 64-65.

Fulbright blasts pressure groups who were responsible for preventing Firestone from building a plant in Rumania.

446 "The First Call." *Time,* 1 January 1951, 11.

Fulbright questions Charles Wilson, director of U.S. mobilization, before the Joint Committee on Defense Production about mobilization plans.

447 "First to Be Shot." *Time,* 1 January 1951, 10-11.

The story concerns Harry Truman's defense of Secretary of State Dean Acheson amid demands for Acheson's removal from office. It includes Fulbright's explanation of his statement regarding the ouster issue.

448 "Foreign Policy." *The New Republic,* 17 November 1958, 12.

This editorial advocates a strong role for Congress in the realm of foreign affairs. The editor also sees an opening for Fulbright, as a senior Foreign Relations Committee member, to exercise a leadership role.

449 "The Freshmen Assist." *Time,* 5 February 1945, 26-27.

The article concerns a letter written by freshman senators to President Franklin D. Roosevelt urging the early formation of an international peace-keeping organization and early U.S. participation in postwar peace plans. Senators Fulbright and H. Alexander Smith initiated the effort.

450 Fried, Richard M. *Men Against McCarthy.* Contemporary American History Series, edited by William E. Leuchtenburg. New York: Columbia University Press, 1976, 94n, 158, 185, 189-90, 199, 239, 261-62, 269-70, 276, 293, 295-97, 299, 307-8, 310.

The author notes the senator's clashes with Joseph R. McCarthy over such issues as Fulbright's defense of Secretary of State Dean Acheson, the nomination of Philip C. Jessup as a delegate to the United Nations, and the Fulbright scholar program hearings. He also mentions Fulbright's lone vote against appropriations for McCarthy's Permanent Investigations Subcommittee and his work with Senator Ralph Flanders on the McCarthy censure resolution.

451 Fritchey, Clayton. "Washington Insight: Who Belongs to the Senate's Inner Club?" *Harper's Magazine* 234 (May 1967): 104, 106, 108, 110.

In an article about the men who run the Senate, the author notes Fulbright's position and examines the reasons that he was not a member of the Inner Club.

452 "From Capitol Hill." *Newsweek,* 29 January 1945, 17.

The item includes a short note concerning the reunion of Fulbright and Claude Pepper in the Senate. Senator Pepper was Fulbright's law professor at the University of Arkansas in the mid-twenties.

453 "From Capitol Hill." *Newsweek,* 5 February 1945, 19.

The item includes a short note concerning Fulbright's part in drafting a letter from freshman senators to Franklin D. Roosevelt supporting the Dumbarton Oaks plan.

454 "From Capitol Hill." *Newsweek,* 18 June 1945, 23.

The item includes a short note regarding Fulbright's position on efforts to repeal the Johnson Act.

455 "Fulbright and Foreign Policy." *America,* 29 January 1972, 79-80.

Reflecting on President Richard Nixon's trips to Peking and Moscow, the editors call for a serious discussion of U.S. foreign policy. They cite Fulbright's remarks in the January 8 issue of the *New Yorker* as an "opener" for such a debate. In those comments Fulbright warned against an ideological approach to international relations.

456 "Fulbright Cites AHE Housing Resolutions." *College and University Bulletin* 7, No. 13 (1955): 1-2.

The article concerns Fulbright's proposed amendment to Title IV of the Housing Act of 1950 to expand the college and university housing and construction loan program.

457 "Fulbright Finds de Gaulle 'Puzzling.'" *Freedom and Union* 18 (February 1963): 11.

Fulbright takes President Charles de Gaulle to task for his failure to cooperate with the United States and European allies to strengthen economic and defense ties.

458 "Fulbright Has a Vision." *National Review,* 4 February 1972, 83-84, 86.

Answering Fulbright's article in the January 8 issue of the *New Yorker,* the writer analyzes the senator's thesis regarding President Truman's role in "institutionalizing" the cold war.

459 "Fulbright vs. Truman." *Arkansas Alumnus,* n.s. 4 (June 1951): 2, 4.

In a letter to W.J. Lemke, Douglas Smith explains the story surrounding the publication of Fulbright's suggestion that President Truman resign in 1946 when the Republicans gained control of Congress in the midterm elections.

460 "The 'Get Dulles' Campaign." *Newsweek,* 4 February 1957, 21-22.

The article concerns John Foster Dulles's appearance before a joint hearing of the Foreign Relations and the Armed Services committees and includes an account of Fulbright's attack on the secretary of state's foreign policy. It also mentions the senator's position on the Middle East resolution.

461 Goldman, Eric F. "The Presidency as Moral Leadership." *The Annals of The American Academy of Political and Social Science* 280 (March 1952): 37-45.

The author quotes Fulbright on the criteria of ethical conduct in government.

462 "Go-Slow Roadblocks." *Time,* 28 April 1958, 18.

The article concerns Republican efforts to foil antirecession spending by the Democrats. It focuses on congressional strategies associated with Fulbright's community facilities bill.

463 Griffith, Robert. *The Politics of Fear: Joseph R. McCarthy and the Senate.* Lexington: University Press of Kentucky, 1970, 148, 150, 172, 206, 239, 280, 282, 285, 289-90, 295-96, 298, 301-2, 304-5, 315.

The author notes Fulbright's clash with Joseph R. McCarthy over Philip C.

Jessup's nomination as a delegate to the United Nations and his lone vote against appropriations for McCarthy's Permanent Subcommittee on Investigations. The writer also notes Fulbright's role in the McCarthy censure movement, particularly his introduction of six charges in the form of amendments to the resolution.

464 "Gruenther on NATO Deeds and Needs." *Freedom and Union* 11 (July-August 1956): 5-8.

The article consists of excerpts from General Alfred M. Gruenther's testimony, including questions and answers, at the Senate Foreign Relations Committee hearing regarding NATO on May 31, 1956. Fulbright questions are included.

465 Grundy, Kenneth W. "The Apprenticeship of J. William Fulbright." *The Virginia Quarterly Review* 43 (Summer 1967): 382-99.

In an article about Fulbright's first ten years on the Foreign Relations Committee, from 1949 until 1959, the author examines the senator's role as critic of U.S. foreign policy during President Eisenhower's tenure and focuses on his relationship with John Foster Dulles, particularly their clash over the Eisenhower Doctrine. Fulbright became chairman of the committee on February 6, 1959.

466 Hale, William Harlan. "The Man from Arkansas Goes After Mr. Dulles." *The Reporter,* 18 April 1957, 30-33.

The author traces Fulbright's encounters with Secretary of State John Foster Dulles before the Foreign Relations Committee concerning U.S. policy in the Middle East and evaluates the senator's efforts to secure a complete accounting from the State Department of the situation in the region. The senator was chairman of the subcommittee that examined U.S. policy in the Middle East in the spring of 1957.

467 Hamer, Helen B. "Atlantic Union Resolution Re-introduced." *Freedom and Union* 6 (February 1951): 8-9.

The article concerns the reintroduction of the Atlantic Union resolution and its bipartisan support in both houses of Congress. Fulbright was one of the sponsors.

468 "Herter and Fulbright Talk Foreign Policy." *The New York Times Magazine,* 3 May 1959, cover.

Secretary of State Christian A. Herter and the senator are featured on the cover. An article on Herter begins on page 6.

469 "Honor of the Corps." *Newsweek,* 13 August 1951, 78.

This article about the cheating scandal at West Point includes Fulbright's recommendation that intercollegiate football be eliminated at the military academies.

470 "How to Win." *Newsweek,* 27 August 1956, 30-31.

This is a photo essay featuring Adlai Stevenson on how to capture the presidential nomination. A photograph of Stevenson with Fulbright is included.

471 "'If Wine Is Not Desired.'" *Newsweek,* 3 April 1961, 28, 32.

The article regards Secretary of State Dean Rusk's training course for ambassadors. It mentions Fulbright as lecturer on issues related to Congress.

472 "Irritated Man." *Time,* 19 February 1951, 18.

The article concerns Harry Truman's outbursts of temper and includes his attack on Fulbright's subcommittee report concerning the White House and the Reconstruction Finance Corporation. The story concludes with a review of the Truman-Fulbright relationship and includes the president's pointed remarks regarding the senator's Oxford education.

473 "Is This Bad? Figures Say No—And Ike Acts to Aid Laggards." *Newsweek,* 11 January 1954, 57-58.

The article concerns President Eisenhower's antirecession program and includes Fulbright's criticism of the president's policy of diverting defense appropriations to areas of high unemployment.

474 Johnson, Walter. *How We Drafted Adlai Stevenson.* New York: Alfred A. Knopf, 1955, 113, 141, 149, 151.

This book about the nomination of Adlai Stevenson as the Democratic presidential candidate in 1952 is dedicated to Fulbright.

475 ——, ed. *The Papers of Adlai E. Stevenson.* Vol. 4, *"Let's Talk Sense to the American People,"* *1952-1955.* Boston: Little, Brown and Company, 1974, 27, 125, 186, 445, 519-20.

The fourth volume of Stevenson's papers includes incidental references to Fulbright.

476 ——, ed. *The Papers of Adlai E. Stevenson.* Vol. 5, *Visit to Asia, the Middle East, and Europe, March-August 1953.* Boston: Little, Brown and Company, 1974, 371, 483.

The fifth volume of Stevenson's papers includes incidental references to the senator.

477 ——, ed. *The Papers of Adlai E. Stevenson.* Vol. 6, *Toward a New America, 1955-1957.* Boston: Little, Brown and Company, 1976, 21n, 154, 158, 170, 361, 384-85, 434-35, 453-54, 471.

The sixth volume of Stevenson's papers includes several letters to Fulbright concerning Stevenson's interest in the presidency of the University of California, Eisenhower's proposed Middle East resolution of 1957, the Fulbright exchange program, and John Erickson's assistance with the Stevenson presidential campaign of 1956. Incidental references to the senator are found on pages 27, 125, 186, 445, and 519-20 of the fourth volume and on pages 371 and 483 of the fifth volume of the Stevenson papers.

478 Kamm, Henry. "Listening In on Radio Free Europe—The Station That Fulbright Wants to Shut Down." *The New York Times Magazine,* 26 March 1972, 36-37, 112-15.

In an article supporting Radio Free Europe, the author opposes Fulbright's efforts to stop congressional funding of the station.

479 Kaplan, Lawrence S. *The United States and NATO: The Formative Years.* Lexington: University Press of Kentucky, 1984, 8, 49-50, 52, 55-57, 67, 71, 75-76, 78, 89, 91-92, 99-102, 131, 133, 177-78, 247n, 249n.

The author incorporates Fulbright's position on European unity into his treatment of the United States's relationship with the North Atlantic Treaty Organization.

480 "Kefauver's Reply to the State Department: Fifth in Kefauver Memorial Series." *Freedom and Union* 19 (March 1964): 20-24.

In a speech on March 13, 1950, Senator Estes Kefauver responds to the State Department, with the intervention of Senators Fulbright, Douglas, and Flanders supporting his attack on the department's position on Atlantic unity.

481 Kelly, Frank K. *Court of Reason: Robert Hutchins and the Fund for the Republic.* New York: Macmillan Publishing Company, Free Press, 1981, 217, 226, 228, 249, 280, 292-94, 296, 298-99, 301, 325, 328, 347-48, 376, 469, 505-7.

The author mentions several events concerning Fulbright's association with the Fund for the Republic and its brainchild, the Center for the Study of Democratic Institutions.

482 Kemler, Edgar. "Democratic Giveaway: The Natural Gas Bill." *The Nation,* 4 February 1956, 84-86.

The author examines the Senate debate surrounding the natural gas bill and mentions Fulbright as one of the floor leaders of the bill to remove regulations from the natural gas producers.

483 Kendrick, Frank J. "McCarthy and the Senate." Ph.D. diss., University of Chicago, 1962, 108, 112, 117-18, 269-70, 273, 281, 286, 288, 295, 301.

In this study of the Senate's reaction to McCarthyism, the author notes Fulbright's lone vote against appropriations for Joseph R. McCarthy's Permanent Investigations Subcommittee and his role in the censure of the Wisconsin senator.

484 "The Kennedy Non-Papers." *Newsweek,* 9 August 1971, 24-25.

In an article about the opening of the John F. Kennedy Papers, the president's consideration of Fulbright for secretary of state is noted.

485 "Knight of the Bald Iggle." *Time,* 12 August 1957, 16.

The story concerns Fulbright's exchange with Maxwell Gluck during hearings before the Foreign Relations Committee concerning Gluck's nomination as U.S. ambassador to Ceylon. Despite Fulbright's opposition to the appointment, Gluck was confirmed.

486 "Last Travels." *Newsweek,* 10 November 1952, 27-28.

The article is an account of presidential candidate Adlai E. Stevenson's campaign travels filed by *Newsweek's* Hobart Rowen. It mentions Fulbright's pinch hitting for Stevenson in Maryland, West Virginia, and Delaware during the final days of the campaign.

487 "Leaks and Innuendoes." *Newsweek,* 9 October 1961, 49-50.

The article includes Fulbright's remarks on the joint responsibility of the Soviet Union and the West for the Berlin crisis.

488 "Levels of Thinking." *Time,* 3 December 1945, 28.

The article examines the different levels of thinking of British, American, and Russian leaders on the issue of strengthening the United Nations Organization. The positions of Senators Fulbright and Carl A. Hatch are noted.

489 "Look Homeward, Angel." *The Nation,* 7 April 1951, 312-13.

The editorial concerns the moral problems revealed by the congressional investigation of Joseph R. McCarthy's campaign against Millard Tydings of Maryland. The editors praise Fulbright's speech calling for a commission to consider the problems and suggest that Fulbright start with a cleanup of the Senate.

490 McCarry, Charles. "Mourning Becomes Senator Fulbright." *Esquire* 73 (June 1970): 116-19, 178-79.

In a profile of the senator, the author focuses on Fulbright's legislative record on domestic issues, particularly civil rights. He also treats his relationship with presidents, including his break with Lyndon Johnson over U.S. policy in the Dominican Republic and Vietnam. Additionally, he notes Fulbright's reputation with the Old Left and the New Left.

491   McConaughy, James L., Jr. "The World's Most Exclusive Clubmen: Its Characters Give the U.S. Senate Variety and Special Flavor." *Life,* 19 April 1954, 111-16.

The author spotlights key senators and includes Fulbright, noting his professorial demeanor.

492   McGee, Gale W. *The Responsibilities of World Power.* Washington, D.C.: National Press, 1968, 139, 158, 168, 206, 208-10, 257.

The author examines thoughts that Fulbright expressed in an article in the fall 1961 issue of the *Cornell Law Quarterly* on the need for strong executive leadership in the conduct of foreign affairs.

493   McPherson, Harry. "The Senate Observed: A Recollection." *The Atlantic Monthly* 229 (May 1972): 76-82, 84, 86, 89-92.

The article consists of sketches drawn from observing senators, both Democratic and Republican, and includes Fulbright.

494   Meador, Allison. "J. William Fulbright and the Truman-MacArthur Controversy." *The Ozark Historical Review* 15 (Spring 1986): 12-19.

The author examines Fulbright's defense of Harry Truman in the wake of the president's dismissal of General Douglas MacArthur. She concludes that the senator's position in the controversy says something about his concept of U.S. foreign policy and about his style as a legislator.

495   "Middle East Debate (Contd.)." *Time,* 4 February 1957, 13-14.

The article pertains to John Foster Dulles's appearance before Senate committees on U.S foreign policy in the Middle East. Fulbright expresses concern about the effect of the secretary's policies on relations with Britain and France and calls for a white paper on Dulles's conduct of U.S. policy in that region.

496   "The Mideast Debate." *The New Republic,* 4 February 1957, 3-4.

In an editorial about John Foster Dulles and the Eisenhower Doctrine, the writers criticize the Democrats for trying to combine policy issues with the question of Dulles's fitness to remain in office. The editors recommend that Congress endorse the Eisenhower Doctrine and then institute a full-scale inquiry into U.S. policies in the Middle East.

497   Moley, Raymond. "By-passing Congress." *Newsweek,* 1 March 1954, 84.

Moley reviews the legislative history of amendments to the Defense Production Act sponsored by Senators Fulbright and Homer Ferguson. The amendments concerned U.S. participation in the International Materials Conference.

498   ———. "Money for Tourists." *Newsweek,* 22 March 1965, 100.

Moley scolds Fulbright for holding the view that Americans can help the balance-of-payments problem by traveling within the United States instead of going abroad.

499   ———. "The Unsinkable REA." *Newsweek,* 19 August 1963, 84.

In a column opposing subsidies for the Rural Electrification Administration, Moley reproves Fulbright for his stand on the REA and its critics.

500 "More Inflation? The Yen to Spend." *Newsweek,* 10 November 1958, 55-56.

The article mentions Fulbright's community facilities bill.

501 Morford, Richard. "Coexistence." *New World Review* 33, No. 6 (1965): 60-61.

The item includes an excerpt from Fulbright's statement at the *Pacem in Terris* convocation in New York on coexistence.

502 "'Most Disappointed.'" *Time,* 10 June 1957, 19, 21.

Fulbright comments on this country's China policy in the wake of the British announcement to ease economic restrictions against Peking.

503 "Mr. Ambassador." *The New Republic,* 15 June 1974, 8-9.

This editorial mentions Fulbright's letter to the Department of State recommending reforms of the system of political appointments to high Foreign Service posts.

504 "Mrs. Roosevelt, and Others." *Time,* 31 December 1945, 14.

Fulbright questions the qualifications of President Truman's five alternate delegates to the General Assembly of the United Nations in London. Senators Joseph Ball and Wayne Morse support his position.

505 "Nasty Job." *Newsweek,* 21 September 1964, 30-31.

The article includes Fulbright's remarks reproving Congressman William E. Miller for his attack on Hubert Humphrey.

506 "New Frontierland: The Big Wheels." *Look,* 2 January 1962, 46-49.

This is a photo essay of President John F. Kennedy's assistants and includes Fulbright. It notes the harmony of the two men's world views.

507 "New Team at U.N." *Time,* 9 August 1954, 14.

The article notes Fulbright's nomination by President Eisenhower to be U.S. Representative to the ninth session of the United Nations General Assembly.

508 "The New Word." *The Nation,* 1 February 1965, 98.

The editorial concerns the currency of the word "neo-isolationism" and mentions Walter Lippmann and Fulbright as two whose thoughts harmonize with the new philosophy concerning foreign policy.

509 "Newsmakers." *Newsweek,* 10 March 1969, 64.

The item reports Fulbright's presence at an intramural basketball game at George Washington University to watch a team named the "Fulbrights" play.

510 "Newsmakers." *Newsweek,* 11 October 1971, 50.

The item mentions Fulbright's remarks concerning Vice President Spiro Agnew's visit to Greece.

511 "The Obsolescence of Bipartisanship." *The Nation,* 16 August 1958, 61.

The editors praise Fulbright for his remarks in the Senate regarding the failure of U.S. leadership in foreign policy.

512 "Oleo's Day." *Newsweek,* 30 January 1950, 15.

The article concerns the repeal of federal taxes on oleomargarine and notes Fulbright's position on the issue.

513 "On the South Side." *Time,* 18 April 1955, 25.

The article concerns Fulbright's 1952 amendment to the Walsh-Healey Act and its effect on southern manufacturers in the cotton, silk, and synthetic textile plants. The amendment allowed the courts to review minimum wage orders established by the U.S. Department of Labor pursuant to the Walsh-Healey Public Contracts Act.

514 "Operation Rooney." *Time,* 6 January 1961, 15.

The article includes a note about Fulbright's visit to Palm Beach to confer with President-elect Kennedy on a proposal to increase the minimum wage.

515 Oshinsky, David M. *A Conspiracy So Immense: The World of Joe McCarthy.* New York: Macmillan, Free Press, 1983, 178, 210-12, 219, 316, 319, 361, 474, 475n, 477, 487, 492n.

The author notes the senator's clash with Joseph R. McCarthy over Philip C. Jessup's nomination for a United Nations post, Fulbright's exchange with the Wisconsin senator over appropriations for the Fulbright program, and the senator's role in the censure of McCarthy.

516 "The Painful Search." *Newsweek,* 19 December 1960, 17-18.

The article notes the outlook for Fulbright's appointment to the cabinet post of secretary of state.

517 "People." *Sports Illustrated,* 15 September 1969, 93.

The senator talks about the benefits of playing golf.

518 "People." *Time,* 7 March 1969, 40.

Fulbright attends an intramural basketball game at George Washington University and cheers for the squad named for him.

519 "People of the Week." *U.S. News and World Report,* 8 February 1957, 18.

The senator calls for a complete accounting by the secretary of state of U.S. policy in the Middle East.

520 "A Pet Bill for Every Man on the Hill." *Newsweek,* 4 September 1961, 19.

Fulbright introduces a bill to repeal the excise tax on croquet balls and mallets.

521 "Peyton Boswell Comments: Bill S. 2439." *The Art Digest,* 15 April 1948, 7.

Boswell's column concerns the bill introduced by Fulbright providing for the temporary retention and exhibition in the United States of 202 German paintings recovered by the U.S. military from a salt mine near Merkers. A reprint of the bill is included.

522 "Picking the Men." *Time,* 19 December 1960, 15-16.

The story concerns President-elect Kennedy's task of choosing his cabinet and includes a note regarding the decision to switch from Fulbright to Dean Rusk for secretary of state.

523 "Picking the Team." *Time,* 12 December 1960, 17.

The story concerns President-elect Kennedy's consideration of Fulbright for the office of secretary of state and the primary drawback associated with the senator, his record in Arkansas on racial issues.

524 "President Expresses Views on Mutual Security Program." *The Department of State Bulletin,* 6 October 1958, 546-49.

This is an exchange of letters between President Eisenhower and the Senate Foreign Relations Committee on proposed reform of the mutual security program.

525 "President: Loser's Stand." *Newsweek,* 18 November 1946, 36.

President Truman rejects Fulbright's suggestion that he appoint a Republican secretary of state and resign, allowing a Republican to succeed in the wake of the Democratic losses in the midterm elections.

526 Prochnow, Herbert V., and Herbert V. Prochnow, Jr. *The Toastmaster's Treasure Chest.* New York: Harper and Row, 1979, 375.

The volume includes a quotation by Fulbright in the chapter "Great Thoughts of Distinguished Americans."

527 Purvis, Hoyt, and Steven J. Baker, eds. *Legislating Foreign Policy.* A Westview Special Study. Boulder, Colo.: Westview Press, 1984, 24-25, 30, 42-45, 51, 68, 109, 113, 117-18, 121, 190.

The editors discuss the reversal of the senator's belief that the president should have more control over foreign policy than the Senate. They also discuss the evolution of Fulbright's thought regarding the Truman Doctrine.

528 Reeves, Thomas C. *The Life and Times of Joe McCarthy: A Biography.* New York: Stein and Day, Publishers, 1982, 115, 388-91, 408, 414, 460, 491, 504, 507, 539, 605, 641-44, 646-47, 655, 663, 668.

The author discusses the senator's clash with Joseph R. McCarthy over the Philip C. Jessup nomination and Fulbright's role in the censure of the Wisconsin senator.

529 "Resolved: No Action: The Thomas Report—2." *Freedom and Union* 5 (November 1950): 24-25.

Freedom and Union presents a compendium of the remaining four resolutions considered in part 2 of the Thomas Report: Senate Resolution 133 (the Sparkman resolution or the "ABC" proposal), Senate Concurrent Resolution 66 (the Taylor or "World Constitution" resolution), Senate Concurrent Resolution 12 (the Fulbright-Thomas or "European Federation" resolution), and Senate Concurrent Resolution 72 (the Ferguson resolution). See the October issue of *Freedom and Union* for the report on the first three. The seven resolutions concerned the United Nations Charter, Atlantic Union, and world federation.

530 "Revival of Learning?" *The Commonweal,* 7 February 1958, 475-76.

The editorial focuses on the Fulbright idea that restructuring education and restoring a respect for learning are the key to meeting the challenge from the Soviet Union.

531 "The Role of the Maverick." *The Nation,* 16 November 1974, 485.

The editorial contrasts Fulbright's November 2 foreign policy address at Westminster College in Fulton, Missouri, with Winston Churchill's 1946 "Iron Curtain" speech. Using the speech as a base, the editors assess the senator's importance to the nation as a thinker and dissenter and the void left by his departure from the Senate. They incorrectly cite the date of the speech as November 3.

532 Rostow, Eugene V. "The Cost of Fealty." *The Department of State Bulletin,* 15 April 1968, 493-500.

In an address before the Manchester, New Hampshire, Chamber of Commerce on March 22, the undersecretary of state includes a critique of Fulbright's view of the role of the United States in the world.

533   Rourke, John. *Congress and the Presidency in U.S. Foreign Policymaking: A Study of Interaction and Influence, 1945-1982.* Boulder, Colo.: Westview Press, 1983, 93, 95, 98, 103-4, 108-11, 113, 127, 142-44, 148, 151-53, 163, 169, 176-77, 181, 184, 188, 192, 194-95, 200, 204-6, 208-10, 214-16, 222, 224-27, 230, 232, 234, 239, 243, 250, 252, 262, 289, 298, 300, 304, 309.

Fulbright figures in the writer's study of the scope of congressional influence in postwar policy formation, particularly as regards such issues as foreign aid, Middle East diplomacy, and the Foreign Relations Committee's China hearings. He also treats Fulbright's break with President Johnson.

534   Rovere, Richard H. "Letter from Washington." *The New Yorker,* 26 March 1960, 138-47.

This article concerns the Senate filibuster associated with the 1960 civil rights legislation. The author notes the absence of a champion of southern views and values in the Senate and profiles prominent southern senators, including Fulbright, noting their contributions to the filibuster.

535   Rozzell, Forrest. "Labeling Senator Fulbright." *The Journal of Arkansas Education* 34 (October 1961): 44.

The author discusses the failure of attempts to label the senator and the reasons that he cannot be easily categorized.

536   "Rural Educators, Meeting in Wichita, Are Optimistic About Their Future." *The Kansas Teacher* 71 (November 1962): 22-23.

The article includes excerpts from Fulbright's address before the National Education Association's Department of Rural Education on October 13, 1962. The senator's remarks begin on page 21 of this issue of the *Kansas Teacher.*

537   Schlesinger, Arthur [M.], Jr. "Congress and the Making of American Foreign Policy." *Foreign Affairs* 51 (October 1972): 78-113.

In an article about the congressional role in foreign policy, the author includes references to Fulbright, and quotations, which document the reversal of his belief in a strong presidency in foreign affairs.

538   ———, ed. *The Dynamics of World Power: A Documentary History of United States Foreign Policy, 1945-1973.* Vol. 2, *Eastern Europe and the Soviet Union.* Edited by Walter LaFeber. New York: Chelsea House Publishers in association with McGraw-Hill Book Company, 1973, 484-93, 573-78.

This is question-and-answer testimony of Secretary of State John Foster Dulles before the Senate Foreign Relations Committee in the spring of 1954 explaining his policy of massive retaliation and discussing the Eisenhower Doctrine. Questions by Fulbright are included.

539   "Secretary of State." *The New Republic,* 14 November 1960, 3-7.

This editorial evaluates the front runners for the office of secretary of state in the Kennedy administration. Fulbright is included.

540   "The Secretary's Defense." *Time,* 5 March 1956, 17-18.

Fulbright questions Secretary of State John Foster Dulles before an open session of the Foreign Relations Committee on the Middle East and the Soviet Union.

541 Seib, Charles B., and Alan L. Otten. "Fulbright: Arkansas Paradox." *Harper's Magazine* 212 (June 1956): 60-66.

In an outline of Fulbright's legislative record, the authors examine the inconsistencies in his political profile and the impossibility of categorizing him. They review his idea of the role of the legislator in a democratic society and conclude that this concept accounts for the inability to label his voting record.

542 "The Senate." *Newsweek,* 12 November 1956, 66, 73.

The article mentions Fulbright as one of the impressive young senators on the Foreign Relations Committee.

543 "Senate Committee Weighs Atlantic Convention Call—Dulles Opens New Way." *Freedom and Union* 10 (September 1955): 6-13.

The article concerns the Foreign Relations Committee hearings on Senate Concurrent Resolution 12 proposing a convention of delegates from the Western democracies to consider the formation of an Atlantic Union. It includes a picture of Fulbright with his colleagues. The senator was an early advocate of European federation.

544 "Senator Fulbright, a National Leader." *The Ozarks Mountaineer* 9 (December 1961): 15.

This is an editorial praising Fulbright's work in foreign relations.

545 "Senators for Federation." *Freedom and Union* 3 (February 1948): 19.

Senators Fulbright and Elbert Thomas call for the political federation of Europe.

546 "Senators Kefauver and Fulbright Reply to Wilson." *The Nation,* 18 August 1951, 140.

These are letters to the editor related to H.H. Wilson's article, "The Pressure to Buy and Corrupt," in the July 21 issue of the *Nation.*

547 "Senators Learn About Atlantic Union." *Freedom and Union* 4 (July-August 1949): 9-15.

The article consists of excerpts from testimony of officers of the Atlantic Union Committee before the Senate Foreign Relations Committee at hearings in May 1949 on Atlantic unity. Fulbright questions are included.

548 "Shifting the Load." *Newsweek,* 21 November 1960, 28-29.

Fulbright is mentioned as a possible appointment to the Kennedy cabinet as secretary of state.

549 "Shifts and Middle Ground." *Time,* 7 May 1951, 23-24.

The article concerns the debate over President Truman's dismissal of General Douglas MacArthur from the Far East command after differences in points of view on policy and includes Fulbright's defense of the president.

550 "Should Fulbright Be Muzzled?" *National Review,* 24 August 1965, 718.

The editors defend the Young Americans for Freedom from Fulbright's charge that they behaved unconstitutionally regarding Firestone's efforts to build synthetic rubber plants in Rumania.

551 "Sickness." *Time,* 13 December 1954, 14.

Fulbright reads to his colleagues from some of the abusive letters received from supporters of Joseph R. McCarthy.

552 "Socony-Vacuum and Freedom." *Saturday Review,* 19 February 1955, 23.

In a letter to the editor, Socony-Vacuum Oil Company responds to Fulbright's reference in his speech, "The Mummification of Opinion," to their pamphlet, "So You Want a Better Job." The company official discusses the revised edition of the pamphlet and includes remarks concerning the place of young people in the business community. The senator's speech appeared in the February 12 issue of *Saturday Review*.

553 "Speaking of Books: For the Joy of It." *The New York Times Book Review,* 4 July 1965, 2.

The editor asks a number of people, including Fulbright, to talk about the kinds of books they read for enjoyment.

554 "A Special Report: *Pacem in Terris III:* A National Convocation to Consider New Opportunities for United States Foreign Policy." *Center Report* 6 (December 1973): 15-24.

This is a review of *Pacem in Terris III,* the national convocation of the Center for the Study of Democratic Institutions, held in Washington, D.C., in October 1973. It includes press coverage of Fulbright's participation in the meeting. The senator's remarks were published in the January-February 1974 issue of the *Center Magazine* under the title "What Is the National Interest?"

555 "Standing Alone." *Newsweek,* 19 October 1964, 11, 16.

In a letter to the editor, the writer notes Fulbright's position on Senator Dirksen's efforts to frustrate the Supreme Court's ruling on reapportionment of state legislatures.

556 "State of the Union." *The Commonweal,* 13 April 1951, 3-4.

This is an editorial pertaining to the moral problems revealed by the Kefauver crime committee's investigations. It includes Fulbright quotations reflecting his concern and notes his recommendation that a commission be appointed to consider the problems.

557 Stein, Emanuel. "The Dilemma of Union Democracy." *The Annals of The American Academy of Political and Social Science* 350 (November 1963): 46-54.

The author quotes Fulbright on the difficulties facing the political community in a democracy.

558 "Storm Center." *Newsweek,* 2 October 1961, 18, 20.

In an article about the UN in the wake of Dag Hammarskjöld's death, Fulbright urges the United States to concentrate more on the Atlantic community and instrumentalities like the North Atlantic Treaty Organization and less on the United Nations.

559 Streit, Clarence. "Balanced Atlantic Forces—Another Maginot Blunder." *Freedom and Union* 5 (July-August 1950): 2-5.

The article includes question-and-answer testimony from hearings on the North Atlantic Treaty in the spring of 1949 in which Fulbright questions the absence of voting procedures in the Atlantic Council.

560 "Sun Hot? Earth Round?" *Newsweek,* 29 July 1957, 29.

The article includes Fulbright's remarks regarding President Eisenhower's overture to Marshal Georgi K. Zhukov, defense minister of the Soviet Union.

561 T.R.B. "Capital Portraits." *The New Republic,* 7 May 1966, 4.

The column consists of T.R.B.'s candid notes drawn from observing five prominent Americans on the Washington speaking circuit: J. William Fulbright, Robert McNamara, John Kenneth Galbraith, Hubert Humphrey, and Dean Acheson.

562 ———. "The Heart of the Contest." *The New Republic,* 10 February 1958, 2.

The writer uses Fulbright's speech on federal aid to education as the springboard for this item on the importance of education.

563 ———. "Washington Wire." *The New Republic,* 7 February 1955, 2.

The item concerns Fulbright's speech attacking the one-party press in the United States.

564 "The Talk of the Town." *The New Yorker,* 28 April 1973, 29-34.

The writer incorporates interviews with Mike Mansfield, John Sherman Cooper, Clark Clifford, Edmund Muskie, Donald E. Santarelli, and J. William Fulbright concerning the constitutional questions surrounding Watergate.

565 "The Tangled Web." *Time,* 9 April 1945, 23-24.

The article concerns the secret agreement of the Big Three at Yalta regarding voting in the assembly of the proposed United Nations. It includes Fulbright's criticism of the arrangement.

566 "Target: A Senator." *Newsweek,* 2 March 1959, 6.

This is a letter to the editor concerned with Fulbright's remarks about John Foster Dulles. The writer also comments on the senator's civil rights position.

567 "Till the Boys Come Home." *Time,* 12 March 1945, 18-19.

The story regards Fulbright's resolution proposing that treaties be approved by a simple majority in both houses of Congress. The Senate responded by tabling the resolution.

568 "A Time for Daring: Senate Hearings on S.C.R. 57." *Freedom and Union* 5 (June 1950): 22-26.

The article concerns the Foreign Relations Committee hearings on Senate Concurrent Resolution 57 proposing a convention of delegates from the Western democracies to consider the formation of an Atlantic Union. Fulbright poses a question about the economic benefits accruing from such a union.

569 "Truman v. Congress." *Time,* 14 January 1946, 15-16.

The article concerns President Truman's battle with Congress over his proposed economic program and includes Fulbright's remarks on fact-finding and labor unions.

570 "25th Anniversary Year Opens with Greetings from All over Atlantica." *Freedom and Union* 26 (October 1971): 8-9, 12-13.

The article includes congratulations from Fulbright to *Freedom and Union* on its twenty-fifth anniversary.

571 "UNESCO." *The School Executive* 66 (October 1946): 69-74.

Fulbright is recognized as one of the "UNESCO Personalities" for his contributions toward the reconstruction of educational and cultural institutions in war-torn nations. Fulbright was chairman of the U.S. delegation to the Allied Ministers of Education Conference in London in April 1944.

572 "United Nations: Battlefield of Peace." *Time,* 29 September 1961, 20-24.

The article mentions Fulbright's proposal of an international community of free nations to be pursued primarily outside the United Nations, starting with the existing institutions of the North Atlantic Treaty Organization and the Organization for Economic Cooperation and Development. The senator's article in the October 1961 issue of *Foreign Affairs* is quoted.

573 "Unwelcome . . ." *Newsweek,* 11 February 1957, 26-28.

The article notes Fulbright's proposal for a full-scale inquiry into U.S. foreign policy in the Middle East and its intended effect on President Eisenhower's Middle East resolution.

574 "A U.S.E.?" *Time,* 28 April 1947, 26.

The article mentions Fulbright's pending resolution favoring the political unification of Europe.

575 Viorst, Milton. "Portrait of a Man Reading: J. William Fulbright, U.S. Senator from Arkansas." *The Washington Post Book World,* 24 March 1968, 2.

In an interview with Milton Viorst, Fulbright talks about the books that have influenced him, the role of the Senate Foreign Relations Committee as educator, China, Vietnam, and political leaders concerned with their place in history.

576 Walton, William. *The Evidence of Washington.* New York: Harper and Row, Publishers, in association with Chanticleer Press, 1966, facing page 100, 105, 123.

The book includes a photograph of Fulbright by Evelyn Hofer.

577 "What's It Worth?" *Newsweek,* 1 July 1957, 68.

The article lists Fulbright as a board member of the Archives of American Art.

578 White, William S. "Senate Shapers of Foreign Policy." *The New York Times Magazine,* 1 February 1953, 8-9.

The article profiles six new members of the Senate Foreign Relations Committee and features Fulbright as a minority member specializing in Europe, the Near East, and Africa.

579 "Who for the Cabinet?" *Time,* 21 November 1960, 18-19.

Fulbright is among those listed as possibilities for the office of secretary of state.

580 "Why Mr. Truman Doesn't Quit; Refusal to Change Rules by Fiat, or to Run Out on Job and Party." *The United States News,* 15 November 1946, 34.

The article centers around Fulbright's suggestion that President Truman appoint a Republican secretary of state and resign, giving control of the executive and the legislative branches to the Republican party. Fulbright's proposal came in the wake of Republican victories in the midterm elections.

581 "Why the Republicans Are Mad at Democrats—and Friend." *Newsweek,* 22 February 1954, 27.

The article includes a quotation by Fulbright on the difficulties of a democratic society in dealing with public officials who engage in abusive behavior. The excerpt is from an address in the Senate on February 2, 1954, on the Bricker amendment.

582 "Why U.S. Senators Are Raising Questions About the U.N." *U.S. News and World Report,* 16 April 1962, 56-57.

The article reviews key senators' concerns about the United Nations and its effect on U.S. foreign policy and cites Fulbright's article, "For a Concert of Free Nations," which appeared in the October 1961 issue of *Foreign Affairs.*

583 "Wing Shot." *Newsweek,* 25 March 1963, 60.

Fulbright responds to a news report of former President Eisenhower's hunting trip in Mexico. The senator criticizes Eisenhower for the number of birds taken, asserting that such practices affect duck hunting in Arkansas.

584 Wooten, Paul. "Capital Views and Previews." *Dun's Review and Modern Industry* 76 (December 1960): 83-84.

In a column devoted primarily to Fulbright remarks on meeting the communist challenge, the senator calls for economic cooperation between the United States and Latin America and the federation of Europe as strategies for competing economically with the communists. Fulbright also notes the importance of domestic economic decisions on foreign policy.

585 "Worldgram: From the Capitals of the World." *U.S. News and World Report,* 14 August 1961, 59.

The item regards West Berlin's response to Fulbright's remarks about East German refugees.

586 "Worldgram: From the Capitals of the World." *U.S. News and World Report,* 8 July 1963, 55-56.

Fulbright mentions France's performance in World War II and notes its effect on U.S.-French relations.

587 "Yellow Supremacy." *Newsweek,* 23 January 1950, 18-19.

The article concerns the debate in the Senate between the butter and the oleomargarine interests and notes Fulbright's support of the repeal of taxes on margarine.

BANKING AND CURRENCY COMMITTEE, 1945-1960

588 "Bad Weather for Bulls." *Time,* 21 March 1955, 88-90.

The article concerns the stock market hearings conducted by Fulbright's Banking and Currency Committee.

589 Beatty, Jerome. "Washington's Cleanup Man." *American Magazine* 151 (June 1951): 26-27, 104-6, 108-9.

The author uses Fulbright's Banking and Currency Committee's investigation of the activities of the Reconstruction Finance Corporation as the springboard for a profile of the senator.

590 Bibby, John, and Roger Davidson. *On Capitol Hill: Studies in the Legislative Process.* New York: Holt, Rinehart and Winston, 1967, 102, 173-76, 178-79, 188, 200-201, 203-6, 217.

The authors examine the Senate Banking and Currency Committee and Fulbright's leadership style as chairman from 1955 until 1959. They also examine the legislative background of the Depressed Areas Act and Fulbright's battle with Paul Douglas over it in committee.

591　"Birth of a Scandal." *Newsweek,* 12 February 1951, 18.

The article concerns the Fulbright banking subcommittee report on Reconstruction Finance Corporation activities and includes highlights of charges of wrongdoing.

592　"Chairmen of Top Committees: 19 Who Will Shape the Laws in the New Congress." *U.S. News and World Report,* 5 December 1958, 38-40.

The article consists of vignettes of nineteen men in Congress who will head the key committees and features Fulbright as chairman of the Banking and Currency Committee.

593　"Charge of Politics in 'Biggest Bank': Troubles for Directors of the RFC." *U.S. News and World Report,* 16 February 1951, 40-43.

The article concerns the difficulties of the Reconstruction Finance Corporation in the light of an investigation by Fulbright's Banking and Currency subcommittee concerned with RFC activities.

594　"The Clamor Goes On." *Newsweek,* 6 June 1955, 78, 80.

The article concerns the Banking and Currency Committee's majority and minority reports of findings on the stock market.

595　"Dawson on the Carpet." *Newsweek,* 21 May 1951, 26-27.

The article concerns presidential assistant Donald Dawson's testimony before the Banking and Currency Committee hearings associated with the Reconstruction Finance Corporation.

596　"Down and Up; 'We Are in a Box.'" *Time,* 28 March 1955, 80.

The article concerns the stock market investigation conducted by Fulbright's Banking and Currency Committee and features William McChesney Martin, Jr., chairman of the Federal Reserve Board, and George Humphrey, secretary of the treasury, as witnesses. Note is also made of Fulbright's exchange with Homer Capehart.

597　Dunar, Andrew J. *The Truman Scandals and the Politics of Morality.* Columbia: University of Missouri Press, 1984, 78-96, 108, 141.

The author reviews Fulbright's role in the Banking and Currency Committee's investigation of the activities of the Reconstruction Finance Corporation and also assesses the impact of the interim and final reports of the committee.

598　"End of the Hunt?" *Newsweek,* 4 April 1955, 74, 76.

This article concerns the conclusion of the Senate Banking and Currency Committee's hearings on the stock market.

599　"Fair Deal Low Tide." *Newsweek,* 26 March 1951, 25.

The article notes the Fulbright subcommittee investigation of the Reconstruction Finance Corporation and President Truman's acceptance of its proposed reorganization plan for the agency.

600　"Five Ex-Bank Presidents Are Among the Members of the House and Senate

Banking and Currency Committees: Former Governors of States, Professors Most Numerous Among the Lawmakers." *Finance,* 10 September 1945, 40-42, 61-63.

The article includes a sketch of Fulbright's family background in banking.

601 "A 'Friendly' Check on the Stock Market." *U.S. News and World Report,* 4 March 1955, 70, 72-73.

The article concerns Fulbright's proposed investigation of Wall Street activities and outlines his plans for conducting the study. It includes a biographical sketch.

602 "The 'Friendly' Findings." *Time,* 6 June 1955, 93-94.

The article concerns the report prepared by the Senate Banking and Currency Committee on the stock market.

603 "A 'Friendly' Look-See." *Newsweek,* 14 February 1955, 69-70.

The article concerns the Banking and Currency Committee's study of the stock market.

604 "Fulbright Changed RFC Plan . . . and President's Mind." *U.S. News and World Report,* 2 March 1951, 37-38.

The article concerns Fulbright's differences with President Truman over how the Reconstruction Finance Corporation should be organized and managed. It focuses on the Fulbright subcommittee investigation of the RFC and President Truman's reversal of his position on the restructuring of the agency.

605 "Fulbright Group Splits Four Ways." *Business Week,* 28 May 1955, 178.

The article concerns the Banking and Currency Committee report on the stock market investigation. It also notes the various dissenting opinions of the Republicans.

606 "Fulbright Pauses for Breath." *Business Week,* 26 March 1955, 154-56.

The article concerns the Banking and Currency Committee hearings on the activities of the stock market and the deterioration of the hearings into a political quarrel between Senators Fulbright and Homer Capehart.

607 "Fur and Odor." *Newsweek,* 12 March 1951, 21-22.

The article pertains to the Reconstruction Finance Corporation scandal and investigation.

608 "The Hazards of Whizzing." *Time,* 31 March 1958, 10-11.

The article focuses on Lyndon Johnson's efforts to push Fulbright's community facilities bill through the Banking and Currency Committee and the ensuing battle with Paul Douglas over the committee agenda, including Douglas's bill to aid depressed areas.

609 "Head Banking Committees." *The National Savings and Loan Journal* 10 (January 1955): cover.

The journal features Fulbright on the cover as the new chairman of the Banking and Currency Committee.

610 "Headliner." *Time,* 5 March 1951, 89.

This is an article about the visibility captured by NBC's *Meet the Press.* It mentions the interview with Fulbright in which he discussed charges of irregularities associated with the Reconstruction Finance Corporation.

611 "Hot Spot for Lustron." *Newsweek,* 23 January 1950, 60, 65.

The article concerns Fulbright's plans to investigate Lustron Corporation of Columbus, Ohio, and the Reconstruction Finance Corporation.

612 "'In the Public Interest.'" *Newsweek,* 14 March 1955, 75-76.

The article concerns the Banking and Currency Committee hearings on the stock market.

613 "The Joy of Public Money." *American Affairs* 12 (July 1950): 154-58.

The article examines the Reconstruction Finance Corporation's loan to Texmass Petroleum Company and includes Fulbright's exchange with RFC directors during hearings before the Banking and Currency Committee. The senator was chairman of the subcommittee investigating RFC loan policy.

614 "Lecture for a Senator." *Time,* 4 April 1955, 84-85.

The article focuses on Bernard Baruch's testimony before Chairman Fulbright's Senate Banking and Currency Committee on the stock market. Fulbright also questions Ralph Demmler, Securities and Exchange Commission chairman, and Benjamin Fairless, U.S. Steel Corporation chairman.

615 Lindley, Ernest K. "Kefauver and Fulbright." *Newsweek,* 2 April 1951, 25.

Columnist Lindley comments on Fulbright's reasons for wanting to halt the Banking and Currency Committee's investigation of the Reconstruction Finance Corporation.

616 "People of the Week." *U.S. News and World Report,* 11 February 1955, 18.

The article concerns Fulbright's plans for a review of the stock market and includes a biographical sketch. The senator was chairman of the Banking and Currency Committee from 1955 until 1959.

617 Pettit, Lawrence K., and Edward Keynes, eds. *The Legislative Process in the U.S. Senate.* Rand McNally Political Science Series. Chicago: Rand McNally and Company, 1969, 14, 94n, 119, 124, 135n, 153-59, 167, 262.

In an analysis of the Banking and Currency Committee, the writer compares the leadership style of Chairman Fulbright with the style used by A. Willis Robertson, who succeeded Fulbright in 1959.

618 "Playing Post Office." *Newsweek,* 5 March 1951, 66, 69-70.

The article concerns the Senate Banking and Currency Committee hearings on the Reconstruction Finance Corporation. It notes Fulbright's response to President Truman's examination of correspondence between Congress and the RFC.

619 "Politics and a Parody." *Newsweek,* 13 June 1955, 84.

The article concerns a parody of Fulbright's investigation of the stock market by the Bond Club of New York.

620 "Pro and Con." *Time,* 7 May 1951, 27.

After his investigation of the Reconstruction Finance Corporation, Fulbright defends the agency and calls for a revamped RFC to help small businesses far from major financial centers.

621 "Report on Influence." *Newsweek,* 27 August 1951, 61-62.

The article concerns Fulbright's report on the investigation of the Reconstruction Finance Corporation by the Banking and Currency Committee.

622 "RFC Under Fire." *Newsweek,* 4 July 1949, 57, 60.

The article concerns Fulbright's criticism of the Reconstruction Finance Corporation's lending policies.

623 "S. and P. Reply to Fulbright Poll." *The Outlook,* 28 February 1955, back cover
and page 918.

This is a reprint of questions and answers associated with Fulbright's Banking and
Currency Committee's survey of the stock market. The questions focus primarily on
the reasons for the rise in market prices. The *Outlook* is a Standard and Poor's
publication concerned with business and market trends.

624 "Sen. Fulbright Goes to Bat for His Over-the-Counter Bill." *Business Week,* 21
January 1956, 78.

Fulbright makes a case for his proposed legislation calling for regulation of the
over-the-counter market by the Securities and Exchange Commission.

625 "Sen. J.W. Fulbright . . . Moving In on Unlisted Shares." *Business Week,* 9 July
1955, 52-54, 57.

In an article about the unlisted securities market, the writer considers the impact
of Fulbright's proposed regulation of the market by the SEC.

626 "The Shape of Things." *Newsweek,* 21 March 1955, 25-26.

The article pertains to the Banking and Currency Committee hearings on the
stock market.

627 "Start on Cleanup." *Newsweek,* 26 February 1951, 16-17.

The article highlights the reforms instituted by the Reconstruction Finance Corporation chairman to correct practices criticized by Fulbright's subcommittee and also
notes President Truman's acceptance of the subcommittee's reorganization plan for
the agency.

628 "The Stock Market: Watchdog's Bark." *Newsweek,* 17 January 1955, 63-64.

This article mentions Fulbright's proposed study of the stock market.

629 "Stocks: A Real Boom but Not for All." *Newsweek,* 18 July 1955, 67-68.

The article focuses on the state of the stock market after the Banking and Currency Committee hearings.

630 "Stocks in '57: How Will the Bird Fly?" *Newsweek,* 7 January 1957, 55-56.

The article mentions the Fulbright committee report on the stock market and
notes its findings concerning institutional stock buying.

631 "Strictly Legal." *Newsweek,* 9 April 1951, 18-19.

The article concerns the Fulbright subcommittee's findings regarding investment
in surplus tankers.

632 T.R.B. "Washington Wire." *The New Republic,* 4 April 1955, 2.

This item describes Bernard Baruch's appearance before Fulbright's Banking and
Currency Committee hearings on the stock market.

633 "Talking About the Market." *Business Week,* 5 March 1955, 30.

The article regards Fulbright's Banking and Currency Committee inquiry into stock market activities and his strategy for examining the sharp rise of stock prices.

634 "Texmass Mess?" *Time,* 24 April 1950, 100, 102.

The story concerns Fulbright's Senate banking subcommittee investigation of the Reconstruction Finance Corporation's loan to Texmass Petroleum Company.

635 "That 'Friendly' Study." *Newsweek,* 21 March 1955, 26-27.

The article concerns Fulbright's study of the stock market and includes highlights of the testimony.

636 "These Fourteen Men Will Shape Your Future." *Nation's Business* 43 (March 1955): 84-86.

The article regards the chairmen of the key committees in the Eighty-fourth Congress and features Fulbright as head of the Banking and Currency Committee, along with a brief committee agenda.

637 "Thorny Money." *Time,* 30 January 1950, 82.

The article mentions Fulbright's call for an investigation of the Reconstruction Finance Corporation's loan policy.

638 "Tighter Rein on Speculation Isn't Likely to Hurt Prices." *Newsweek,* 2 May 1955, 65.

The article features highlights from *Factors Affecting the Stock Market,* a book prepared by the staff of Fulbright's Banking and Currency Committee.

639 "Time for a Moral Spring Cleaning?" *Newsweek,* 9 April 1951, 17-18.

Fulbright calls for a moral cleanup of the government in the light of the findings of the Banking and Currency Committee's investigation of activities of the Reconstruction Finance Corporation. He further notes that the moral health of the country has implications for the United States in its foreign relations.

640 "Tooling Up for Senate Probe." *Business Week,* 12 March 1955, 184, 186, 189-90, 192, 194.

This is the story of how Fulbright's Banking and Currency Committee's stock market inquiry took form, how Fulbright and the committee prepared themselves for the study, and how they assembled the staff and prepared for the witnesses. Fulbright and the committee staff are featured on the cover.

641 Turner, Jean. "Corruption in Government: The Reconstruction Finance Corporation Scandal, 1950-1951." *The Ozark Historical Review* 6 (Spring 1977): 36-41.

The article traces the waning of the Reconstruction Finance Corporation, beginning in February 1950 with the investigation of RFC activities by a Banking and Currency subcommittee chaired by Fulbright, continuing in early 1951 with more hearings and suggestions for reorganization, and culminating in July 1951 with the final report calling for a National Commission of Ethical Standards.

642 "Week in Business." *Newsweek,* 24 January 1955, 77-78.

This item notes the Senate Banking and Currency Committee's intention to investigate the stock market.

643 "What Fulbright Really Meant." *Newsweek,* 17 January 1955, 22.

Fulbright responds to questions by *Newsweek* concerning his proposed study of the stock market.

644 "What Investment Bankers Think." *Newsweek,* 28 March 1955, 75-76.

The article concerns investment bankers' opinions regarding the effect of the Banking and Currency Committee's hearings on the stock market. It includes Fulbright's clash with Homer Capehart.

645 "When the Market Is High." *Time,* 14 March 1955, 94-95.

The story concerns the study of the stock market undertaken by Fulbright's Banking and Currency Committee.

646 "Where the Sugar Is You Will Find the Flies: Jesse Jones on the RFC." *American Affairs* 12 (July 1950): 158-59.

This is a letter to Fulbright from Jesse H. Jones expressing his thoughts about the Reconstruction Finance Corporation. Jones was the first RFC chairman, from 1932 until the end of the war.

CHAIRMAN, FOREIGN RELATIONS COMMITTEE, 1959-1974

647 "The Ablest Men in the Senate and House: 50 Top Washington Correspondents Rate Them." *Newsweek,* 20 June 1960, 35.

Fulbright appears on the list of Senate Democrats with eighteen votes, after Lyndon Johnson, who had forty-one, and Mike Mansfield, who had twenty-six.

648 "The Absentee." *Newsweek,* 3 January 1966, 15-16.

The article regards Fulbright's absence from President Johnson's state dinners for visiting foreign dignitaries. It centers on the widening breach between the president and the senator over foreign policy issues.

649 "Access to the Suez Canal." *The New Republic,* 16 May 1960, 5-6.

This editorial takes Fulbright to task for his remarks about the Senate vote favoring the Douglas-Keating rider to the foreign aid bill. The amendment called for withholding U.S. economic aid from Egypt for closing the Suez Canal to Israeli shipping.

650 "Admiral Burke Speaks Out About 'Muzzling' the Military." *U.S. News and World Report,* 21 August 1961, 85-86.

The senator's memorandum on the political activities of the military inspired these remarks by Admiral Arleigh A. Burke before the National Press Club in Washington, D.C., on August 3, 1961.

651 "Admiral Harlin's Open Letter to Senator Fulbright on Defense Seminars: ROA President Urges Full Debate of Issues Before American People." *The Officer* 37 (October 1961): 15-16.

The president of the Reserve Officers Association summarizes the association's experience with defense strategy seminars and outlines the organization's beliefs on the issue. This letter from Admiral John E. Harlin was written in response to Fulbright's memorandum on political and educational activities of the military.

652 "After-Dinner Speech." *Newsweek,* 5 July 1971, 47-48.

The article concerns Premier Chou En-lai's remarks on U.S.-Chinese relations and mentions Fulbright's Foreign Relations Committee hearings on China policy.

653 "Aftermath of the U-2—The Argument Goes On—Findings of Investigating Committee . . . Views of Individual Senators." *U.S. News and World Report,* 11 July 1960, 88-90.

The article concerns the consequences of the U-2 reconnaissance flight over the Soviet Union and consists of excerpts from the Foreign Relations Committee report and separate statements of three committee members: Homer E. Capehart, Frank J. Lausche, and Alexander Wiley. It also includes excerpts from Fulbright's speech criticizing President Eisenhower's handling of the situation and a rejoinder by Senator Wiley.

654 ". . . All Those Sugar Lobbyists Go Tweet Tweet Tweet." *Newsweek,* 30 July 1962, 21.

The article regards the sugar bill signed by President Kennedy and the related lobbying activities on the part of a number of sugar-producing countries. It mentions Fulbright's concern about the influence of foreign lobbyists.

655 Alsop, Stewart. "The Lessons of the Cuban Disaster." *The Saturday Evening Post,* 24 June 1961, 26-27, 68-70.

In an analysis of the Cuban invasion at the Bay of Pigs, the author notes Fulbright's opposition to the operation.

656 Ambrosius, Lloyd E. "The Goldwater-Fulbright Controversy." *The Arkansas Historical Quarterly* 29 (Autumn 1970): 252-70.

The author examines the Fulbright-Barry Goldwater argument over U.S. foreign policy options in terms of their assessment of the character of the communist challenge, their differing sets of foreign policy objectives, and their choice of means for attaining those objectives. Fulbright and Goldwater speeches and writings on the cold war from the period 1959-1964 make up the text for this study.

657 "Americans Off-Limit [*sic*]?" *Newsweek,* 17 October 1960, 56, 58.

Fulbright's contributions are noted in an article about the American delegation to the Inter-Parliamentary Union meeting in Tokyo.

658 "Anti-Missive Missive." *Newsweek,* 6 February 1967, 32.

The article notes Fulbright's position on the U.S.-Soviet consular treaty.

659 "Are We Muzzling Those Who Know Red Tactics Best?" *The Saturday Evening Post,* 4 November 1961, 82.

The editorial blasts Fulbright's memorandum on the military. It defends the Foreign Policy Research Institute's role as consultant to military officers and leaders as well as its "forward-strategy" program. For another view, see H.M.'s article, "Grand Strategy: The Views of the Administration and the Cold War College Do Not Seem to Coincide," in the August 25, 1961, issue of *Science.*

660 "Arms Sales." *The New Republic,* 30 June 1973, 7.

This editorial concerns foreign military assistance and focuses on the bill introduced by Fulbright to stress sales rather than grants. It examines the effects of the bill on the Nixon administration's sales policy.

661 "As Fulbright Sees U.S. Policy Abroad." *U.S. News and World Report*, 13 February 1959, 87.

The article includes excerpts from Fulbright's speeches and press conferences concerning a number of subjects: U.S. foreign policy, the Soviet Union, U.S. overseas bases, the cold war, foreign aid, the Middle East, and China.

662 "As Tensions Ease, a Time to Look Inward." *Newsweek*, 20 April 1964, 49-50.

The article explores the consequences of the easing of the cold war for the United States, the Soviet Union, and the rest of the world. It focuses on two speeches, one by Fulbright and the other by Premier Nikita S. Khrushchev, expressing the idea that domestic interests should take precedence over foreign concerns. The article includes excerpts from both speeches.

663 Ascoli, Max. "Charity Begins Abroad." *The Reporter*, 7 October 1965, 24.

This is an editorial critiquing Fulbright's speech on the Johnson administration's intervention in the Dominican Republic. The writer takes issue with Fulbright's ideas regarding the forces of social revolution in Latin America.

664 "At Home: Senator Strom Thurmond . . . " *National Review Bulletin*, 9 January 1962, 4-5.

Assessing the impact of the Fulbright memorandum on the military, the writer expresses concern about the effect of the Edwin A. Walker case on Senator Thurmond's investigation of the senator's memorandum.

665 "At War with the Military." *Time*, 22 August 1969, 13.

The article examines amendments to the Pentagon's appropriations request, noting restrictions sponsored by Fulbright on the military's research funds.

666 "Atavistic Yearning." *Time*, 10 November 1967, 26.

The article concerns the Senate's consideration of Fulbright's national commitments resolution.

667 Bales, James D. *Senator Fulbright's Secret Memorandum*. Searcy, Ark.: Bales Bookstore, 1962.

This booklet examines Fulbright's memorandum to the secretary of defense concerning the military's role in troop and public education programs on issues related to the cold war. The author argues that qualified military officers should be allowed to participate in such programs. The typescript of the booklet is housed with the Bales Papers in the Special Collections Division of the University of Arkansas Libraries, Fayetteville.

668 Barth, Heinz. "Herschensohn v. Fulbright." *National Review*, 23 June 1972, 682.

The editorial supports Bruce Herschensohn of the United States Information Agency in his clash with Fulbright over the domestic showing of documentaries produced by the USIA.

669 "Bedtime Thoughts." *Time*, 1 December 1967, 14.

The article concerns the unanimous approval by the Senate Foreign Relations Committee of a report regarding proposed congressional restraints on executive power to make foreign military commitments.

670 Ben, Philip. "The New Russia." *The New Republic*, 19 September 1964, 7-8.

The article includes a quotation from Fulbright's *Prospects for the West.* The statement pertains to his reading of a change in the direction of Soviet foreign policy toward moderation.

671   "Best Hope for Peace: The U.N.—Or the U.S.?" *Newsweek,* 2 April 1962, 19-20.

The article features the thoughts of Senators Fulbright and Henry M. Jackson in a reappraisal of the role of the United Nations in the foreign policy of the United States.

672   "Bill's Baedeker." *Time,* 12 March 1965, 23.

In a Senate speech about foreign aid, Fulbright also talks about the relationship of U.S. tourism to the balance-of-payments problem.

673   Blanchard, William H. *Aggression American Style.* Santa Monica, Calif.: Goodyear Publishing Company, 1978, 77-78, 110, 122-23, 128-31, 133n, 144-51, 160, 167-68, 180, 292, 303n.

This book includes an exchange between Fulbright and Secretary of State Christian Herter concerning the wisdom of continuing intelligence flights before the summit conference with the Soviet Union, the senator's position on the American-backed invasion of Cuba at the Bay of Pigs, and materials associated with Fulbright's support of the Tonkin Gulf resolution and his opposition to U.S. intervention in the Dominican Republic.

674   "Blunderball." *Newsweek,* 8 August 1966, 19.

The article concerns the letter from CIA Director Richard Helms to the *St. Louis Globe-Democrat* commending an editorial attacking Fulbright for his effort to expand the congressional committee monitoring the CIA.

675   "Both Sides of Great Debate over Nuclear Weapons." *U.S. News and World Report,* 3 July 1972, 58-63.

The article concerns the arguments for and against agreements with the Soviet Union for the control of nuclear weapons and includes excerpts from the testimony of William P. Rogers, Gerard C. Smith, Melvin R. Laird, and Thomas H. Moorer before the Foreign Relations Committee on U.S.-Soviet arms agreements. Fulbright remarks are also included.

676   Bradshaw, Larry L. "The Genesis of Dissent." *The Southern Speech Communication Journal* 38, No. 2 (1972): 142-50.

The writer examines Fulbright's failure to establish an enthymematic relationship between himself and his listeners on the issue of U.S. intervention in the Dominican Republic. He discusses the significance of the speech in terms of the beginning of Fulbright's dissent from Johnson policies in Latin America and Southeast Asia.

677   Brandon, Henry. *The Retreat of American Power.* Garden City, N.Y.: Doubleday and Company, 1973, 141-44, 148, 152, 288, 353.

The author notes the senator's change from a champion of presidential power in foreign policy to one of its most important critics. In chapter 9 he discusses the reasons for the reversal of Fulbright's position.

678   "Break It Up!" *The Nation,* 15 February 1965, 153-54.

This is an editorial supporting Fulbright's proposal to effect changes in the foreign aid program, including the separation of military and economic components.

679   Buckley, William F., Jr. "On Tormenting Fulbright." *National Review,* 1 July 1969, 662.

The writer answers Fulbright's charges regarding President Nixon's earlier address, particularly the president's remarks about neoisolationists.

680   ———. "Sheriff Fulbright." *National Review,* 28 April 1972, 484-85.

The column concerns the controversy surrounding efforts to show USIA film producer Bruce Herschensohn's documentary, *Czechoslovakia, 1968,* and Fulbright's opposition to the domestic showing of materials produced by the agency. See also Heinz Barth's article, "Herschensohn v. Fulbright," in the June 23, 1972, issue of the *National Review.*

681   Burnell, Elaine H., ed. *Asian Dilemma: United States, Japan and China: A Special Report from the Center for the Study of Democratic Institutions.* Santa Barbara, Calif.: Center for the Study of Democratic Institutions, October 1969, 12, 81-85, 88, 90, 97-98, 116-17, 137-39, 192-93, 217-19.

This report is a distillation of position papers and transcripts of working sessions of participants from the United States and Japan at a two-day conference arranged by the Center for the Study of Democratic Institutions on China policy. It includes comments and statements by Fulbright regarding a number of subjects, including the character of Chinese aggression, the Vietnam War, East-West security, the recognition of China, and trade and development. He concludes by calling for a new approach to the solution of problems associated with Asia. The senator points to Japan as an example of a modern nation following a nonmilitary course in its international relations.

682   Burnett, John H. "J.W. Fulbright, Chairman of the Senate Foreign Relations Committee." *The Arkansas Historical Quarterly* 20 (Winter 1961): 318-30.

In a profile of Fulbright as chairman of the Foreign Relations Committee, the author focuses on the senator's ideas regarding the role of the Senate in the formulation and conduct of foreign policy.

683   "A Challenge to the Myth-Minded." *The Churchman* 178 (May 1964): 4.

This editorial praises the ideas expressed in the senator's "Old Myths and New Realities" speech and highlights his thoughts on the Soviet Union and China.

684   Chandler, David Leon. *The Natural Superiority of Southern Politicians: A Revisionist History.* Garden City, N.Y.: Doubleday and Company, 1977, 179, 267, 270, 295, 298-99, 336.

The author examines the reasons that Fulbright was not a member of the Senate Club and assesses his importance as chairman of the Foreign Relations Committee.

685   "CIA Chief vs. Fulbright: Helms's Letter Irks Senate." *U.S. News and World Report,* 8 August 1966, 16.

Richard Helms, CIA director, apologizes to Fulbright for writing a letter to the *St. Louis Globe-Democrat* applauding an editorial titled "Brickbats for Fulbright." The editorial concerned the rejection by the Senate of Fulbright's resolution to enlarge the committee overseeing the CIA.

686   "Closer Ties for LBJ and Fulbright?" *U.S. News and World Report,* 27 June 1966, 15.

The article speculates about the increasing number of meetings between President Johnson and Fulbright and the future of the relationship between the two.

687 "Comedy of Errors." *Newsweek,* 17 April 1967, 32-34.

The article recounts President Johnson's efforts to get congressional support for a $1.5 billion promise to Latin America for the promotion of economic integration and notes the role of Fulbright's Foreign Relations Committee in rejecting the pledge and thwarting his preparations for the Punta del Este conference.

688 Commager, Henry Steele. "Can We Limit Presidential Power?" *The New Republic,* 6 April 1968, 15-18.

Professor Commager mentions Fulbright's national commitments resolution in his article on executive power and concludes that it holds little hope of restraining the president.

689 Cook, Fred J. "Juggernaut: The Warfare State: Face of the Radical Right." *The Nation,* 28 October 1961, 321-28, 330-34.

This is part 7 of an eight-part series regarding the issue of civilian control of the military in the presence of a growing military-industrial complex. The author includes a discussion of issues raised by Fulbright's memorandum on the political activities of the military. He also examines some of the freedom forums, seminars, programs, and conferences alerting the public to the dangers of communism. The series makes up the October 28, 1961, issue of the *Nation.*

690 ———. "Memo to Vice President Spiro T. Agnew: 'There Is No Eastern Intellectual Elite; There Is No Eastern Liberal Press.'" *Lithopinion* 7, No. 2, Issue 26 (1972): 8-15.

The author challenges Spiro Agnew's assertions about the power of the intellectual community and the danger of the liberal press in the East. The article includes a Fulbright quotation on the exercise of the right of dissent in the United States. Invited comments from Emile de Antonio, Bernard Fensterwald, Jr., Sidney Hook, and the senator, all mentioned in the story, appear at the end of the article.

691 ———. "Their Men in Washington." *The Nation,* 30 March 1964, 311-30.

The writer examines the record of Fulbright's Foreign Relations Committee investigation into the lobbying activities of agents working for foreign governments and evaluates the committee's suggested changes in the Foreign Agents Registration Act of 1938.

692 "Correspondence: Fulbright." *The Reporter,* 14 July 1966, 6, 8.

Readers respond to Henry Fairlie's article, "Old Realities and New Myths," in the June 16 issue of the *Reporter.*

693 "The Crackdown." *The Nation,* 11 October 1965, 205-6.

This editorial expresses concern for the crackdown on dissent in the United States and profiles leading dissenters, including Fulbright.

694 Crawford, Kenneth. "Be Kind to China." *Newsweek,* 4 April 1966, 34.

In a column inspired by Fulbright's hearings before the Foreign Relations Committee on U.S. policy toward China, Crawford examines the senator's position. Included are quotations from a March 22 speech at the University of Connecticut, Storrs.

695 ——. "Courage to Be Wrong." *Newsweek,* 7 February 1966, 27.
Columnist Crawford examines Fulbright's foreign policy ideas.

696 ——. "Democratic Dialogue." *Newsweek,* 13 April 1964, 32.
The column concerns the primarily favorable reaction to the senator's speech of March 25, 1964, challenging long-standing myths associated with U.S. foreign policy.

697 ——. "Fulbright Converted?" *Newsweek,* 7 September 1970, 34.
This is a critique of Fulbright's speech proposing a peace plan for the Middle East.

698 ——. "Fulbright on de Gaulle." *Newsweek,* 11 November 1963, 49.
Crawford reviews Fulbright's Senate speech on President Charles de Gaulle and France's performance as a member of the North Atlantic Treaty Organization.

699 ——. "Fulbright vs. Meany." *Newsweek,* 18 August 1969, 29.
Crawford reviews the exchange between Fulbright and George Meany before the Senate Foreign Relations Committee concerning the AFL-CIO's sponsorship of trade unionism abroad and the organization's relationship with President Johnson. Crawford compares the committee transcript with a committee record from the Joseph R. McCarthy period.

700 ——. "Fulbright's Revenge." *Newsweek,* 30 December 1968, 24.
The column concerns Fulbright's national commitments resolution.

701 ——. "Fulbright's Rightness." *Newsweek,* 16 October 1961, 32.
Crawford discusses Fulbright's record of being right in his thinking regarding unpopular issues. He cites the Bay of Pigs invasion and the military's sponsorship of public meetings principally related to highly controversial political issues as examples and wonders whether Fulbright will be right in his thinking on Berlin.

702 ——. "'Neo-isolationism.'" *Newsweek,* 21 April 1969, 40.
Columnist Crawford examines Fulbright's national commitments resolution and its implications for neoisolationism.

703 ——. "Politics and the Brass." *Newsweek,* 21 August 1961, 24.
Crawford mentions Fulbright's efforts to curtail the political activities of the military.

704 ——. "Replacement Needed." *Newsweek,* 10 October 1966, 44.
Crawford calls for Fulbright's resignation as chairman of the Foreign Relations Committee.

705 ——. "Unquiet on the Potomac." *Newsweek,* 15 May 1961, 38.
Columnist Crawford notes the senator's advice to the president regarding the invasion at the Bay of Pigs in Cuba.

706 "Darkening Shadows of Crisis." *Newsweek,* 9 March 1959, 29-30.
The article mentions the senator's stand on the Berlin crisis.

707 Davis, Forrest. "The Immaturity of J.W. Fulbright." *National Review,* 9 May 1959, 43.
The author expresses concern for the new Foreign Relations Committee

chairman's view of U.S. foreign policy, particularly his proposals for dealing with the communist world. He also expresses concern for the position that the senator holds among those guiding U.S. policy toward the Soviet Union.

708   "A Day to Remember." *Newsweek,* 9 February 1959, 29-30.

The story concerns Fulbright's elevation to the chairmanship of the Foreign Relations Committee and its implications for Secretary of State John Foster Dulles and Senate Majority Leader Lyndon Johnson.

709   "Debate on Berlin." *Time,* 9 March 1959, 11-13.

The article concerns the debate in the Senate on the Berlin crisis. Fulbright tangles with Thomas J. Dodd on the issue of morality in foreign policy.

710   Deer, Lewis H. "The Military and Politics: Fulbright Memorandum." *Social Action News Letter* 25 (October 1961): 2.

The writer applauds Fulbright's efforts to curtail right-wing political activities of military personnel. The article appears in the publication of the United Christian Missionary Society, Indianapolis, Indiana.

711   "The Dilettante." *The Nation,* 7 September 1970, 166.

The editors take issue with Dean Acheson for his characterization of Fulbright as a "dilettante" and for his opposition to Fulbright's appointment as secretary of state.

712   "Diplomats on the Spot." *Newsweek,* 23 February 1959, 36.

The article is concerned with the issue of envoys' qualifications for posts abroad and focuses on the nomination of Ogden R. Reid as ambassador to Israel.

713   "'Dirksen's Bombers.'" *Time,* 9 April 1965, 25-26.

The article focuses on Everett Dirksen's influence in the Senate on legislation sponsored by the Democrats, specifically the president's civil rights bill. It also notes Foreign Relations Committee action to check Fulbright's attempt to divide the foreign aid bill into separate military and economic packages.

714   "The Disinvited Guest." *Time,* 31 December 1965, 14.

The article concerns Fulbright's conspicuous absence from President Johnson's social engagements for visiting statesmen, a situation set in motion by the senator's criticism of administration foreign policy. The article concludes with a defense of the president.

715   "Division on Berlin." *Time,* 16 March 1959, 20.

Adlai E. Stevenson, Dean Acheson, and Fulbright discuss their positions on the Berlin crisis. Fulbright calls for regular summit sessions with Nikita Khrushchev and negotiated disengagement from Central Europe.

716   Dobriansky, Lev E. "Wanted: An Apparatus for the Cold War." *The Ukrainian Quarterly* 20 (Spring 1964): 22-32.

The writer challenges Fulbright's analysis of U.S. foreign policy in his "Old Myths and New Realities" speech, particularly his ideas regarding the Soviet Union. He calls for the creation of an agency concerned with the task of clarifying the issues of Soviet cold warfare.

717   Douth, George. "Senatorial Spotlight: Senators from Arkansas." *City East: A Magazine for New Yorkers* 1 (June 1968): 10-11, 26-30.

In this profile of Fulbright, the author touches upon the senator's role as foreign policy critic and his use of the Foreign Relations Committee as a forum for discussion and debate.

718 "'Doves' and 'Hawks'—New Clash." *U.S. News and World Report,* 17 March 1969, 8.

Senators Fulbright and Richard Russell express divergent views on the nonproliferation treaty.

719 Draper, Theodore. "Senator Fulbright and U.S. Foreign Policy." Appendix in *Castroism: Theory and Practice,* 223-45. New York: Frederick A. Praeger, Publishers, 1965. (First published in *The New Leader,* 13 April 1964, 6-10, under the title "Fulbright and Cuba"; and 27 April 1964, 3-9, under the title "Senator Fulbright's Cuban Options"; the articles were adapted for the essay in the appendix.)

Responding to Fulbright's "Old Myths and New Realities" speech, the author challenges the senator's position on Cuba, particularly his premise that the political and economic boycott was not successful, and questions his views concerning the mission and meaning of the boycott strategy. In the second part of his analysis, the writer takes issue with Fulbright's presentation of three policies for dealing with Castro: invasion of Cuba, boycott of the island, and "acceptance" of the Castro regime. He questions the senator's treatment of the first two as alternative policies and objects particularly to the third. The author expands his analysis of Fulbright's Cuban position in the appendix to include the senator's revised and reconsidered views in his book, *Old Myths and New Realities and Other Commentaries,* and his remarks in an article in the May 16, 1964, issue of the *Saturday Evening Post.*

720 Dudman, Richard. "Military Seminars: The Mongers Return." *The Nation,* 23 January 1967, 101-5.

In an article about the Freedom Studies Center near Culpeper, Virginia, the author reviews Fulbright's role in exposing right-wing political activities of military officers during the early sixties.

721 "Duel in the Dark." *Newsweek,* 25 July 1966, 20-21.

The article concerns Fulbright's clash with Richard Russell over the proposed expansion of the panel monitoring the CIA to include three members of the Foreign Relations Committee.

722 "A Duel of Chairmen." *Time,* 22 July 1966, 21.

The article pertains to Fulbright's efforts to expand the congressional committee overseeing the CIA to include representatives from the Foreign Relations Committee. It notes the debate between Fulbright and Richard Russell and the fate of the Fulbright resolution in Russell's Armed Services Committee.

723 Dunham, Barrows. "When Thoughts Are Unthinkable." *The Nation,* 27 April 1964, 411-13.

The author elaborates on the philosophical context in which Fulbright places his "unthinkable thoughts" regarding U.S. foreign policy. Calling the problem of unthinkable thoughts universal, he describes the predicament of the dissenter in terms of the distinction drawn by social organizations between orthodoxy and heresy.

724 "Early Warning: Back to the Drawing Boards: Nth Round in the Arms Race." *Center Report* 5 (April 1972): 6-7.

The article consists of a collection of statements regarding President Nixon's request for appropriations for an Undersea Long-Range Missile System and its effect on the arms race. Fulbright argues that the country is impoverishing itself by appropriating large military budgets.

725 "Eight of the Political Hammers of Washington." *Vogue,* 15 November 1969, 107-13.

The article features short profiles of J. William Fulbright, Warren E. Burger, William McChesney Martin, Jr., Melvin R. Laird, Strom Thurmond, Henry Kissinger, William P. Rogers, and Wilbur D. Mills.

726 Eller, J.N. "Spooks Need Course in Ghostwriting." *America,* 13 August 1966, 151.

A letter to the *St. Louis Globe-Democrat* from CIA Director Richard Helms applauding an editorial titled "Brickbats for Fulbright" inspired this article about the letter-writing habits of congressmen. The editorial concerned the rejection by the Senate of Fulbright's resolution to enlarge the committee overseeing the Central Intelligence Agency.

727 "Erratic Attack." *Time,* 24 September 1965, 44.

This is a response to Fulbright's speech criticizing the Johnson administration for its intervention in the Dominican Republic. It concludes with an evaluation of U.S. policies in Latin America.

728 "Excerpt from a Letter of March 12, 1970, from H.G. Torbert, Jr., Acting Assistant Secretary for Congressional Relations, to Senator J. William Fulbright, Chairman of the Senate Committee on Foreign Relations, Concerning State Department Views on Proposals to Repeal Certain Congressional Resolutions, Including the Middle East Resolution." In *The Arab-Israeli Conflict: Volume III: Documents,* edited by John Norton Moore, 678-81. Princeton, N.J.: Princeton University Press in association with the American Society of International Law, 1974. (First published in *The Department of State Bulletin,* 6 April 1970, 468-71, under the title "Department Gives Views on Proposal to Repeal Certain Congressional Resolutions.")

The letter contains comments by the Department of State on Senate Joint Resolution 166 to rescind resolutions regarding Formosa, the Middle East, Cuba, and the Tonkin Gulf.

729 "Eyes Front." *Newsweek,* 31 July 1961, 26.

The article concerns Fulbright's memorandum to the Department of Defense reproving the military for right-wing political activities and includes the Defense Department's response.

730 "Fair Play for Gen. Walker." *Life,* 6 October 1961, 4.

In an editorial supporting General Edwin Walker, the writers take Fulbright to task for wanting to restrict the involvement of military officers in strategy seminars and public education programs on the perils of the cold war.

731 Fairlie, Henry. "At Home and Abroad: Old Realities and New Myths." *The Reporter,* 16 June 1966, 19-21.

The author compares Fulbright's "Old Myths and New Realities" speech of March 25, 1964, with his Christian A. Herter Lectures at Johns Hopkins University in the spring of 1966. Although Fairlie charges the senator with "self-plagiarism" in his use of passages from the earlier speech, the author focuses his attention on the differences between the 1964 and the 1966 versions of Fulbright's ideas concerning U.S. foreign policy. He concludes his analysis of the "arrogance of power" lectures with a challenge to the senator to rise above the role of Cassandra.

732 "Fed Up with Aid?" *The New Republic,* 10 April 1965, 6.

The editorial examines the reasons for the growing disenchantment with foreign aid in Congress and the country. Fulbright's position is examined.

733 Findley, Paul. *They Dare to Speak Out: People and Institutions Confront Israel's Lobby.* Rev. and updated ed. Chicago: Chicago Review Press, Lawrence Hill Books, 1989, 93-97, 130, 169, 320.

Congressman Findley assesses Fulbright's role as a dissenter and traces his criticism of U.S. policies toward Israel.

734 Finney, John. "Fulbright and Friend." *The New Republic,* 15 April 1972, 11-12.

The article explores the relaxation of the Senate Foreign Relations Committee in its attempt to restore the balance of power between the executive and the legislative branches in the area of foreign policy. It examines the efforts of the Nixon administration, particularly Secretary of State William P. Rogers, to neutralize the effectiveness of the committee.

735 "Foreign Affairs Debate: Are Our Policies Turning Obsolete?" *Business Week,* 4 April 1964, 28-29.

This article about the foreign policy debate inspired by Fulbright's "Old Myths and New Realities" speech includes a congressional profile of the senator titled "Senate's Scholarly Dissenter."

736 "Foreign Aid: Debating Its Doom." *Time,* 8 November 1963, 23-24.

The article concerns the foreign aid debate in the Senate and Fulbright's efforts to effect changes in the overall foreign aid program.

737 "Foreign Aid: The Dawn of a New Era." *Newsweek,* 15 November 1971, 40-41.

The article concerns the Senate's rejection of the president's foreign aid package and focuses on senators' efforts to reform the overall aid program. Fulbright remarks are included.

738 "Foreign Policy and the Senate." *The Commonweal,* 13 February 1959, 510.

This editorial focuses on speculation about Fulbright's elevation to the chairmanship of the Senate Foreign Relations Committee and its meaning for the conduct of U.S. foreign policy.

739 "Foreign Policy Changes? Fulbright Has Some in Mind." *U.S. News and World Report,* 1 February 1965, 20.

The article focuses on Fulbright's role as chairman of the Foreign Relations Committee and his campaign for rethinking U.S. foreign policy.

740 "Former ROA National President Forces into Open Long-Smouldering 'Anti-Anti-Communist' Fight." *The Officer* 37 (October 1961): 14.

The article concerns Strom Thurmond's opposition to Fulbright's military memorandum.

741 "Fraternal Fencing." *Newsweek,* 7 August 1961, 18-19.

The article pertains to the Fulbright-Barry Goldwater debate on foreign policy.

742 "Free-Nations Council? Fulbright Backs the Idea." *U.S. News and World Report,* 3 September 1962, 19.

Fulbright supports Herbert Hoover's peace-keeping proposal for a Council of Free Nations and thinks the new plan would reinforce the United Nations. See also the senator's article, "For a Concert of Free Nations," in the October 1961 issue of *Foreign Affairs.*

743 "From Senator Fulbright: How Not to Fight the Reds." *U.S. News and World Report,* 10 July 1961, 14.

Citing the Bay of Pigs invasion and U.S. policy in Laos as errors, Fulbright urges that the United States exercise greater care in selecting its commitments in the struggle against communism. Remarks are drawn from a June 29 Senate speech.

744 Frye, Robert L. "Project Alert." *The Nation,* 23 December 1961, 504-5.

The article examines Project Alert, a program warning Americans about the communist threat. It also reviews the significance of Fulbright's memorandum to the Department of Defense on the military's political activities.

745 "Fulbright." *The Reporter,* 14 July 1966, 6, 8.

These are letters to the editor concerning Henry Fairlie's article, "Old Realities and New Myths," in the June 16 issue of the *Reporter.*

746 "Fulbright and Bowles." *The New Republic,* 15 June 1959, 3-4.

This editorial praises Fulbright and Congressman Chester Bowles for their leadership in recommending changes in the military component of the foreign aid program.

747 "Fulbright and Foreign Policy." *Newsweek,* 27 April 1964, 4.

This is a set of letters written in response to the Fulbright article in the April 6 issue of *Newsweek* regarding foreign policy.

748 "Fulbright and Myths." *The Commonweal,* 17 April 1964, 101-2.

This is an editorial responding to Fulbright's "Old Myths and New Realities" speech in the Senate on March 25, 1964.

749 "Fulbright Criticizes Foreign Policy." *The Christian Century,* 8 April 1964, 452-53.

The article praises the ideas expressed in Fulbright's "Old Myths and New Realities" speech on U.S. foreign policy and predicts that his critique will achieve a consensus.

750 "Fulbright DSR-TKA's 'Speaker-of-the-Year.'" *Spectra,* June 1966, 1, 4.

The article concerns the selection of Fulbright as the 1965 winner of the "Speaker-of-the-Year Award," an honor bestowed by the Delta Sigma Rho-Tau Kappa Alpha Society for his efforts to educate the public and encourage open discussion of foreign policy issues. *Spectra* is a bimonthly publication of the Speech Association of America.

751 "Fulbright Flays Administration on Dominican Policy." *New World Review* 33, No. 10 (1965): 11-12.

The item concerns the senator's speech criticizing the Johnson administration for its intervention in the Dominican Republic and includes Fulbright remarks.

752 "Fulbright: No Accident." *National Review,* 5 October 1965, 859.

The editorial assails Fulbright for his September 15 Senate speech critiquing U.S. intervention in the Dominican Republic.

753 "The Fulbright Proposal . . . Mythology . . . and More Mythology." *America,* 11 April 1964, 500-501.

This article challenges the senator's "Old Myths and New Realities" speech on March 25, 1964, calling for a review of U.S. foreign policy. The writer takes issue with Fulbright's views regarding the communist world, the cold war, and détente.

754 "Fulbright Under the Glass." *National Review,* 12 July 1966, 662-64.

The editors praise Henry Fairlie's article, "Old Realities and New Myths," in the June 16 issue of the *Reporter.* Fairlie scrutinized the senator's foreign policy speech in the Senate on March 25, 1964, and his Christian A. Herter Lectures at Johns Hopkins University in the spring of 1966 in that article.

755 "Fulbright vs. Birds." *Armed Forces Journal,* 18 October 1969, 12.

The article concerns Fulbright's efforts to cut funds from the Defense Department's procurement bill for research and development and for Freedom Fighter aircraft for Asian allies. It focuses on his battle with L. Mendell Rivers over congressional committee jurisdiction of military assistance programs.

756 "Fulbright's Advice: 'Go Slow' on Nuclear Fleet." *U.S. News and World Report,* 30 November 1964, 17.

The article concerns Fulbright's suggestions regarding plans for a nuclear fleet under the jurisdiction of the Western Alliance.

757 "Fulbright's Firing Line." *Time,* 17 August 1970, 9-10.

The article pertains to charges by Fulbright of presidential domination and usurpation of legislative power. The two immediate issues fueling the charges are the renewal agreement with Spain regarding the use of military bases in that country and President Nixon's increasing use of television to communicate with the American people.

758 "Fulbright's Leadership." *The New Republic,* 4 May 1959, 5-6.

This is an editorial lauding Fulbright, in his new position as chairman of the Foreign Relations Committee, for his recommendations to amend the foreign aid legislation.

759 "Fulbright's New Order." *Playboy* 15 (October 1968): 9-10.

In letters to the editor, readers respond to Fulbright's article, "For a New Order of Priorities at Home and Abroad," in the July 1968 issue of *Playboy.* Among the correspondents are Senator Stephen M. Young and playwright Arthur Miller.

760 "Fulbright's Plan to Win 'Cold War.'" *U.S. News and World Report,* 21 September 1959, 6.

Fulbright urges President Eisenhower to spend more money on domestic programs, defense, and foreign assistance in order to win the cold war with the Soviet Union. Remarks are drawn from a Senate speech of September 9 on administration policy.

761   "Fulbright's Progress." *The Nation,* 13 April 1964, 357-58.

This editorial concerns Fulbright's landmark speech calling for a review of U.S. foreign policy and examines his intentions for making such a speech in an election year.

762   "'Fulbright's Revenge.'" *Newsweek,* 14 April 1969, 38.

The article concerns the revival of Fulbright's 1967 national commitments resolution and the accompanying majority report prepared by the Foreign Relations Committee. The committee passed the resolution on March 12 by a vote of 14-1.

763   "A Furor over 'Muzzling' the Military." *U.S. News and World Report,* 14 August 1961, 70-71.

The article concerns Fulbright's memorandum on the political activities of the military and includes the senator's recommendations for restricting troop indoctrination and public education programs regarding the dangers of communism. It includes quotations from the memorandum.

764   Gambrell, Leonard Lee. "The Influence of the Senate Foreign Relations Committee Chairman in the Making of United States Foreign Policy: A Case Analysis." Ph.D. diss., University of Virginia, 1971, 1, 3, 40, 64, 68, 149, 218-325, 328-39, 341-45.

This study concerns the influence of the chairman of the Senate Foreign Relations Committee on the development of postwar foreign policy and features three senators: Arthur H. Vandenberg, Tom Connally, and Fulbright. The author concludes that all three chairmen had an important impact on the shaping of policy. The analysis of Fulbright's tenure is focused on the Mutual Security Act of 1959, foreign aid legislation of 1961 and 1966, the Cuban missile crisis, the Gulf of Tonkin resolution, the expansion of the Vietnam War, U.S. intervention in the Dominican Republic, and Foreign Relations Committee hearings in 1966 and 1968 on the Vietnam War.

765   Garay, Ronald. *Congressional Television: A Legislative History.* Contributions in Political Science, No. 111. Westport, Conn.: Greenwood Press, 1984, 65-69.

The book includes a review of Fulbright's efforts to secure equitable television air time for Congress by amending the Communications Act of 1934. His proposed amendment died in the Senate Commerce Committee's communications subcommittee.

766   Gardner, Frank J. "Watching the World: Gazelle, Anyone?" *Oil and Gas Journal* 71, No. 22 (1973): 43.

The author praises Fulbright's speech of May 21 in which he addresses the issues of a possible oil boycott by the Persian Gulf states and the role of the United Nations in effecting a Middle East peace agreement.

767   Gardner, Lloyd C., ed. *American Foreign Policy, Present to Past: A Narrative with Readings and Documents.* Urgent Issues in American Society Series. New York: Macmillan Publishing Company, Free Press, 1974, 40-41, 63-69, 79-85, 90-91, 95-96.

Fulbright figures prominently in the narrative, particularly in the sections concerning the Vietnam War controversy, U.S. intervention in the Dominican Republic in 1965, and George F. Meany's appearance before the Foreign Relations Committee on the trade union movement in Latin America.

768   "General Walker Speaks." *Newsweek,* 25 December 1961, 19-20.

General Edwin A. Walker speaks out on several subjects, including Fulbright's memorandum to the Department of Defense on right-wing political activities of the military.

769 Goldbloom, Maurice J. "The Fulbright Revolt." *Commentary* 42 (September 1966): 63-69.

The writer examines the reversal of Fulbright's thinking concerning the role of the Foreign Relations Committee and the Senate in the realm of foreign affairs from submissiveness to assertiveness.

770 "Goldwater Speaks Out About Senator Fulbright." *U.S. News and World Report,* 16 May 1966, 23.

In a speech criticizing President Johnson's foreign and domestic policies, Barry Goldwater calls for Fulbright's resignation as chairman of the Foreign Relations Committee.

771 Greenberg, D.S. "Space: Senator Fulbright Steps into Lunar Landing Controversy." *Science* 142, No. 3591 (1963): 470.

The article includes Fulbright's critique of the arguments supporting an expanded space program.

772 "Growing Foreign-Policy Row: Two Top Democrats Urge Changes." *U.S. News and World Report,* 6 April 1964, 19.

Mike Mansfield criticizes the U.S. position in Southeast Asia, and Fulbright, in his "Old Myths and New Realities" speech, calls for reshaping U.S. policy toward Panama, Cuba, and China.

773 H.M. "Grand Strategy: The Views of the Administration and the War College Do Not Seem to Coincide." *Science* 134, No. 3478 (1961): 543-45.

The author uses the Fulbright memorandum on political activities of the military as the base for an examination of the views and activities of three organizations associated with research on foreign policy questions: the Institute for American Strategy, the Foreign Policy Research Institute at the University of Pennsylvania, and the Richardson Foundation. Fulbright discussed the relationship of the Joint Chiefs of Staff and the National War College with these groups in the second part of his memorandum.

774 Halper, Thomas. *Foreign Policy Crises: Appearance and Reality in Decision Making.* Merrill Political Science Series, edited by John C. Wahlke. Columbus, Ohio: Charles E. Merrill Publishing Company, 1971, 30-33, 66, 77, 81n, 82-83, 85-92, 95n, 99, 104-6, 171, 215.

The author treats Fulbright's opposition to the Bay of Pigs invasion, his support of the Tonkin Gulf resolution in the Senate, and his subsequent role as a critic of administration policy in Vietnam.

775 Hamilton, Harry. "The Senate Lets L.B.J. Down." *America,* 16 July 1966, 56.

The author discusses the Senate's discontent with administration measures in both domestic and foreign affairs. He focuses on the role of Fulbright and the Foreign Relations Committee in obstructing the passage of the president's foreign aid bill.

776 Hanks, Robert J. "Against All Enemies." *Proceedings of the United States Naval Institute* 96, No. 3 (1970): 22-29.

In an article about the campaign against the U.S. military, the writer examines the dissent of leading critics, including Fulbright, and proposes ways of countering the attack. The senator mentions this essay in his book, *The Pentagon Propaganda Machine.*

777 "The 'Hard Line' Policy Pays Off." *U.S. News and World Report,* 13 April 1964, 6.

article concerning a series of victories for the United States in Latin America
Fulbright remarks about the permanence of the Castro regime. Critics of
~~ıgıt~~'s position respond.

778 Hazlitt, Henry. "Where We Are Now." *Newsweek,* 16 November 1959, 94.

The U.S. Development Loan Fund's "Buy American" stand inspired this article on
the U.S. foreign aid program. Fulbright's position on the DLF policy is noted.

779 "The Heat's on the U.S." *Newsweek,* 1 February 1960, 46.

The article mentions Secretary of State Christian A. Herter's private appearance
before Fulbright's Foreign Relations Committee on the matter of deteriorating U.S.-
Cuban relations.

780 Hinckle, Warren, with Milton Viorst and Sol Stern. "A Profile in Courage: J.
William Fulbright." *Ramparts* 5 (June 1966): 11-18.

This essay examines Fulbright's dissent from Johnson administration policies in
Vietnam and the Dominican Republic and includes an assessment of his challenge
of cold war assumptions on the national consensus in the president's foreign agenda.
A sketch of Fulbright is on the cover.

781 "Hopeful Beginning." *Newsweek,* 22 May 1961, 53.

The article includes the senator's remarks on economic aid funds for Latin America.

782 Hughes, Emmet John. "The Contagion of Hope." *Newsweek,* 4 October 1965, 23.

Columnist Hughes discusses the jolting effects of new realities on old premises in
an informed view of U.S. relations with the Soviet Union and with Third World
revolutionary movements. He talks about the leaders who ignore the new realities
and the leaders, like Fulbright and U.N. Ambassador Arthur Goldberg, who do not.

783 ———. "The Spoiled Spring." *Newsweek,* 31 May 1965, 17.

The column includes comments on Fulbright's speech at the University of Vienna on
the process of harmonizing relations between the free world and the communist world.

784 Hyman, Sidney. "The Advice and Consent of J. William Fulbright." *The Reporter,* 17 September 1959, 23-25.

This is a report of an interview in which the senator talks about the role of the
Senate in the formulation and implementation of foreign policy, President Eisenhower on domestic affairs, and the president's practice of "personal diplomacy," specifically the forthcoming visit of Nikita Khrushchev.

785 ———. "Fulbright: The Wedding of Arkansas and the World." *The New Republic,*
14 May 1962, 19-26.

In a thoughtful profile of Fulbright, the author discusses the senator and the Little
Rock integration crisis, Fulbright's efforts to redefine the roles of the president and
the Senate in the foreign policy realm, President Kennedy's consideration of the
senator for secretary of state, the main points of the Fulbright memorandum advising
the president against the Bay of Pigs invasion, and his memorandum to the Department of Defense regarding right-wing political activities of the military.

786 "'If Flag of Surrender Is Waved Before Castro . . .'" *U.S. News and World
Report,* 13 April 1964, 6.

This is a letter from Emilio Nuñez Portuondo, former president of the United Nations Security Council, in which he addresses Fulbright's position regarding Castro's Cuba and calls for U.S. assistance in overthrowing Castro.

787 "Influence Is a Two-Way Street." *Extension*, November 1963, 6.

In an editorial about the nuclear test ban treaty, the writer praises Fulbright for his wisdom in advising the United States to use the period of improved relations with the USSR to influence the Soviets in the direction of a new relationship. *Extension* is the national publication of the Catholic Church.

788 "Is America Going Isolationist? Size-up by Key Senators." *U.S. News and World Report,* 28 June 1971, 24-31.

Responding to questions by *U.S. News and World Report* staff, twelve key senators, including Fulbright, from the Foreign Relations Committee and the Armed Services Committee discuss U.S. foreign and defense policies.

789 "The Israel Lobby." *Newsweek,* 12 August 1963, 24.

Senate Foreign Relations Committee hearings concern the intricate system involving the Jewish Agency-American Section and the American Zionist Council and their efforts to influence Israeli policy in the United States.

790 Jackson, Henry M. "Détente and Human Rights." *The Center Magazine* 7 (January-February 1974): 62-63.

In an excerpt from a statement made at the *Pacem in Terris III* convocation in Washington in October 1973, Senator Jackson challenges Fulbright's position on détente with the Soviet Union. Jackson argues in behalf of his effort to link U.S. trade concessions to Soviet acceptance of a policy of free emigration.

791 "The Job of the Military." *The Nation,* 2 September 1961, 109.

In an editorial concerning the role of the military in American society, Fulbright's memorandum calling for an end to right-wing political activities of military officers is cited. The editors advise the Department of Defense to listen to the senator.

792 Johnson, Gerald W. "The Imperial Role." *The New Republic,* 12 December 1970, 9.

The article is a critical analysis of Fulbright's view that the United States has had no preparation, historically, for the role of an imperial power.

793 Johnson, Haynes, Manuel Artime, José Pérez San Román, Erneido Oliva, and Enrique Ruiz-Williams. *The Bay of Pigs: The Leaders' Story of Brigade 2506.* New York: W.W. Norton and Company, 1964, 68-69, 232.

The authors discuss the ambiguity of Fulbright's position at President John F. Kennedy's April 4, 1961, meeting of the National Security Council. Their account of the meeting differs from the one presented in *The Cuban Invasion: The Chronicle of a Disaster* by Karl E. Meyer and Tad Szulc.

794 Kaplan, Morton A. "Old Realities and New Myths." *World Politics* 17 (January 1965): 334-47, 349, 351, 353, 355, 357, 359, 361, 363, 365, 367. (Later published in *Great Issues of International Politics: The International System and National Policy.* 1st and 2d eds., edited by Morton A. Kaplan, 259-79, 266-86. Chicago: Aldine Publishing Company, 1970, 1974.)

The author acknowledges the necessity of Fulbright's effort to bring about a reexamination of long-standing foreign policy beliefs but concludes that he fails to achieve that goal in his book, *Old Myths and New Realities and Other Commentaries.* Instead, he says that the senator only confuses old realities and promotes countermyths. He challenges Fulbright's analysis of the Soviet system regarding foreign policy under Stalin and Khrushchev and questions his views concerning China and Europe, particularly NATO. He also wonders why the senator did not consider the myths surrounding such issues as foreign aid, German unity, the United Nations, and Atlantic Union. The review includes a consideration of Fulbright's use of psychological generalizations in his analysis of politics. For other Kaplan remarks on the senator and social science, see his article, "A Psychoanalyst Looks at Politics: A Retrospective Tribute to Robert Waelder," in the July 1968 issue of *World Politics.*

795 Karnow, Stanley. "Henry and Bill: The Kissinger-Fulbright Courtship." *The New Republic,* 29 December 1973, 15-18.

The author examines the warm relationship between Fulbright and Secretary of State Henry Kissinger and the reasons for their mutual approbation. He continues with a review of Fulbright's legislative record and an analysis of the senator's leadership style as Foreign Relations Committee chairman as well as his concept of the committee itself.

796 ———. "Secretary Kissinger." *The New Republic,* 22 September 1973, 19-21.

The author points out the ambiguities in the hearings conducted by the Senate Foreign Relations Committee on the nomination of Henry Kissinger as secretary of state.

797 Kelly, George A. "Officers, Politics, Ideology." *Army* 12 (January 1962): 30-33.

In an article about the politics of military officers, the author cites Fulbright's prescription for meeting the communist challenge.

798 Kempton, Murray. "The Washrooms of Power: Those Anonymous Propaganda Peddlers." *The New Republic,* 3 August 1963, 9-13.

The article concerns Fulbright's hearings before the Foreign Relations Committee on the activities of lobbyists working for foreign governments and focuses on the lessons coming out of the hearings.

799 Kenworthy, E.W. "Fulbright Becomes a National Issue." *The New York Times Magazine,* 1 October 1961, 21, 89, 92, 96-97.

In a lucid treatment of Fulbright's foreign policy ideas, the author reviews the senator's thoughts regarding the use of national power and the requirements for establishing a "national style." He focuses on Fulbright as a target of the Barry Goldwater-Strom Thurmond forces, following his opposition to the Bay of Pigs invasion and his memorandum to the secretary of defense recommending revision of the military's indoctrination program. The author also discusses the significance that a Fulbright defeat in the upcoming May primary would have for the Goldwater forces.

800 ———. "The Fulbright Idea of Foreign Policy." *The New York Times Magazine,* 10 May 1959, 10-11, 74, 76, 78.

In a profile of the new chairman of the Foreign Relations Committee, the writer examines Fulbright's views of the role of the Senate in the foreign policy realm. The article includes a biographical sketch in which the writer discusses Fulbright's position on the Little Rock integration crisis.

801 "Killed by Compromise." *Time,* 8 September 1961, 23.

The article concerns the approval by Fulbright's Foreign Relations Committee of a compromise foreign aid agreement.

802 Kopkind, Andrew. "The Speechmaker: Senator Fulbright as the Arkansas de Tocqueville." *The New Republic,* 2 October 1965, 15-19.

The author reviews the senator's speech denouncing the Johnson administration's intervention in the Dominican Republic. He also profiles Fulbright's role in the Senate as leader of the Foreign Relations Committee and examines the senator's thoughts regarding the committee's participation in foreign policy making decisions.

803 Kuhn, Irene Corbally. "Senator Fulbright . . . The Man and the Memo." *The American Legion Magazine,* January 1962, 20-21, 40-45.

The author takes the senator to task for his memorandum alerting the Department of Defense to political and educational activities of military personnel and recommending revision of the military's troop indoctrination program. In an assessment of the senator and the memorandum, she concludes that the implementation of the Fulbright directive resulted in much harm to the military and the country.

804 Lawrence, David. "'Arrogance of Power.'" *U.S. News and World Report,* 20 February 1967, 120.

Lawrence questions the intervention of Democratic members of the Senate Foreign Relations Committee into the foreign policy making process and charges them with practicing "arrogance of power."

805 ———. "'Guaranteeing' a Mideast Peace." *U.S. News and World Report,* 7 September 1970, 80.

Lawrence questions Fulbright's proposal for a bilateral treaty guaranteeing the territorial integrity of Israel as a way of supplementing any Mideast peace settlement reached by the United Nations.

806 ———. "Responsible and Irresponsible Criticism of Foreign Policy." *U.S. News and World Report,* 23 May 1966, 124, continues on page 123.

Lawrence responds to ideas expressed by Fulbright in his "arrogance of power" lectures at Johns Hopkins University.

807 Lazo, Mario. *Dagger in the Heart: American Policy Failures in Cuba.* New York: Funk and Wagnalls, 1968, facing title page, 265, 269.

A quotation from the memorandum that Fulbright sent to President John F. Kennedy on March 30, 1961, expressing his reservations about the proposed Cuban invasion inspired the title of this book.

808 Lehman, John. *The Executive, Congress, and Foreign Policy: Studies of the Nixon Administration.* Praeger Special Studies in U.S. Economic, Social, and Political Issues. New York: Praeger Publishers, 1976, 9-11, 14, 25, 31, 41-42, 47, 50, 61-62, 64-65, 73, 88, 92-93, 96-98, 102-3, 114, 120-21, 124, 128-30, 133-35, 139-40, 144, 147-48, 150, 152-59, 185, 192-93, 195-98, 200, 202-3, 208-9, 226.

The book includes materials associated with the senator's roles in the Vietnam War controversy, the Spanish base agreements, the Symington subcommittee investigation into U.S. security agreements and commitments overseas, and the debate over the 1970 supplemental foreign assistance request for Cambodia.

809   Lindley, Ernest K. "Campaign '60—Danger." *Newsweek,* 11 July 1960, 38.

Columnist Lindley evaluates the Foreign Relations Committee hearings on the U-2 incident and the subsequent committee report. He also reviews Fulbright's conclusions regarding the event.

810   ———. "Senator Fulbright, Chairman of the Foreign Relations Committee." *The American Oxonian* 47 (April 1960): 51-55.

In a profile of Fulbright, the author treats the senator's beliefs regarding the Foreign Relations Committee and its function, his experience on the committee, and his support of a "nonpartisan" approach to foreign policy. He also discusses Fulbright's usefulness, primarily as a teacher, in encouraging the examination and discussion of basic policy questions.

811   Lindsay, John J. "The Case of Gen. Walker." *The Nation,* 14 October 1961, 245-48.

The article includes a reference to Fulbright's memorandum alerting the president and the secretary of defense to the military's political and educational activities.

812   Lippmann, Walter. "A Senator Speaks Out." *Newsweek,* 13 April 1964, 19.

Responding to Fulbright's Senate speech of March 25, 1964, Lippmann praises the senator for addressing long-standing myths associated with the conduct of U.S. foreign policy and for inspiring public discussion. A summary of Fulbright's public record is included.

813   Lisagor, Peter. "When Friends Fall Out." *Nation's Business* 54 (June 1966): 23-24.

The author discusses the attack upon consensus in President Johnson's domestic and foreign agendas and examines the exit of important administration and congressional figures, including Fulbright.

814   "Little Was Lost But . . . " *Newsweek,* 13 June 1960, 32.

The article regards the Senate Foreign Relations Committee investigation of the U-2 incident and the preparation of the committee report.

815   Lomax, Sir John. "The Day the Cold War Changed." *The Nation,* 6 July 1963, 10-12.

The author examines the unspoken pact between Moscow and Washington concerning the Berlin crisis in the fall of 1961. He bases his interpretation of the events on a statement by Fulbright extending the possibility of an agreement with the Soviets for a peaceful resolution of issues surrounding Berlin and West German rearmament.

816   McCracken, Daniel D. *Public Policy and the Expert: Ethical Problems of the Witness.* New York: Council on Religion and International Affairs, 1971, 24, 26-28, 30-33, 35-38, 44-47, 55, 63, 70, 91-92, 120-21.

Using the ABM hearings of 1969 as a springboard for his essay, the author examines the ethical issues raised by specialists as witnesses and by legislators as judges of their information. His remarks include extensive quotations from Fulbright's contribution to the debate. Commentators are Bruce Arden, Victor C. Ferkiss, and Roger L. Shinn.

817   Masse, Benjamin L. "Mr. Meany Replies to Sen. Fulbright." *America,* 30 August 1969, 111.

This article supports George Meany and the AFL-CIO in its quarrel with Fulbright over payments by the Agency for International Development to the organization for the promotion of the free trade union movement in Latin America, Africa, and Asia.

818   "A Matter of Mutual Advantage." *Time,* 3 February 1967, 19-20.

The article concerns Dean Rusk's testimony before the Foreign Relations Committee in support of a consular treaty with the Soviet Union.

819   Meany, George. "A Return to Appeasement?" *The American Federationist* 71 (May 1964): 1-2.

The editor criticizes the ideas expressed by Fulbright in his "Old Myths and New Realities" speech in the Senate on March 25, 1964, particularly his thoughts concerning changes in the character of the cold war and in the monolithic nature of the communist bloc. The editorial appears in the official monthly magazine of the American Federation of Labor and Congress of Industrial Organizations.

820   "Men and the Woman." *Newsweek,* 27 April 1959, 36.

The article concerns the hearings before the Senate Foreign Relations Committee on the nomination of Clare Boothe Luce as ambassador to Brazil.

821   Meyer, Karl E., and Tad Szulc. *The Cuban Invasion: The Chronicle of a Disaster.* New York: Frederick A. Praeger, 1962, 110-12.

The authors discuss the senator's position on the Bay of Pigs invasion, focusing on his memorandum to the president outlining proposed U.S. policies toward Cuba. They note Fulbright's presence at the April 4, 1961, meeting of the National Security Council called by the president. This account of the meeting differs from the one given by Haynes Johnson in *The Bay of Pigs: The Leaders' Story of Brigade 2506.* The senator's memorandum is reproduced in chapter 7 of Meyer's book, *Fulbright of Arkansas: The Public Positions of a Private Thinker.*

822   "The Mideast Peace Talks Begin: The Central Challenge: How to Leave Everybody Equally Dissatisfied." *Newsweek,* 7 September 1970, 37-38.

The article concerns the opening of the Arab-Israeli peace talks in New York and notes Fulbright's Senate speech outlining his proposal for a Middle East peace settlement.

823   "The Military in Politics." *The Progressive* 25 (September 1961): 3-4.

The editorial warns against the military's involvement in political activities and defends Fulbright for calling attention to their strategy seminars and public education programs.

824   Miller, Judith. "The Senate Surrenders." *The Progressive* 37 (January 1973): 30-31.

In an interview conducted by Judith Miller, Washington Bureau news chief of the Pacifica radio stations, Fulbright discusses the waning of the senatorial role in foreign policy and the problems facing a democracy, including war, the increasing scope of presidential power, a politically divided government, and the relationship of the press with the president.

825   "More Trade with the Soviets? This Is Official U.S. Answer." *U.S. News and World Report,* 13 July 1959, 86.

The article consists of excerpts from a Foreign Relations Committee report regarding State Department policy on issues associated with U.S.-Soviet trade. The State Department disclosed their views in answers to questions posed by Fulbright.

826   Morgenthau, Hans J. "Senator Fulbright's New Foreign Policy." *Commentary* 37 (May 1964): 68-71.

Responding to the senator's "Old Myths and New Realities" speech, the author challenges Fulbright's primary assumption of profound changes in Soviet policies toward the United States. He further challenges the senator on several points regarding his analysis of U.S.-Soviet relations and on his failure to include U.S. alliance policies in his inquiry.

827   "A Move to Restore the Senate's Power." *U.S. News and World Report,* 14 August 1967, 10.

The article concerns Fulbright's national commitments resolution.

828   "'Muzzling the Military'—Another Example?" *U.S. News and World Report,* 21 August 1961, 13.

The item notes Fulbright's memorandum on the military.

829   "Myth and Reality II." *Newsweek,* 27 September 1965, 27.

The article reviews Fulbright's speech criticizing U.S.-Latin American policies, particularly U.S. intervention in the Dominican Republic in April 1965.

830   Nelson, Bryce. "The Senate Revolt: Protesting U.S. Overcommitment Abroad." *Science* 154, No. 3750 (1966): 751-53.

The article focuses on Fulbright's role in legitimizing criticism of U.S. foreign policies by his personal example and rallying dissent in the Senate and the country through his use of educational hearings.

831   "The New Debate on China." *Newsweek,* 21 March 1966, 25-26.

The article regards Fulbright's Foreign Relations Committee hearings on U.S. policy toward China and notes the testimony of A. Doak Barnett and John K. Fairbank.

832   "A New Weapon for Fulbright." *Newsweek,* 3 January 1972, 9.

The item notes the proviso in the foreign aid legislation that required the approval of State Department funds by Fulbright's Foreign Relations Committee.

833   "News and Ethics." *Newsweek,* 26 August 1963, 2, 5.

This is a letter to the editor associated with the article titled "Something Newsy" in the July 22 issue of *Newsweek.* The letter is from Don Frifield, one of the journalists mentioned in the story about lobbyists for foreign countries.

834   Niebuhr, Reinhold. "Prisoner of the South." *The New Leader,* 27 April 1964, 16-17.

The writer discusses the plight of southern "liberals," like Fulbright and Richard Russell, and the importance of regional interests, including the race issue, in preventing them from achieving higher national office. In critiquing the senator's "Old Myths and New Realities" speech, he notes that the address was a contribution to the filibuster against civil rights legislation.

835   "No Consensus." *Newsweek,* 6 September 1965, 33.

Fulbright defends the Foreign Relations Committee staff from charges by Thomas J. Dodd that they slanted the staff study regarding the Dominican Republic intervention against the Johnson administration.

836 "'Nobody Dropped Dead.'" *The Progressive* 30 (May 1966): 3-5.

The editorial praises Fulbright's Foreign Relations Committee hearings on U.S. policy toward China and calls for setting aside the old policy of isolation and containment in favor of a new one. Primary comments concern the country's positive reaction to the hearings.

837 Oberdorfer, Don. "Noninterventionism, 1967 Style." *The New York Times Magazine,* 17 September 1967, 28-31, 102-9, 111-12.

The author discusses the growing Senate concern over U.S. intervention abroad and examines the views of Senators John C. Stennis, Milton R. Young, Mike Mansfield, Thruston B. Morton, and others, including Fulbright.

838 "On 'Imposing' Peace in the Middle East and Southeast Asia." *War/Peace Report* 10 (October 1970): 12-13.

The editors challenge Fulbright's plan to force a peaceful solution in the Middle East through UN intervention and offer their own proposal.

839 "On Name-Calling." *The Officer* 37 (October 1961): 4.

The editorial criticizes Fulbright's memorandum alerting the president and the secretary of defense to educational and propaganda activities of the military.

840 "On the Couch." *Time,* 3 June 1966, 20-21.

The article is a review of Fulbright's hearings before the Foreign Relations Committee regarding the application of psychology to U.S. foreign policy. Witnesses included Jerome Frank and Charles Osgood.

841 "One Way to Learn." *Newsweek,* 18 May 1964, 47.

The article concerns the Cyprus mission undertaken by Fulbright for President Johnson. The trip included stopovers in London, Athens, and Ankara to discuss the quarrel between the Greek and Turkish Cypriots.

842 "Open Up!" *The Nation,* 12 April 1965, 377-78.

This editorial reproves the Foreign Relations Committee for its vote to override Fulbright's proposal to divide the foreign aid program into separate military and economic packages and to disclose information about disbursements of economic assistance in other countries.

843 "Out Come the Knives." *Newsweek,* 23 March 1959, 28.

The article mentions Fulbright's objections to the foreign aid program.

844 "Oversell? Overkill?" *Newsweek,* 7 July 1969, 18.

The story concerns the flap over Secretary of Defense Melvin Laird's testimony before the Senate Foreign Relations Committee regarding predictions of Soviet missile capabilities. It concludes with a note about the passage and significance of Fulbright's national commitments resolution.

845 "Peking's Other Enemy." *Newsweek,* 4 April 1966, 47.

In an article about Fulbright's hearings before the Foreign Relations Committee on China, witnesses advocate a complete restructuring of U.S. foreign policy toward Peking. It also notes the impact of the hearings on the Johnson administration, particularly on Secretary of State Dean Rusk.

846 Phillips, Cabell. "Dozen Key Men in Congress." *The New York Times Magazine,* 3 January 1960, 6-7.

Chairman Fulbright is featured as one of the twelve key members of Congress at the beginning of the decade.

847 "Pick Your Senator." *Newsweek,* 4 September 1961, 3.

These letters to the editor regard the article in the August 7 issue of *Newsweek* about the Fulbright-Barry Goldwater debate on foreign policy.

848 "Piece Work." *Newsweek,* 22 November 1971, 40, 43.

The article concerns the efforts of Congress to put together a substitute foreign aid bill after an earlier Senate vote to scuttle the administration's aid program. It reviews the strategy designed by Fulbright's Foreign Relations Committee to regain support for the legislation.

849 "Piqued Plea." *Time,* 11 August 1967, 10.

This article pertains to Fulbright's "sense of the Senate" resolution calling for the agreement of both the executive and legislative branches in matters concerning military commitments to other governments. It was reintroduced and passed by the Senate in 1969.

850 "Powerful Quartet from Arkansas." *U.S. News and World Report,* 13 February 1959, 24.

The article features four powerful chairmen from Arkansas: J. William Fulbright, Senate Foreign Relations Committee; John McClellan, Senate Government Operations Committee; Wilbur Mills, House Ways and Means Committee; and Oren Harris, House Interstate and Foreign Commerce Committee.

851 "President Comments on DLF Proposals by Senator Fulbright." *The Department of State Bulletin,* 22 June 1959, 926-28.

The article consists of Eisenhower-Fulbright correspondence regarding the senator's proposed reform of the Development Loan Fund.

852 "President Eisenhower's Lieutenants—Plus a Pair of Democrats." *U.S. News and World Report,* 4 May 1959, 21.

Fulbright appears with President Eisenhower in a photograph taken on the occasion of Christian Herter's swearing-in as secretary of state. Lyndon Johnson is the other Democrat in the photograph.

853 "Probing the Bungle." *Newsweek,* 6 June 1960, 30-31.

The article concerns the Senate Foreign Relations Committee investigation of the U-2 incident.

854 "Professor Einstein to Dr. Freud: 'Can We Eliminate War?'" *Avant Garde,* March 1968, 32-36.

The article mentions Fulbright's interest in the application of psychology to the analysis of international politics.

855 "Purse-String Answer." *Time,* 1 September 1967, 12-13.

The article concerns the constitutional powers of Congress in initiating war and influencing its conduct. It mentions Fulbright's efforts in behalf of his "sense of the

Senate" resolution regarding military commitments to foreign governments. It also notes his position on the passage and repeal of the Tonkin Gulf resolution.

856 "Reading the Dragon's Mind." *Time,* 18 March 1966, 27A.

The story concerns Fulbright's committee hearings on China.

857 "Reason for Hope." *Newsweek,* 5 June 1961, 24, 31.

The article includes the senator's remarks concerning Fidel Castro's proposal to exchange captives from the Bay of Pigs invasion for five hundred tractors.

858 "Report on Washington." *The Atlantic Monthly* 213 (June 1964): 4, 6, 8.

The column includes a short note regarding the origin of Fulbright's "Old Myths and New Realities" speech, which the senator delivered in the Senate on March 25, 1964.

859 "Report on Washington: The Foreign Aid Squabble." *The Atlantic Monthly* 204 (September 1959): 4, 8, 10.

The column includes an item concerning Fulbright's efforts to secure long-term funding for the Development Loan Fund.

860 "Reshaping Policy." *The Commonweal,* 10 April 1964, 75-76.

This editorial critiques Fulbright's Senate speech on March 25, 1964, titled "Old Myths and New Realities." The editors take issue with some of the senator's ideas regarding communist countries, particularly Cuba.

861 Reston, Richard. "Report on Washington: Fulbright Pro and Con." *The Atlantic Monthly* 218 (October 1966): 4, 6, 8, 10, 12.

The writer discusses the positive and the negative sides of the senator's role as foreign policy critic of the Johnson administration. He also reflects on Fulbright's break with the president.

862 "Rethinking the Unthinkable." *The Reporter,* 21 September 1967, 14, 16.

The article concerns the reversal of Fulbright's belief that the president should have more control over the conduct of foreign policy than Congress. Using the senator's national commitments resolution as a base, the writer questions the change from one extreme position to the other. He also looks at the parallels between the issues raised by Fulbright in the congressional debate on the national commitments resolution and those raised by Senator Robert Taft sixteen years earlier during the Korean War.

863 Ritchie, Donald A. "Making Fulbright Chairman: Or How the 'Johnson Treatment' Nearly Backfired." *Society for Historians of American Foreign Relations Newsletter* 15, No. 3 (1984): 21-28.

The author recounts Lyndon Johnson's role in securing the resignation of Theodore Francis Green as chairman of the Foreign Relations Committee. Based on committee and oral history transcripts, the article documents the strategy used by the Senate majority leader and the Senate staff to elevate Fulbright to the chairmanship in early 1959.

864 "Roadblock for Kennedy in Congress?" *U.S. News and World Report,* 9 January 1961, 56-59.

The article concerning President Kennedy and Congress includes a picture of Fulbright and a summary of the Foreign Relations Committee agenda.

865   Rogers, Jimmie Neal. "An Investigation of Senator J. William Fulbright's Attitudes Toward President Lyndon B. Johnson as Demonstrated in Selected Foreign Policy Addresses: An Evaluative Assertion Analysis." Ph.D. diss., Florida State University, 1972.

The study concerns the origin of the discord and the eventual break in the friendship between the senator and Lyndon Johnson. Using evaluation assertion analysis, the author examines important foreign policy speeches for evidence of changes in Fulbright's attitude toward President Johnson for the two-year period from March 25, 1964, the date of "Old Myths and New Realities," to May 10, 1966. Fifteen speeches make up the text of the study. The dissertation includes a biographical sketch emphasizing significant encounters and achievements in the senator's twenty-four-year congressional career, up to 1966.

866   Rogers, Jimmie N., and Theodore Clevenger, Jr. "'The Selling of the Pentagon': Was CBS the Fulbright Propaganda Machine?" *The Quarterly Journal of Speech* 57 (October 1971): 266-73.

The writers examine the parallelism between CBS's special report, "The Selling of the Pentagon," on February 23, 1971, and Fulbright's earlier exposé. See chapter 9 in William C. Berman's *William Fulbright and the Vietnam War: The Dissent of a Political Realist* for additional information.

867   Roper, Elmo. "A Tale of Two Senates." *Lithopinion* 3, No. 2, Issue 10 (1968): 19-25.

The writer compares the Senate of 1968 with the Senate of 1850. He includes Fulbright among the men of prominent intellectual standing.

868   Rovere, Richard H. "Letter from Washington." *The New Yorker,* 11 April 1964, 149-55.

The author includes a critique of Fulbright's "Old Myths and New Realities" speech, specifically the senator's treatment of the monolithic nature of the communist bloc and his failure to address the NATO issue.

869   "The 'Safeguard' Debate Opens." *Newsweek,* 31 March 1969, 24-25.

The article concerns Secretary of Defense Melvin Laird's appearance before Senate committees on the Safeguard ABM system and the ensuing argument between Laird and senators over Soviet missile capabilities. Fulbright's clash with the secretary is noted.

870   Safran, Nadav. "Middle East: The Fleeting Opportunity." *The Nation,* 5 April 1971, 425-28.

The author analyzes the prospects for peace in the Middle East, calling for a mutual defense treaty between the United States and Israel. He outlines the advantages of such a treaty and cites Fulbright's proposal of a U.S. security guarantee to Israel. He also discusses the differences between Fulbright's suggested unilateral guarantee and his proposed mutual defense treaty.

871   Schlesinger, Arthur M., Jr., ed. *The Dynamics of World Power: A Documentary History of United States Foreign Policy, 1945-1973.* Vol. 5, *The United Nations—Subsaharan Africa.* Edited by Richard C. Hottelet and Jean Herskovits. New York: Chelsea House Publishers in association with McGraw-Hill Book Company, 1973, 824-66.

The volume includes testimony from hearings before Fulbright's Foreign Relations Committee in June 1970 on U.S. security agreements and commitments with Ethiopia.

872 Sclanders, Ian. "The Quiet Spokesman for Sanity in the U.S. Senate." *Maclean's*, 9 September 1961, 81.

This is a friendly profile of the senator which includes Fulbright statements on war, Cuba, Berlin, American values, and the use of communist tactics against the communists.

873 "Scrub It Up, Don't Wipe It Out." *The New Republic,* 13 November 1971, 5-7.

This editorial consists of a scenario of the debate and defeat of foreign aid legislation in the Senate on October 29, 1971, and a defense of the internationalists in Congress working to reform the program. The editorial includes remarks by Fulbright.

874 "Sec. Def. Says Military Men, Resources 'Are Not Instruments of Social Change.'" *Army, Navy, Air Force Journal and Register,* 21 September 1963, 8, 30.

This is an exchange of correspondence between Fulbright and Secretary of Defense Robert McNamara in which the senator voices his objections to the Defense Department's directive of July 26, 1963, titled "Equal Opportunity in the Armed Forces."

875 "Secret Agreements." *The New Republic,* 26 July 1969, 5-6.

This is an editorial concerning secret executive agreements with Spain and Thailand and the Department of State's response. Fulbright discovered the secret agreements during the preparation of his national commitments resolution.

876 "Secretary Rusk's News Conference of March 27, 1964." *The Department of State Bulletin,* 13 April 1964, 570-76.

The secretary of state's press conference includes responses to questions inspired by Fulbright's "Old Myths and New Realities" speech.

877 "Sections to Debate Controversial Issues in Honolulu: Senator Fulbright to Speak at Joint Section Luncheon." *American Bar News* 12, No. 5 (1967): 5.

This item announces Fulbright's address, "The Price of Empire," before the Sections of General Practice and International and Comparative Law on August 8 and includes brief biographical information.

878 "The Senate vs. the White House." *Newsweek,* 22 March 1971, 19.

The item centers on the efforts of the Foreign Relations Committee to get information on U.S. bases in Greece.

879 "Senate's Amen Corner on U.S. Hegemony." *Freedom and Union* 21 (September 1966): 20.

This is an excerpt from the official report of question-and-answer testimony of General Lauris Norstad and Fulbright at the Senate hearing on U.S. policy toward the European and Atlantic communities on June 23, 1966.

880 "The Senator and Castroism." *Life,* 10 April 1964, 2.

The editors disagree with Fulbright's position on Cuba in his "Old Myths and New Realities" speech.

881 "Senator Fulbright Dissents." *The Nation,* 4 October 1965, 177-78.

This editorial concerns Fulbright's speech criticizing U.S. intervention in the Dominican Republic. It laments the failure of the Johnson administration to listen to the dissenters.

882 "Senator Fulbright Gets Top Foreign-Policy Post." *U.S. News and World Report,* 6 February 1959, 21.

The article features Fulbright as the new chairman of the Foreign Relations Committee and includes a biographical sketch.

883 "Senator Fulbright Hits at Ike's 'Summit' Views." *U.S. News and World Report,* 15 June 1959, 24.

The article concerns Fulbright's disagreement with President Eisenhower's position regarding summit conferences. It also notes other Fulbright disagreements with the administration over foreign policy.

884 "Senator Fulbright's Call for New Foreign Policy." *New World Review* 32, No. 5 (1964): 3-5.

The item reviews thoughts expressed by Fulbright in speeches advocating a reassessment of U.S. foreign policy and challenging long-standing myths in foreign affairs.

885 "Senator's Turnabout." *Newsweek,* 1 June 1959, 23.

The article concerns Wayne Morse's switch on the nomination of Ogden R. Reid as ambassador to Israel and its effect on Fulbright's plan to test the State Department's policy of naming political appointees to diplomatic posts.

886 Shannon, William V. "Fulbright's Guerrilla War." *The Commonweal,* 8 September 1967, 544-45.

In an article inspired by the senator's national commitments resolution, the writer challenges Fulbright's positions on overseas commitments and foreign aid. For a defense of the senator, see Rory V. Ellinger's letter to the editor in the September 29 issue of the *Commonweal.*

887 ———. "New Myths for Old." *The Commonweal,* 17 April 1964, 102-3.

The author critiques Fulbright's Senate speech of March 25, 1964, titled "Old Myths and New Realities." Shannon challenges the senator's ideas regarding the monolithic nature of the communist bloc, Cuba, and China.

888 Shearer, Lloyd. "The Plight of American Youth: No More Heroes." *Parade Magazine,* 29 October 1967, 4-5.

Fulbright ranks second behind Robert F. Kennedy in a poll of 2,100 people between the ages of sixteen and twenty-three.

889 "Signs of an End to Castro's Isolation." *U.S. News and World Report,* 5 August 1974, 30.

The article concerns Pat M. Holt's trip to Cuba to meet with Fidel Castro and other Cuban officials and mentions Fulbright's role in securing the State Department's approval. Holt was chief of staff of the Senate Foreign Relations Committee from 1974 until 1977.

890 "The Silent Liberals." *The Progressive* 29 (November 1965): 3-4.

The editors discuss the significance of the senator's speech criticizing U.S. intervention in the Dominican Republic. Praising his forward-looking approach to foreign policy issues, they deplore the silence of all but three progressives in the Senate: Wayne Morse, Joseph Clark, and Eugene McCarthy.

891 Smith, Beverly Waugh, Jr. "Egghead from the Ozarks." *The Saturday Evening Post*, 2 May 1959, 31, 115-16, 118.

In this profile of the new chairman of the Foreign Relations Committee, the writer looks at Fulbright's general make-up and background for indications of the direction of the committee under his leadership.

892 Smith, Jessica. "The Meaning of the US-USSR Agreements to Both Peoples." *New World Review* 41, No. 3 (1973): 10-12.

The item includes Fulbright remarks expressing opposition to the Jackson amendment to the trade bill with the Soviet Union. See also Fulbright's speech, "Getting Along with the Russians," in the September 15, 1973, issue of *Vital Speeches of the Day.*

893 "'Something Newsy.'" *Newsweek*, 22 July 1963, 27-28.

Fulbright's Foreign Relations Committee investigates the lobbying activities of the Hamilton Wright Organization.

894 "Southerners in Senate—A Group with Real Power." *U.S. News and World Report*, 21 March 1960, 86-88.

The article concerns the power of the southern Democrats, particularly the nine who chair Senate committees, and their control over a broad range of legislation, including civil rights and foreign aid. The group includes two chairmen from Arkansas: Fulbright of the Foreign Relations Committee and John L. McClellan of the Government Operations Committee.

895 "'Speaker of the Year' Award." *Speaker and Gavel* 3 (May 1966): 100.

In his acceptance statement, Fulbright comments on the importance of effective communication, particularly for senators. Delta Sigma Rho-Tau Kappa Alpha, national honorary forensic society, presented the award.

896 "Standards to Maintain." *Time*, 1 June 1959, 14-15.

The article concerns the Foreign Relations Committee hearings on the nomination of Ogden R. Reid as U.S. ambassador to Israel. It concludes with a harsh assessment of the new Foreign Relations Committee chairman.

897 Stanford, Neal. "Should U.S. Envoys Be Professionals?" *Foreign Policy Bulletin*, 1 July 1959, 155.

The article examines the reasons for the Senate's tougher standards for candidates seeking ambassadorial posts. It notes Fulbright's efforts to increase the number of professional appointees.

898 "The State of 'Chassis.'" *The Nation*, 19 March 1960, 238-39.

This editorial examines Fulbright's Senate speech of March 4, 1960, expressing concern about the threat of communism.

899 Stone, I.F. "Can Congress Stop the President?" *The New York Review of Books*, 19 April 1973, 19-26.

In a trenchant analysis of the war powers legislation, Stone cites Fulbright's "Additional Views" of the Senate report on the Javits-Stennis-Eagleton bill, in which the senator warns against the loopholes in the bill. Stone examines the failure of the Fulbright committee to attach the Church-Case bill to the foreign aid bill and also the failure of the committee to question Secretary of State William P. Rogers about administration commitments to resume bombing in the Southeast Asian war.

900 ———. "The Washington Power Game: War Curbs: How the Senate Flunks." *The New York Review of Books,* 19 July 1973, 20-21.

Stone examines the loopholes in the Javits-Stennis-Eagleton war powers bill, quoting extensively from Fulbright's dissenting "supplemental views," which accompanied the Senate report on the legislation. Stone also compares the Senate bill with the House bill and investigates the absence of a provision against first strike attacks, noting Fulbright's argument for an amendment regarding the use of nuclear weapons.

901 "Storm Signals." *Newsweek,* 8 February 1965, 23-24.

The article includes Fulbright's announcement that he would not act as floor manager for the administration's foreign aid bill.

902 "Storm Signals for Foreign Aid in '65." *U.S. News and World Report,* 4 January 1965, 8.

Calling for a restructuring of the foreign assistance program, Fulbright announces that he will not manage the administration's foreign aid bill in the Senate.

903 "Strange Story of a Senate Committee." *U.S. News and World Report,* 4 April 1966, 32, 35.

The article concerns Fulbright as chairman of the Foreign Relations Committee and includes a look at his voting record and his foreign policy views.

904 "Sugar Blues." *Newsweek,* 29 April 1963, 23.

The article concerns Fulbright's investigation of the lobbying activities of agents working for foreign governments and focuses on the activities of John A. O'Donnell.

905 "Support for Fulbright." *The Commonweal,* 29 September 1967, 618-19.

In a letter to the editor, Rory V. Ellinger defends Fulbright against criticism leveled by William V. Shannon in the September 8 issue of the *Commonweal.* Citing the senator's book, *The Arrogance of Power,* the writer argues that Fulbright has his priorities regarding overseas commitments and foreign aid in order.

906 "Sweet and Sour." *Newsweek,* 16 July 1962, 63-64.

The article regards President Kennedy's sugar bill and related lobbying activities on the part of a number of sugar-producing countries. It mentions Fulbright's plans to conduct an investigation into lobbyists' impact on legislation.

907 T.R.B. "Dirksen and Fulbright." *The New Republic,* 4 April 1964, 2.

The item concerns Everett Dirksen on civil rights and Fulbright on foreign policy. T.R.B. reviews Fulbright's comments regarding myths in U.S. policies toward Panama, Cuba, Latin America, the Soviet Union, and China.

908 ———. "Faubus for Fulbright?" *The New Republic,* 9 February 1959, 2.

T.R.B. asks whether Fulbright will use his new power as chairman of the Foreign Relations Committee. He also wonders whether Fulbright will be forced out of the Senate by Orval Faubus in the 1962 election.

909 ———. "Quack, Quack, Quack." *The New Republic,* 4 September 1961, 2.

T.R.B. mentions the clash between Barry Goldwater and Fulbright over the military's sponsorship of public meetings principally related to highly controversial political issues.

910 ——. "Senate Spectacular." *The New Republic,* 4 February 1967, [6].

The column focuses on Fulbright and two Senate Foreign Relations Committee hearings, one on the U.S.-Soviet consular treaty and the other on the foreign policy of the United States as a great power.

911 "Target." *Newsweek,* 25 May 1959, 33.

The article concerns Ogden R. Reid's nomination as ambassador to Israel and Fulbright's position on the appointment.

912 "The Thaw." *The Progressive* 28 (May 1964): 3-4.

In a review of Fulbright's "Old Myths and New Realities" speech, the editors praise the senator for helping to create a favorable environment for the open discussion of foreign policy questions.

913 "Think." *America,* 16 May 1964, 660.

In a letter to the editor, the writer disagrees with the position of the magazine regarding the senator's "Old Myths and New Realities" speech of March 25, 1964, and commends Fulbright for urging his compatriots to think and for giving the country something to think about. The article which inspired the letter appeared in the April 11 issue and begins on page 500 under the title "The Fulbright Proposal."

914 "Thinking About Destiny." *Newsweek,* 23 September 1963, 26-27.

The article concerns the nuclear test ban treaty and highlights Fulbright's remarks about U.S.-Soviet relations.

915 "Three Senatorial 'Secretaries of State.'" *U.S. News and World Report,* 23 October 1961, 22.

The article features Hubert Humphrey, Mike Mansfield, and Fulbright expressing their views on Berlin.

916 "Time for a Deeper Debate." *Business Week,* 4 April 1964, 120.

The editors commend Fulbright's attempt to discuss necessary changes in U.S. foreign policy in his "Old Myths and New Realities" speech but maintain that additional realities will have to be confronted. They also quarrel with his position on Cuba and China.

917 "'The Time Has Come.'" *Time,* 9 February 1959, 15.

The article concerns the resignation of Theodore Francis Green as chairman of the Senate Foreign Relations Committee and the succession of Fulbright to the position. It includes a brief sketch of Fulbright's career.

918 Toffler, Al. "How Congressmen Make Up Their Minds." *Redbook* 118 (February 1962): 56-57, 126-31.

In a *Redbook* survey of Congress, Fulbright ranked fifth among the five most influential senators. He also ranked among the top five most admired among Senate Democrats. He used the results of this survey in his campaign for a fourth term in 1962.

919 "Tomorrow." *U.S. News and World Report,* 7 September 1970, 9.

The article explains Fulbright's proposal for a treaty insuring the preservation of Israel's borders. It also examines his idea that a Mideast settlement would revive the United Nations and improve U.S.-Soviet relations.

920 "Tracking the Iceberg." *Time,* 27 May 1966, 19.

The story concerns the Foreign Relations Committee resolution calling for the expansion of the congressional committee monitoring the activities of the Central Intelligence Agency. Fulbright was the leader of the effort to establish legislative oversight of the agency.

921 "Tube Power." *Newsweek,* 17 August 1970, 61.

The article regards the power of television in politics and efforts to get Congress an equitable allotment of air time for discussion and debate. It notes Fulbright's proposal in the form of an amendment to the Communications Act and includes reaction by Congress and the media.

922 "Underlining China." *Time,* 8 April 1966, 26.

The article concerns the Senate Foreign Relations Committee hearings associated with China and includes excerpts from testimony of leading Sinologists. The views of Hans Morgenthau, Walter H. Judd, Robert A. Scalapino, and George Taylor are reviewed.

923 "Unity on Berlin." *Time,* 16 March 1959, 19.

The story mentions President Eisenhower's appearance before the foreign and military affairs committees to brief chairmen and ranking members in the Senate and the House on the Berlin situation. It includes questions by Fulbright.

924 "U.S. Policy: Old Myths, Mixed Voices." *Newsweek,* 6 April 1964, 17-18.

The article reviews the senator's speech separating myth from reality in foreign affairs, particularly in U.S. relations with the communist world, and includes reactions of Republicans and Democrats. It also includes excerpts from Fulbright's speech.

925 "U.S. Senators Visit Brazil." *The Department of State Bulletin,* 23 August 1965, 332.

This State Department announcement concerns the visit of a U.S. delegation, including Fulbright, to Brazil to discuss a program associated with the Alliance for Progress and the Organization of American States.

926 "Victimizing Foreign Aid." *The New Republic,* 11 June 1966, 6.

This editorial examines the action taken by the Foreign Relations Committee to effect changes in the foreign aid program. It also looks at Fulbright's position.

927 "A Victory for Russell; Fulbright Loses CIA Wrangle." *U.S. News and World Report,* 25 July 1966, 19.

The article concerns the defeat in the Senate of Fulbright's resolution to enlarge the committee monitoring CIA activities.

928 "Warfare by Witchcraft." *Time,* 31 May 1968, 13-14.

During the Senate's consideration of the defense budget, Fulbright questions the Pentagon's research spending on such mysterious studies as the practices of Congolese witchcraft.

929 "Was U.S. Wrong in Dominican Crisis?" *U.S. News and World Report,* 27 September 1965, 20.

The article concerns the controversy sparked by Fulbright's September 15 Senate speech condemning U.S. intervention in the Dominican Republic and includes Fulbright remarks. Senators Thomas J. Dodd and Frank J. Lausche defend administration policy.

930 Wechsler, James A. "Propaganda in the Press: A Study in Suppression." *The Progressive* 27 (August 1963): 10-15.

In an article based largely on transcripts of Fulbright's committee hearings titled "Activities of Nondiplomatic Representatives of Foreign Principals in the U.S.," the author examines the role of the press in the management of news and opinion. He focuses on the activities of the U.S. Press Association, the Hearst International News Service, and the Special Services Bureau of United Press International, noting how little notice the committee findings received in the press.

931 ———. "Senator Arbuthnot Takes a Stand." *The Progressive* 28 (May 1964): 31-32.

Senator Arbuthnot takes a consistently middle-of-the-road position in this "interview" inspired by Fulbright's "Old Myths and New Realities" speech.

932 "What Is So Rare?" *Newsweek*, 23 August 1965, 45-46.

The article concerns a trip by senators and administration officials to Brazil to talk with the president and his planning minister. It includes Fulbright's remarks linking the upcoming Brazilian presidential election with the prospects of U.S. private investment.

933 "'Who Is Mr. Shepley?'" *Newsweek*, 29 August 1960, 19.

The article pertains to charges surrounding the use of funds provided by the Joseph P. Kennedy, Jr. Foundation for the air transportation of African students to the United States. President Richard Nixon appointed James Shepley to handle the matter, and Fulbright demanded to know who he was.

934 "Who's for Fulbright?" *Newsweek*, 18 October 1965, 2.

These are letters responding to the article "Myth and Reality II" in the September 27 issue of *Newsweek*.

935 "Whose Foreign Policy?" *Newsweek*, 23 December 1968, 27-28.

The article concerns the struggle between the executive and legislative branches over the conduct of U.S. foreign policy. It focuses on Fulbright's efforts to secure passage of his national commitments resolution.

936 "Whose Myth? Whose Reality?" *Time*, 3 April 1964, 23-24.

This is a review of Fulbright's Senate speech separating myth from reality in foreign affairs. The magazine takes exception to his view of reality and to his suggestions regarding U.S. foreign policy toward Cuba and China. Included also are reactions to the speech by Lyndon Johnson and Dean Rusk.

937 "William the Terrible." *Newsweek*, 8 August 1966, 18-19.

The article regards Fulbright's opposition to the Johnson administration's foreign aid bill.

938 "Winter Term." *Newsweek*, 13 February 1967, 35-36.

The article concerns Fulbright's hearings before the Foreign Relations Committee on U.S. foreign policy and features witnesses George F. Kennan and Edwin Reischauer on dealing with the communist world.

939   Witze, Claude. "The Contradictions Exist." *Air Force and Space Digest* 47 (May 1964): 13-14.

The writer challenges the ideas expressed by Fulbright in his "Old Myths and New Realities" speech concerning the threat of communism.

940   ———. "Who Said the Cold War Is Over?" *Air Force and Space Digest* 53 (October 1970): 12-15.

The author notes Fulbright's proposed U.S. security guarantee to Israel in an article concerned primarily with the Senate debate over the Pentagon's authorization bill for Fiscal 1971. Fulbright's amendments are also noted. Witze concludes with a description of the Foreign Relations Committee chairman, which turns out to be an account of Senator William E. Borah by Selig Adler in *The Isolationist Impulse*.

941   "Work for the 'Fabulous' 89th." *The Nation,* 8 November 1965, 317.

The editors spell out an agenda for Congress, proposing that the legislators conduct a painstaking review of U.S. foreign policy. Pointing out congressional ineffectiveness in international affairs, they note the futility of Fulbright's efforts to discuss foreign policy problems.

942   "Worldgram: From the Capitals of the World." *U.S. News and World Report,* 7 September 1970, 37-38.

The item examines Fulbright's three-point proposal for a Middle East settlement and evaluates its chances of effecting a permanent peace.

943   Wyden, Peter. *Bay of Pigs: The Untold Story.* New York: Simon and Schuster, 1979, 122-23, 146-51, 165, 305, 323.

The author notes the senator's memorandum to the president outlining proposed U.S. policies toward Cuba. He also discusses Fulbright's presence at the April 4, 1961, meeting of the National Security Council called by the president. For other accounts of the meeting, see *The Bay of Pigs: The Leaders' Story of Brigade 2506* by Haynes Johnson and *The Cuban Invasion: The Chronicle of a Disaster* by Karl E. Meyer and Tad Szulc.

VIETNAM WAR

944   Abt, John J. "The World of Senator Fulbright." *New World Review* 35, No. 6 (1967): 9-12.

This is a critical review of Fulbright's *Arrogance of Power.* The writer sees a revealing self-portrait of the senator emerging from the book and proceeds to explain how the self-portrait harmonizes with Fulbright's position on the war in Vietnam. The dates of the "arrogance of power" lectures are incorrectly cited as 1964. The lectures were delivered in the spring of 1966 at Johns Hopkins University.

945   "Advice—And Consent." *Newsweek,* 15 May 1961, 30.

The article notes the senator's counsel to the president against a military commitment in Laos.

946   "Advice and Dissent." *Newsweek,* 21 February 1966, 30-31.

The article treats Fulbright in his role as Vietnam War dissenter. It consists of a biographical sketch of the senator and excerpts from *Newsweek* correspondent John Lindsay's interviews with Fulbright.

947 "After the Fall: Reactions and Rationales." *Time,* 12 May 1975, 20, 23.

Fulbright, among others, responds to the news of the communist victory in Vietnam.

948 "After the Pause: Motion or Progress?" *Newsweek,* 14 February 1966, 17-21.

The article notes the growing rift between Fulbright and President Johnson over the conduct of the Vietnam War. It also mentions the senator's Foreign Relations Committee hearings investigating U.S. policy in the region.

949 "Agony, Yes; Arrogance, No." *America,* 28 May 1966, 767.

This editorial takes issue with the thesis of the senator's Christian A. Herter Lectures at the School of Advanced International Studies, Johns Hopkins University, on the "arrogance of power."

950 "AID for Whom?" *The Nation,* 21 February 1966, 198.

This editorial concerns the impact of the U.S. economic aid program in Vietnam and focuses on the testimony of David Bell, the administrator of the Agency for International Development.

951 Alsop, Stewart. "Mr. Dove and Mr. Hawk." *The Saturday Evening Post,* 18 June 1966, 18.

In an editorial based on interviews with both Dean Rusk and Fulbright concerning Vietnam, the writer outlines and comments on the Fulbright plan for achieving a negotiated settlement and concludes that the secretary of state makes the stronger argument.

952 ———. "Mr. Thieu Has His Day." *Newsweek,* 5 January 1970, 64.

The article includes excerpts from an interview with President Nguyen Van Thieu of South Vietnam. Alsop mentions Fulbright's position on the Thieu regime.

953 Amter, Joseph A. *Vietnam Verdict: A Citizen's History.* New York: Continuum Publishing Company, 1982, 59, 61-65, 69-70, 107-23, 127, 216, 233, 236-37, 251.

The author recounts the senator's transition from sponsor of the Tonkin Gulf resolution to major war critic. His focus is on the hearings held by the Foreign Relations Committee in early 1966 on the conduct of the war. Other topics include Fulbright's investigation in 1967 of the August 1964 Tonkin Gulf incidents and the February 20, 1968, hearing with Robert McNamara.

954 "And from the White House—Silence." *Newsweek,* 18 March 1968, 45.

The article regards the debate in the Senate on Vietnam policy and notes Fulbright's argument that the president should consult with Congress before escalating the war.

955 "Apologia pro Verbis Suis." *Time,* 27 May 1966, 70.

The article concerns the controversy created by Fulbright in remarks before the National Press Club in which he referred to Saigon as a "brothel." It also includes his criticism of the media's handling of the statement.

956 "Appointment in Manila." *Newsweek,* 10 October 1966, 36.

The article regards President Johnson's meeting with Asian and Pacific leaders in Manila on Vietnam and includes Fulbright's response to the conference.

957 "The Arrogance of Power." *The Progressive* 37 (February 1973): 3.

In an editorial denouncing the Nixon administration's bombing of North Vietnam, the writers credit the senator with first using the phrase "the arrogance of power" as a characterization of the Johnson administration's conduct of the Vietnam War.

958 Ashmore, Harry S., and William C. Baggs. *Mission to Hanoi: A Chronicle of Double-Dealing in High Places: A Special Report from the Center for the Study of Democratic Institutions*. New York: G.P. Putnam's Sons, 1968, 8-9, 19, 62-72, 78, 118, 172, 179-80, 185, 192, 195-96, 229, 266-67, 269-70, 275-76.

The authors review their efforts to communicate the findings of their meeting in January 1967 with Ho Chi Minh to the Johnson administration. They recall their meeting with State Department officials to draft a response to the North Vietnamese leader and include Fulbright's biting statement about the prospects for a successful session, along with an explanation of "Fulbright's Law" on dealing with the State Department.

959 Austin, Anthony. *The President's War: The Story of the Tonkin Gulf Resolution and How the Nation Was Trapped in Vietnam*. Philadelphia: J.B. Lippincott Company, 1971, 1-2, 4-7, 14-15, 41-43, 54, 56, 64, 68, 78-79, 81-88, 90-91, 93, 95, 102-13, 118, 120-21, 123-25, 128-30, 132, 134-35, 137-39, 151-54, 157-61, 163-64, 166-82, 185-92, 195-96, 199-225, 323, 328-31.

The author profiles Fulbright, noting his role in the passage of the Tonkin Gulf resolution, his subsequent clash with President Johnson, the Foreign Relations Committee's hearings in 1966, the committee's investigation in 1967 of the August 1964 incidents in the Tonkin Gulf, the February 20, 1968, committee hearing with Robert McNamara, and the senator's position on the repeal of the resolution.

960 Bailey, Richard Eugene. "A Rhetorical Analysis of James William Fulbright's Speaking on 'The Arrogance of Power.'" Ph.D. diss., Ohio State University, 1968.

Using the ethical, truth, artistic, and results standards of judgment, the writer undertakes a rhetorical evaluation of Fulbright's "arrogance of power" lectures at Johns Hopkins University in the spring of 1966. His analysis includes an investigation of four rhetorical categories—invention, disposition, style, and delivery—for each of the three lectures. Other features of the study are a biographical sketch; an examination of the components in Fulbright's perspective of a nation; a review of his ideas on discourse; and background information concerning the speeches, including a summary of the Foreign Relations Committee hearings on Vietnam. Speech texts appear in the appendix under the titles "The Higher Patriotism," "Revolution Abroad," and "The Arrogance of Power."

961 Beisner, Robert L. "1898 and 1968: The Anti-Imperialists and the Doves." *Political Science Quarterly* 85 (June 1970): 187-216.

The author compares the anti-imperialist movement of 1898-1900 with the Vietnam War protest movement of 1968, concentrating on the identity of the protesters, their leaders, their activities, and their motives. Fulbright figures prominently in the essay.

962 Berman, William C. *William Fulbright and the Vietnam War: The Dissent of a Political Realist*. Kent, Ohio: Kent State University Press, 1988.

In this in-depth study of the senator and the Vietnam War, the author examines Fulbright's dissent within the context of the realist tradition of foreign policy thought. His primary focus concerns the significance of the Vietnam War in shaping a new Fulbright foreign policy approach regarding the role of the United States in the world. The book is based on extensive research in the Fulbright Papers and incorporates an overview of landmark speeches and writings.

963 "Best Sellers." *Time*, 28 April 1967, 8.

The senator's book, *The Arrogance of Power*, ranks last on the top ten list of nonfiction best sellers.

964 Bradshaw, Leonard Lee. "The Rhetoric of J. William Fulbright: Dissent in Crisis." Ph.D. diss., Southern Illinois University, 1970.

The author uses both synthesis and analysis to examine Fulbright's rhetoric of dissent in selected speeches delivered during the Dominican Republic and Vietnam crises. He introduces the study with a consideration of the senator's philosophy of dissent in a democracy and proceeds to critically evaluate his rhetoric in seven speeches, two regarding U.S. intervention in the Dominican Republic in 1965 and five regarding escalation of U.S. involvement in Vietnam in 1965 and 1966. Texts of the speeches make up the appendix.

965 "Brothels and Hair Spray." *Newsweek*, 23 May 1966, 30.

The article concerns Fulbright's statement in which he referred to Saigon as a "brothel." Secretary of State Dean Rusk and Secretary of Defense Robert McNamara offer rebuttals.

966 Brown, Weldon A. *The Last Chopper: The Denouement of the American Role in Vietnam, 1963-1975*. Port Washington, N.Y.: Kennikat Press, 1976, 26-27, 30, 45-47, 52, 66, 81, 84-91, 95, 104, 112, 134, 146, 154, 166, 176, 225, 232.

The author treats Fulbright's changing role during the course of the Vietnam War, from sponsor of the Tonkin Gulf resolution to major critic of the war.

967 Buckwalter, Doyle Wild. "The Gulf of Tonkin Crisis and Resolution: Myth or Reality?" Ph.D. diss., University of Michigan, 1968, 43, 82, 110, 162-63, 177-78, 188, 189n, 197, 199n, 200n, 202, 212-13, 216-18, 221, 225, 229-32, 241-43, 256-57, 271n, 277-78.

The author examines the August 1964 incidents in the Gulf of Tonkin with the purpose of critically analyzing the crisis decision-making process. He also analyzes the policy formulation and adoption processes associated with the passage of the Tonkin Gulf resolution. The study includes a treatment of Fulbright's role as administration sponsor of the resolution in the Senate.

968 Bullert, Gary Byron, and Francis Michael Casey. "The Foreign Policy of Senator William J. [*sic*] Fulbright: From Cold War Warrior to Neo-Isolationist." *The Journal of Social, Political and Economic Studies* 8, No. 4 (1983): 449-69.

The authors examine the evolution of Fulbright's foreign policy ideas over the forty-year period from 1943, describing his career in terms of the internationalist (1943-1946), the collective security interventionist (1946-1964), and the neoisolationist (1964-1983). They continue with an analysis of his transition from cold warrior to neoisolationist, focusing on the development of his position on Vietnam.

969 Campbell, Alex. "Fulbright on Camera." *The New Republic*, 21 May 1966, 19-22.

This is a critique of Fulbright's foreign policy views, particularly those expressed in his Christian A. Herter Lectures at Johns Hopkins University in the spring of 1966. The author focuses on Fulbright's remarks regarding the relationship of patriotism and dissent and the concept that power engenders arrogance. His positions on Vietnam, China, and Cuba are examined. Concluding remarks concern Fulbright's failure to offer foreign policy alternatives to the policies under criticism.

970 ———. "Fulbright Versus Taylor." *The New Republic*, 25 February 1967, 26-27.

In a comparative review of the senator's *Arrogance of Power* and Maxwell Taylor's

Responsibility and Response, the writer concludes that Taylor is successful in proving Fulbright's thesis.

971 "Can He Be Serious?" *National Review,* 9 August 1966, 757-58.

The editors challenge views expressed by the senator in his July 22 speech on U.S. foreign policy in Asia.

972 "A Captive of Consensus." *Time,* 24 June 1966, 23-24.

The story concerns President Johnson's attempt to achieve a national consensus on the conflict in Vietnam and includes a note regarding White House efforts to patch up differences with Fulbright.

973 Charlton, Michael, and Anthony Moncrieff. *Many Reasons Why: The American Involvement in Vietnam.* New York: Hill and Wang, 1978, 50, 111-13, 163, 167, 177, 180-81, 240-41.

The book is a collection of interviews with people closely associated with the course of the war in Vietnam, policy makers, critics, and others, and includes Fulbright. Responding to questions regarding the Tonkin Gulf resolution and the Geneva Accords, the senator also considers the impact of McCarthyism and the Truman Doctrine on later policies committing the United States to South Vietnam. The book resulted from a series of radio programs written by Michael Charlton and broadcast by BBC Radio Three in the fall of 1977.

974 Compton, Neil. "TV Chronicle." *Commentary* 41 (April 1966): 82-86.

The writer credits Senators Fulbright and Mike Mansfield with inspiring the networks to present differing opinions on the Johnson administration's policies in Vietnam.

975 "A Controversial Senator Surrounded by Controversy." *U.S. News and World Report,* 14 March 1966, 26.

The article concerns the growing breach between President Johnson and Fulbright over U.S. policy toward China and the conduct of the war in Vietnam. It also mentions his vote to repeal the Tonkin Gulf resolution.

976 Crawford, Kenneth. "The Ambitious Senate." *Newsweek,* 27 July 1970, 24.

Crawford charges the Senate with attempting to usurp presidential authority in the realm of foreign policy making. Specifically, he criticizes Fulbright for his efforts to set a schedule for U.S. troop disengagement from Vietnam.

977 ———. "Arrogance of Dissent." *Newsweek,* 18 July 1966, 27.

Crawford's column regards Senator Gale McGee's challenge of Fulbright's criticism of the Johnson administration policy in Vietnam. McGee wonders whether Fulbright's dissent itself is not arrogant.

978 ———. "Back to the War." *Newsweek,* 14 February 1966, 33.

In an article supporting President Johnson's conduct of the Vietnam War, Crawford comments on Senate critics of the administration's war policy. Fulbright is included.

979 ———. "Flight of the Doves." *Newsweek,* 5 July 1965, 28.

Crawford examines the statements of Fulbright, Hans Morgenthau, and Frank Church regarding the Johnson administration's Asian policy and notes the significance of the doves' reconsidered views of the president's position.

980 ——. "Fulbright on Riots." *Newsweek,* 21 August 1967, 28.

Crawford blasts Fulbright's speech linking riots in American cities with the war in Vietnam. He invokes the senator's civil rights record as part of his argument against the senator's thesis.

981 ——. "Is It Constitutional?" *Newsweek,* 4 September 1967, 36.

Crawford discusses the constitutionality of the war in Vietnam. He examines the two lines of argument suggested by the hearings on Fulbright's national commitments resolution, one pursued by the senator and the other by Secretary of State Nicholas Katzenbach.

982 ——. "The Long View." *Newsweek,* 21 March 1966, 36.

In a column about Fulbright's Foreign Relations Committee hearings on the Vietnam War, Crawford notes Senator Russell Long's emotional appeal for support during his appearance before the committee. Crawford also predicts that the dissenters' strength will wane.

983 ——. "Myths and Realities." *Newsweek,* 20 April 1970, 48.

Crawford disputes the thesis of Fulbright's Senate speech concerning "old myths and new realities" associated with U.S. policy in Vietnam.

984 ——. "Nixon's 'Knaves.'" *Newsweek,* 23 June 1969, 38.

Crawford defends President Nixon's address at the Air Force Academy against criticism by his opponents that their views had not been accurately represented.

985 ——. "Now Comes Realism." *Newsweek,* 29 May 1967, 33.

Crawford examines the statement by sixteen dissenting senators, including Fulbright, supporting U.S. military presence in Vietnam until the conclusion of a negotiated settlement.

986 ——. "The Senate Stammers." *Newsweek,* 6 July 1970, 39.

In a column concerning the Senate debate about the constitutional powers of Congress and the president in the war-making realm, Crawford points out inconsistencies in the behavior of senators during the discussion. As an example, he notes Fulbright's changing position on the repeal of the Tonkin Gulf resolution.

987 ——. "'We Put Him In.'" *Newsweek,* 6 February 1967, 42.

Crawford takes issue with Fulbright's views regarding Premier Nguyen Cao Ky of South Vietnam.

988 ——. "Wet-Dry: Hawk-Dove." *Newsweek,* 30 November 1970, 29.

Crawford notes the similarities between the politics associated with Prohibition and the politics associated with the Vietnam War. Fulbright is mentioned.

989 "Debate and Disquiet." *Newsweek,* 6 February 1967, 35-36.

This article is a review of three books associated with U.S. policy in Southeast Asia: *Responsibility and Response* by General Maxwell Taylor, *The Bitter Heritage* by Arthur M. Schlesinger, Jr., and *The Arrogance of Power* by J. William Fulbright.

990 "Demand for a Voice." *Time,* 15 March 1968, 14-15.

The article concerns the Senate debate on the Vietnam War and notes Fulbright's demand that the president consult with Congress before escalating the war. His thoughts are echoed by other senators, including Clifford Case, Jack Miller, and Frank Church. Senators John Tower and Frank Lausche counter the critics.

991 "Dissent and Defeat." *Time,* 11 March 1966, 24.

The story concerns Senate passage of President Johnson's appropriations bill for the war in Vietnam. It includes an account of the dissenters' efforts to repeal the Tonkin Gulf resolution.

992 Dvorin, Eugene P., ed. *The Senate's War Powers: Debate on Cambodia from the Congressional Record.* Markham Political Science Series, edited by Aaron Wildavsky. Chicago: Markham Publishing Company, 1971, 4-9, 12, 24-25, 55, 63-64, 84-89, 129-31, 135-38, 176-77, 183, 185, 192-93, 195-96, 198, 201, 206-7, 210, 212-15, 225-28, 230-32, 237-38.

This is a record of the U.S. Senate debate on the Cooper-Church amendment in May and June of 1970 and includes Fulbright's contributions. The purpose of the amendment to the Foreign Military Sales Act was to restrict military operations in Cambodia.

993 Effros, William G., comp. *Quotations Vietnam: 1945-1970.* New York: Random House, 1970, 41, 43-44, 58, 104, 106, 143, 167, 189, 193, 209, 235, 238.

The Fulbright remarks span the years 1964-1970 and concern the incongruity of ideology in backward, undeveloped nations; the nature of the conflict; the Tonkin Gulf resolution; ways to end hostilities; Laos; and Cambodia.

994 "Exhaustive, Explicit and Enough." *Time,* 25 February 1966, 21-23.

The article concerns the Foreign Relations Committee hearings on U.S. policy in Vietnam and features two administration spokesmen who spell out U.S. aims, General Maxwell Taylor and Secretary of State Dean Rusk. Fulbright and Wayne Morse challenge the Johnson policies.

995 Falk, Richard A., ed. *The Vietnam War and International Law.* Vol. 2. Princeton, N.J.: Princeton University Press in association with the American Society of International Law, 1969, 53, 116, 156n, 243, 257, 287, 603, 649, 675-78, 711n, 750-51, 781, 810, 820, 832, 837n, 931, 1029.

The volume includes materials concerning Fulbright's role in the passage of the Tonkin Gulf resolution in the Senate. It also treats congressional interpretation of intent in the legislative history of the resolution.

996 ———. *The Vietnam War and International Law: The Widening Context.* Vol. 3. Princeton, N.J.: Princeton University Press in association with the American Society of International Law, 1972, 84-85, 189, 302n, 499-502, 505, 552, 553n, 567n, 590-91, 613.

The volume includes materials concerning the senator's national commitments resolution of 1969. It also includes a statement by Fulbright in June 1970 regarding the resolution one year later in the wake of the Cambodian invasion.

997 ———. *The Vietnam War and International Law: The Concluding Phase.* Vol. 4. Princeton, N.J.: Princeton University Press in association with the American Society of International Law, 1976, 28, 180, 318, 406, 643n, 659n, 660n, 684n, 688n, 714-15, 718, 734, 738, 761, 792-96, 801n, 888, 893, 895-98, 906-7, 909-10.

The volume includes materials regarding the Fulbright proviso placing restrictions on U.S. military commitment to Cambodia.

998 Finney, John. "Tonkin Gulf Attack: A Case Study in How Not to Go to War." *The New Republic,* 27 January 1968, 19-22.

The author notes the significance of Fulbright's 1967 inquiry into the Tonkin Gulf incidents of August 1964.

999 "Flap over Fulbright." *The New Republic,* 11 June 1966, 28.

In letters to the editor, readers respond to Alex Campbell's article about Fulbright in the May 21 issue of the *New Republic.*

1000 Fletcher, James. "Vietnam and the Cities: The Politics of Emptiness." *National Review,* 13 February 1968, 133-36, 151.

The author examines the arguments for withdrawal from Vietnam within a rhetorical framework called the "Politics of Emptiness," charging that the war critics do not function in the real world. He criticizes Fulbright's advocacy of a convocation of the Geneva Conference as a "non-solution" and accuses other opponents of the war, including Richard Rovere and Mary McCarthy, of taking the rhetoric still further by their failure to offer an alternative. Disavowing a connection between the war and the cities, he also accuses the critics of having no workable agenda for the domestic front. He concludes that alternative policies are available only through the established constitutional system, not by way of the anarchy set loose by the "Politics of Emptiness."

1001 "Foreign Relations: The Ultimate Self-Interest." *Time,* 22 January 1965, 14-18.

The writer takes up the developing foreign policy debate set in motion in part by Fulbright's "Old Myths and New Realities" speech, with an examination of the argument between advocates of a global system of security and proponents of retrenchment in U.S. commitments abroad. This profile of Fulbright includes a treatment of his position on Vietnam and his thoughts on dealing with the communists and concludes with his prescription for a sound foreign policy. The senator's picture is on the cover.

1002 "A Fretful Congress Confronts Vietnam." *Newsweek,* 17 January 1966, 16-17.

The article mentions Fulbright's concern about U.S. policy in Vietnam and his thoughts about holding public hearings.

1003 "From Fulbright: A Sweeping Attack on LBJ's 'Asian Doctrine.'" *U.S. News and World Report,* 1 August 1966, 12.

The article concerns Fulbright's Senate speech of July 22 assailing President Johnson's July 12 announcement of his "Asian Doctrine" regarding the role of the United States in the Pacific.

1004 "Fulbright: Calling Out the Press." *Newsweek,* 18 March 1968, 17-18.

The article regards Fulbright's thoughts about calling Vietnam War journalists to testify in open session before the Foreign Relations Committee.

1005 "Fulbright on Mythology." *War/Peace Report* 4 (April 1964): 11.

The editors laud Fulbright's "Old Myths and New Realities" speech as a good beginning toward reevaluating U.S. foreign policy. They disagree, however, with the senator's position on Vietnam.

1006 "Fulbright Opposes Spread of War." *New World Review* 33, No. 7 (1965): 3-4.

The editorial comment concerns Fulbright's Senate speech of June 15 related to the war in Vietnam.

1007 "Fulbright Terms Dissent a Patriotic Duty." *New World Review* 34, No. 6 (1966): 5-6.

The item reviews Fulbright's remarks on the relationship of patriotism and dissent and on the concept that power engenders arrogance. It also includes his thoughts on U.S.-Soviet relations in the light of the Vietnam War.

1008 "Fulbright the Undecider." *Life,* 13 May 1966, 4.

The editors review Fulbright's position on Vietnam and reprove him for not offering an alternative to the Johnson administration's Asian policy.

1009 "Fulbright's Dilemma." *Newsweek,* 28 August 1967, 18-19.

The article concerns hearings before the Foreign Relations Committee on the Tonkin Gulf resolution.

1010 "Fulbright's Proposals for Peace." *The Christian Century,* 1 February 1967, 132-33.

The writer commends the Vietnam peace alternatives outlined in Fulbright's book, *The Arrogance of Power,* and urges that the senator's recommendations be given serious attention. The eight points for restoring peace are listed.

1011 Galloway, John. *The Gulf of Tonkin Resolution.* Rutherford, N.J.: Fairleigh Dickinson University Press, 1970, 59-60, 68, 75-78, 80-85, 87-89, 92-94, 97, 100, 102-8, 115, 121-22, 124, 126-28, 132-35, 138-39, 141, 152, 164, 182, 190, 196-97, 211, 224, 238-40, 242-45, 266-82, 284-306, 308, 311-13, 315-27, 329-64, 367, 369-73, 378, 380, 383, 386-88, 391-95, 397, 400-6, 419, 424, 497.

Fulbright figures prominently in this study of the Tonkin Gulf resolution. The author treats the reversal of the senator's position, from administration sponsor to outspoken war critic, in an examination of his role in the 1964 and the 1968 hearings of the Foreign Relations Committee on the resolution. He also notes Fulbright's sponsorship of the national commitments resolution. Appendices consist of speeches by Lyndon Johnson and Wayne Morse, Foreign Relations Committee documents regarding the 1964 and 1968 hearings on the Tonkin Gulf incidents, statements by officials of North Vietnam, and other materials concerning the war.

1012 Garrett, Stephen A. *Ideals and Reality: An Analysis of the Debate over Vietnam.* Washington, D.C.: University Press of America, 1978, 58, 76, 98, 104, 107, 113-14, 125, 130-31, 139-41, 143-44, 146, 161, 176, 214, 217-18, 220-24, 230, 235.

The author includes Fulbright remarks concerning the "fatal impact" of U.S. military operations on South Vietnam, the anthropomorphic view of the state, the impact of the Vietnam War on the American domestic front, the importance of domestic policy on foreign policy, national power and national status, the nature of freedom, China, and revolution in the Third World.

1013 ———. "An Intellectual Analysis of Foreign Policy Arguments: The Vietnam Debate." Ph.D. diss., University of Virginia, 1968, 1, 74-76, 104-6, 111, 115, 139n, 175-76, 178, 192, 195, 200, 206, 208, 234-36, 270, 277-78, 285-86, 299-300, 309, 312-13, 320-21, 328.

The study examines the intellectual features of foreign policy proposals in the debate over U.S. involvement in Vietnam and includes Fulbright remarks on several topics. See the preceding annotation of the published version for a listing of Fulbright references.

1014   Gati, Charles. "Another Grand Debate? The Limitationist Critique of American Foreign Policy." *World Politics* 21 (October 1968): 133-51.

In an essay inspired by literature of the limitationist critics, the writer examines their concept of foreign policy with an evaluation of the alternatives presented in four books: *The Arrogance of Power* by J. William Fulbright; *The Limits of Power: America's Role in the World* by Eugene J. McCarthy; *The Bitter Heritage: Vietnam and American Democracy, 1941-1966* by Arthur M. Schlesinger, Jr.; and *Pax Americana* by Ronald Steel. The article also includes a treatment of the foreign policy ideas of Walter Lippmann, George F. Kennan, and Hans Morgenthau, along with an analysis of U.S. globalism. Gati's concluding remarks about the works under review emphasize the authors' failure to develop a permanent theory regarding policy formulation. For a corresponding conclusion concerning *The Arrogance of Power,* see chapter 6 in Eugene V. Rostow's *Peace in the Balance: The Future of American Foreign Policy.*

1015   Gelber, Lionel. "History and the American Role." *Orbis* 11, No. 1 (1967): 199-209.

In an article about the use of history in the debate over the U.S. role in Vietnam, the writer takes exception to the historical references used by Fulbright and George F. Kennan in the foreign policy hearings before the Senate Foreign Relations Committee in 1966 and 1967. He concludes that the citing of history by these critics has not always served to place critical issues in proper context.

1016   "The Gnawing Debate." *Newsweek,* 14 March 1966, 25-26.

The article notes Secretary of Defense Robert McNamara's appearance before a secret session of the Senate Foreign Relations Committee on U.S. policy in Vietnam.

1017   Goldberg, Ronald Allen. "The Senate and Vietnam: A Study in Acquiescence." Ph.D. diss., University of Georgia, 1972, 15n, 17-18, 115, 118-19, 143-44, 149, 152, 154-57, 170, 174-75, 177.

The study traces the U.S. role in Vietnam from President Truman's initiation to President Johnson's policy of escalation in the summer of 1965. The author notes Fulbright's support of Kennedy and Johnson policies, including his role in the passage of the Tonkin Gulf resolution.

1018   Goulden, Joseph C. *Truth Is the First Casualty: The Gulf of Tonkin Affair—Illusion and Reality.* Chicago: James B. Adler in association with Rand McNally and Company, 1969, 52, 56, 68, 70-76, 163-69, 171-82, 188, 190-91, 193, 195-96, 199-200, 202-12, 214-16, 218-20, 233-36, 243-45, 248, 262-64.

In this comprehensive work on the Tonkin Gulf resolution, the author treats Fulbright's role as administration sponsor of the resolution, his break with President Johnson over U.S. intervention in the Dominican Republic, the 1966 Foreign Relations Committee hearings on the war, the 1967 national commitments resolution, and the 1968 Foreign Relations Committee hearing on the Tonkin Gulf incidents.

1019   "The Grand Alliance." *The Reporter,* 24 February 1966, 16.

The writer discusses the effect of Fulbright's Foreign Relations Committee hearings on Hanoi's resolve to continue the war.

1020   "Growing Dissent." *Newsweek,* 25 March 1968, 33, 36.

The article concerns the appearance of Secretary of State Dean Rusk before the Senate Foreign Relations Committee on Vietnam policy and notes Fulbright's insistence that President Johnson consult with Congress before sending more troops to the area. It also includes a cartoonist's rendering of the Fulbright-Rusk confrontation.

1021 "The Guns of August 4." *Time,* 1 March 1968, 13.

The article concerns the Johnson administration's response to the Tonkin Gulf incident and includes remarks by Fulbright.

1022 Halberstam, David. *The Best and the Brightest.* New York: Random House, 1972, 21, 29-30, 32, 67-68, 145, 174, 316, 373, 404, 409, 415-20, 435, 468, 528-29, 535, 543, 565, 600, 623.

The Fulbright references concern the senator's position in the Kennedy and Johnson administrations, particularly his role in the passage of the Tonkin Gulf resolution, and include a good character sketch. See also Halberstam's book, *The Powers That Be,* for an insightful treatment of the senator's relationship with Lyndon Johnson.

1023 ———. *The Powers That Be.* New York: Alfred A. Knopf, 1979, 48, 352, 443-44, 492-506, 565.

The author examines Fulbright's role in the passage of the Tonkin Gulf resolution and his dissent from White House policy in the Dominican Republic crisis and the Vietnam War. Praising the Fulbright war hearings, the writer analyzes their significance in terms of the educational impact on Congress and the public and the role of the senator in legitimizing dissent.

1024 Hamre, John J. "Congressional Dissent and American Foreign Policy: Constitutional War-Making in the Vietnam Years." Ph.D. diss., Johns Hopkins University, 1978, 5n, 26, 38n, 44n, 45n, 54-61, 63n, 64-71, 73, 75, 91n, 93-97, 101, 103, 106-9, 110n, 124, 137, 141n, 142n, 143, 151n, 152n, 155-56, 160n, 178, 185, 190n, 191, 192n, 224-25, 227, 233n, 245-46, 256, 260n, 270, 284, 297-98, 305.

The study examines the senator's use of the Foreign Relations Committee as a forum for congressional dissent and his use of the national commitments issue as a vehicle for mounting a critique of U.S. policy in Southeast Asia. The author stresses Fulbright's role in bringing constitutional war making into the realm of dissent against the war.

1025 "The Hawaii Conference." *Time,* 11 February 1966, 19-20.

The article concerns President Johnson's Hawaii conference with U.S. military and South Vietnamese leaders. It mentions congressional criticism of U.S. policy in Vietnam, particularly the role played by Fulbright and the hearings conducted by the Foreign Relations Committee on the war.

1026 "'He Is What He Is.'" *Newsweek,* 1 August 1966, 17-18.

This article about Lyndon Johnson includes a note regarding Fulbright's response to the president's July 12 address on the administration's new Asian policy.

1027 "Heat on the Hill." *Time,* 13 October 1967, 26-27.

The article concerns the Senate debate on U.S. policy in Vietnam and focuses on the exchange between Fulbright and Everett Dirksen.

1028 "The High Cost of Allies." *The Progressive* 32 (January 1968): 6.

The editorial includes a Fulbright quotation characterizing allied support of U.S. efforts in Vietnam, particularly the Asian allies.

1029   Hoopes, Townsend. "The Fight for the President's Mind and the Men Who Won It." *The Atlantic Monthly* 224 (October 1969): 97-104, 106-8, 110-12, 114.

In an article drawn from his book, *The Limits of Intervention,* the author, former undersecretary of the Air Force, tells the story of the people in the State Department and the Defense Department who were instrumental in getting the Vietnam escalation policy of the Johnson administration turned around. Included is an account of the hearings conducted by the Senate Foreign Relations Committee on the foreign aid bill, including the military assistance component, in March 1968 and Fulbright's subsequent run-in with the Department of Defense over the declinations of Secretary Clark Clifford and Deputy Secretary Paul Nitze to testify before the committee.

1030   "The Hot Seat." *Newsweek,* 28 February 1966, 18.

The article concerns the appearance of retired General Maxwell Taylor and Secretary of State Dean Rusk before the Senate Foreign Relations Committee on Vietnam policy. It also notes the confrontation between Fulbright and Secretary Rusk.

1031   "How a Dove Was Lost." *Newsweek,* 15 May 1972, 17.

The item focuses on Fulbright's exchange with Secretary of State William P. Rogers before the Foreign Relations Committee and the subsequent loss of Senator George Aiken to the doves' cause.

1032   "How the War Grew—Fulbright vs. McNamara." *U.S. News and World Report,* 4 March 1968, 8.

The article concerns Fulbright's argument with Secretary of Defense Robert McNamara over the August 1964 incidents in the Tonkin Gulf.

1033   "How U.S. Troops Really Behave in Vietnam." *U.S. News and World Report,* 23 May 1966, 57-58, 60-61.

This report on the presence of American troops in Saigon centers around Fulbright's charges that the U.S. military had corrupted the city and disrupted Vietnamese culture. The author disputes the senator's charges, which begin on page 113. The Fulbright remarks which triggered the article were delivered at Johns Hopkins University on May 5, 1966, in the last of three lectures on the "arrogance of power."

1034   Hughes, Emmet John. "The Hollow Dialogue." *Newsweek,* 28 June 1965, 17.

The author discusses the causes of the shallow debate on Vietnam policy. He praises Fulbright's first public statement on Vietnam as the exception and includes quotations.

1035   "The Inquiry." *The New Republic,* 17 July 1971, 9.

This editorial concerns House Resolution 342 pertaining to the establishment of a joint congressional committee to investigate the origins of the Vietnam War. The editors question the appropriateness and usefulness of such an inquiry by Congress.

1036   "Is Compulsory Unionism More Important Than Viet Nam?" *Time,* 11 February 1966, 21.

The article concerns the Senate filibuster associated with Section 14(b) of the Taft-Hartley Act and includes a note about the effect of the filibuster on the Foreign Relations Committee agenda.

1037   Johnson, Marie Evelyn. "The Rhetoric of the 'Doves': A Descriptive Analysis of the Strategies and Techniques Used by Eight Senatorial 'Doves' in 110 Speech

Manuscripts from 1964-1968." Master's thesis, Purdue University, 1969, 2, 10, 16, 18-19, 23-24, 26-29, 36n, 49, 54-56, 60-63, 67-68, 71, 86-89, 91, 94, 96-98, 100n, 101, 104-5, 110, 113, 118-19, 123-24, 131-32, 134, 137-38, 140-42, 146, 147n [sic], 150-51, 156, 159, 170-71, 174-77, 181-83, 197-200, 217, 236-37, 248-49.

Using an analytical method of identifying and describing rhetorical strategies and techniques, the author examines the speeches of eight senators dissenting from U.S. policy in Vietnam during the years 1964-1968. She also examines the feasibility of this method of analysis for significant numbers of speeches and speakers. The senators chosen for the study were Wayne Morse, Ernest Gruening, J. William Fulbright, Frank Church, Eugene McCarthy, Robert Kennedy, Vance Hartke, and George McGovern. For an article drawn in part from research for this thesis, see Marie E.J. Rosenwasser's "Six Senate War Critics and Their Appeals for Gaining Audience Response" in the September 1969 issue of *Today's Speech*.

1038 "Junkets Are Classified." *The New Republic,* 13 June 1970, 8-9.

This editorial concerns two cases of junkets to Vietnam that were classified by the executive branch to mislead Congress. Senators Fulbright and Stuart Symington made the discoveries.

1039 Kail, F.M. *What Washington Said: Administration Rhetoric and the Vietnam War: 1949-1969.* New York: Harper and Row, Publishers, 1973, 194-211.

The author in the final chapter examines five books challenging the administration's argument for Vietnam: *Abuse of Power* by Theodore Draper, *The Bitter Heritage* by Arthur M. Schlesinger, Jr., *The Arrogance of Power* by J. William Fulbright, *American Power and the New Mandarins* by Noam Chomsky, and *Vietnam Crucible* by Carl Oglesby. In a comparative essay, the author reviews these writers' critiques of Washington policies and concludes with a summary of their argument disputing the government's explanation of U.S. involvement in Vietnam.

1040 Kalb, Marvin. "Doves, Hawks, and Flutters in the Foreign Relations Committee." *The New York Times Magazine,* 19 November 1967, 56-58, 60, 63, 66, 68, 70, 73-74, 76, 78, 82.

The author comments on Fulbright's style as Foreign Relations Committee chairman and his use of Sénate hearings on issues concerning Vietnam.

1041 Kalb, Marvin, and Elie Abel. *Roots of Involvement: The U.S. in Asia, 1784-1971.* New York: W.W. Norton and Company, 1971, 20-21, 171-74, 178, 187, 194, 232-33, 255, 274-75, 285, 299, 302.

The authors note Fulbright's role in the passage of the Tonkin Gulf resolution and the Foreign Relations Committee hearings on the Vietnam War.

1042 Kaplan, Morton A. "A Psychoanalyst Looks at Politics: A Retrospective Tribute to Robert Waelder." *World Politics* 20 (July 1968): 694-704.

The author, in this review of Robert Waelder's *Progress and Revolution: A Study of the Issues of Our Age,* discusses the difficulties and dangers of applying psychological generalizations to the analysis of politics. He incorporates a treatment of Fulbright's dissent from the Vietnam War, asserting that the senator personifies Waelder's thesis. His concluding remarks include a suggestion that the Foreign Relations Committee read the book.

1043 Kolodziej, Edward A. "Congress and Foreign Policy: The Timid Political Will." *The Nation,* 14 March 1966, 292-94.

The author examines the reasons for the ancillary role of Congress in the foreign policy process, specifically its slowness to review and hold hearings on the conduct of the war in Vietnam.

1044 LaFeber, Walter. "The Conquest of History: America's Long Dream in Asia." *The Nation,* 6 November 1967, 456-59.

In an article about the imperial history of the United States, the author refutes the "accidental empire" thesis as an explanation of U.S. involvement in Vietnam. He charges the Johnson administration and its critics, including Fulbright, with misreading history, saying that they suffer from "historical myopia." Viewing the clash of American and Asian interests within a historical framework, he discusses the reasons for the presence of the United States in Southeast Asia.

1045 "Laos Debate Heats Up." *Armed Forces Journal,* 21 March 1970, 8-9.

Fulbright expresses his concern about commitment of U.S. military forces in Laos.

1046 Leahy, Stephen M. "Fulbright, the Arkansas Congressional Delegation, and the Vietnam Crisis." Master's thesis, Arkansas State University, 1988.

The author examines Fulbright's dissent within the context of the political dynamics operating inside the Arkansas constituency and the Arkansas congressional delegation and concludes that Fulbright did not jeopardize his Senate seat by opposing the Vietnam War.

1047 "The Legality of United States Participation in the Defense of Viet Nam." *The Department of State Bulletin,* 28 March 1966, 474-89.

This legal memorandum prepared by Leonard C. Meeker for the Department of State spells out the department's defense of the U.S. military operation in Vietnam. It includes Fulbright's response to Gaylord Nelson's proposed amendment to the Tonkin Gulf resolution and also an exchange between Fulbright and John Sherman Cooper regarding Article IV of the Southeast Asia Collective Defense Treaty.

1048 Lemley, Steven Smith. "A Rhetorical Study of the Executive-Legislative Struggle for Influence in Foreign Policy: The Senate Foreign Relations Committee Hearings on America's Role in Southeast Asia, 1964-1971." Ph.D. diss., Ohio State University, 1972, 5, 12-13, 18, 24-25, 36, 40, 42-43, 56-57, 78, 86, 93, 102-11, 118, 121-22, 125-28, 131-39, 144-45, 146n, 148-50, 155-57, 160, 163-68, 173-75, 179-80, 182, 194, 197-99, 204-6, 215-16, 219, 223-25, 229, 231-33, 236-39, 244-52, 254-65, 267-68, 271-73, 275-77, 285-91, 293-94, 296-303, 305-9, 312-15, 317, 319, 322-25, 329, 331-32, 334, 336-37, 342, 345-46.

Using Wayne Brockriede's "Dimensions of the Concept of Rhetoric," the author analyzes the Senate Foreign Relations Committee hearings on Vietnam and Southeast Asia between the years 1964-1971 within the context of a rhetorical-historical movement study. The focus is on the constitutional issue of the division of power between the legislative and the executive branches and the efforts of the Senate to reassert its constitutional powers in policy making, particularly the war power. The study includes a treatment of Fulbright's transition from administration supporter to war critic.

1049 "Live Issue." *Newsweek,* 25 March 1968, 97.

This article regarding the question of live television network coverage notes Fulbright's confrontation with Secretary of State Dean Rusk during the televised war hearings of the Foreign Relations Committee.

1050 McGovern, George. "Why Don't You Speak Out, Senator?" *The New Republic,* 18 March 1967, 10-11.

Senator McGovern replies to letters asking him to speak boldly against the Vietnam War. He recounts the efforts of colleagues, including Fulbright, noting their limited influence on the conduct of the war.

1051 "'Managed News' from Vietnam? Here's What the Pentagon Says." *U.S. News and World Report,* 12 September 1966, 104-5.

The article consists of excerpts from the testimony of Assistant Secretary of Defense Arthur Sylvester before the Foreign Relations Committee on August 31, 1966, on news reports of the Vietnam War. It includes questions by Fulbright.

1052 Manley, John F. "The Rise of Congress in Foreign Policy Making." *The Annals of The American Academy of Political and Social Science* 397 (September 1971): 60-70.

The author includes a profile of Fulbright, noting his role in placing the Vietnam War within the context of executive-legislative relations. He also mentions the senator's national commitments resolution of 1969.

1053 "Mercenaries." *The New Republic,* 7 and 14 August 1971, 10-11.

This editorial concerns U.S. support of mercenaries in Laos. It describes how the Pentagon circumvented the Fulbright amendment to the Defense appropriations bill in order to finance Thai troops in Laos. The Fulbright amendment removed financial assistance for those mercenaries from the Department of Defense budget.

1054 "The Momentum of Power." *The Nation,* 23 May 1966, 602-3.

Inspired by the senator's speech on the "arrogance of power," the editors call for the application of policy, rather than power, as the way to end the war in Southeast Asia.

1055 Mowrer, Edgar Ansel. "The Power of Arrogance." *National Review,* 4 April 1967, 367-68.

This is a review of Fulbright's book, *The Arrogance of Power,* in which the writer disavows the assumptions underpinning the senator's analysis of U.S. foreign policy and presents his own argument.

1056 Nevin, David. "The Dissent: It Questions and Attacks U.S. Involvement in Vietnam." *Life,* 25 February 1966, 56B-60, 62.

In the wake of the Senate Foreign Relations Committee hearings on Vietnam, the author examines the dissent of J. William Fulbright, George F. Kennan, James M. Gavin, Hans Morgenthau, Walter Lippmann, George McGovern, Frank Church, and others.

1057 "New Debate—Is the War 'Immoral'?" *U.S. News and World Report,* 18 December 1967, 11.

Senators Fulbright and Thomas J. Dodd express disharmonious views on the morality of the war in Vietnam.

1058 "The New Realism." *Time,* 18 February 1966, 19-20.

The article concerns the Johnson administration's war aims in Vietnam and mentions Fulbright's reaction to the Honolulu meeting between Nguyen Cao Ky and the president. It also mentions the war hearings before the Foreign Relations Committee.

1059 "The Not-So-Secret War." *Newsweek,* 21 June 1971, 26, 30.

The article concerns a secret session of the Senate called to examine the U.S. military operation in Laos. A Fulbright quotation is included.

1060 "Of Junkets and the USIA." *Time,* 26 August 1966, 43.

The article concerns the testimony before the Foreign Relations Committee of Leonard Marks, USIA chief, regarding the agency's arrangement of paying transportation costs of foreign newsmen to Vietnam.

1061 "On the Subject of Arrogance." *Time,* 13 May 1966, 31.

The article is a review of the last of Fulbright's Christian A. Herter Lectures at Johns Hopkins University entitled "The Arrogance of Power." Rejoinders are by Jacob Javits and Barry Goldwater.

1062 "One-Upmanship." *Newsweek,* 6 July 1970, 37.

The article recounts the successful efforts of the Nixon forces to modify the Cooper-Church amendment and to repeal the Tonkin Gulf resolution. Fulbright's position on the repeal is noted.

1063 "The Oracle Down Under." *Time,* 3 December 1965, 25.

The item concerns Fulbright remarks about Australia's military commitment to Vietnam.

1064 "The Pattern." *The Nation,* 3 October 1966, 299-300.

This editorial lauds Fulbright for his concern about Thailand not becoming another U.S. military commitment.

1065 "Portrait of the Chairman." *Time,* 18 February 1966, 21-22.

This is a profile of the Senate Foreign Relations Committee chairman which examines his role as dissenter.

1066 Powell, Lee Riley. "Fulbright and Vietnam: The Emergence of an Adversary Role." Master's thesis, University of Virginia, 1984.

The author uses the senator's "Old Myths and New Realities" speech as a point of departure for this scholarly analysis of Fulbright's emergence as a major critic of U.S. involvement in Vietnam. The study includes an examination of the reasons for his early support of President Lyndon Johnson and his subsequent disillusionment with Johnson administration policies in Asia. He concludes with a discussion and assessment of the senator's opposition to the war during the period 1966-1968, including the Foreign Relations Committee war hearings in 1966 and 1968 and his "arrogance of power" lectures at Johns Hopkins University in the spring of 1966. The thesis is based on extensive research in the Fulbright Papers and constitutes part 2 of Powell's *J. William Fulbright and America's Lost Crusade: Fulbright's Opposition to the Vietnam War.*

1067 ———. *J. William Fulbright and America's Lost Crusade: Fulbright's Opposition to the Vietnam War.* Little Rock, Ark.: Rose Publishing Company, 1984.

This is a scholarly analysis of the senator's principal foreign policy views from 1945 to 1983. The author examines Fulbright's responses to cold war policies and events of the Truman, Eisenhower, and Kennedy administrations as well as his opposition to the Vietnam War during the Johnson and Nixon years. Included also is an epilogue which concerns postsenatorial activities. The preface is by Fulbright. Part 2 on Vietnam is an expanded version of the author's master's thesis, "Fulbright and Vietnam: The Emergence of an Adversary Role," University of Virginia, 1984. A second edition with a postscript on the Reagan years was published in 1988.

1068 "The Power Akin to Freedom." *Time,* 29 April 1966, 25-26.

The writer takes issue with Fulbright's concept that power engenders arrogance.

The first of the senator's three lectures at the Johns Hopkins School of Advanced International Studies is quoted.

1069 "Psychoanalyzing Vietnam." *Newsweek,* 6 June 1966, 25.

The article concerns the testimony of two psychiatrists and a psychologist before the Senate Foreign Relations Committee on the war in Vietnam.

1070 Pusey, Merlo J. *The Way We Go to War.* Boston: Houghton Mifflin Company, 1969, 2, 11, 29, 32, 94, 107-8, 113, 121, 124-25, 128, 141-44, 171, 185-88.

The author notes the senator's role in the passage of the Tonkin Gulf resolution, his subsequent investigation in 1967 of the August 1964 incidents in the gulf, and his February 20, 1968, Foreign Relations Committee hearing with Robert McNamara.

1071 "The Quid Without the Quo." *Time,* 11 March 1966, 23.

The article is about Fulbright's proposal to settle the war in Southeast Asia by an accord with China.

1072 "Report on Washington: No Consensus on Vietnam." *The Atlantic Monthly* 217 (April 1966): 6, 8, 11-13.

The column includes a short note on Fulbright's relationship with President Johnson.

1073 Reston, James. "Senator Fulbright's 'Teach-In.'" In *Teach-Ins: U.S.A.: Reports, Opinions, Documents,* edited by Louis Menashe and Ronald Radosh, 337-38. New York: Frederick A. Praeger, Publishers, 1967.

This Reston column from the *New York Times* of February 13, 1966, evaluates Fulbright's Vietnam War hearings before the Foreign Relations Committee.

1074 "Rising Pressures." *The Nation,* 7 March 1966, 254.

The editorial evaluates the impact of Fulbright's Vietnam hearings on President Johnson's conduct of the war and on the national political scene.

1075 "The Road Past North C Pier . . ." *Newsweek,* 28 June 1965, 19-20.

The article treats Fulbright's position on the Vietnam War in the early summer of 1965 before his break with President Johnson over foreign policy.

1076 Rosenberg, Michael Paul. "Congress and the Vietnam War: A Study of the Critics of the War in 1967 and 1968." Ph.D. diss., New School for Social Research, 1973, 21, 35-37, 47-48, 54n, 55, 83-91, 100, 110, 113, 118, 125, 135, 143-44, 154, 184, 205.

This study of the congressional opponents of the war, for the period of January 1967 through March 1968, includes an analysis of the Senate Foreign Relations Committee's role in the Vietnam crisis and Fulbright's leadership of the committee.

1077 Rosenwasser, Marie E.J. "Six Senate War Critics and Their Appeals for Gaining Audience Response." *Today's Speech* 17, No. 3 (1969): 43-50.

The author describes the rhetoric of six dissenting senators in terms of five techniques of "direct appeal" used to get endorsement for their views. The senators chosen for the study were Fulbright, Wayne Morse, Frank Church, Eugene McCarthy, Ernest Gruening, and George McGovern. The article is based in part on research conducted by the author for her master's thesis at Purdue University. See also Marie Evelyn Johnson's "The Rhetoric of the 'Doves': A Descriptive Analysis of the Strategies and Techniques Used by Eight Senatorial 'Doves' in 110 Speech Manuscripts from 1964-1968."

1078　Rostow, Eugene V. *Peace in the Balance: The Future of American Foreign Policy.* New York: Simon and Schuster, 1972, 50, 165, 179-97, 240, 320.

This is a critique of the senator's book, *The Arrogance of Power,* in which the reviewer focuses primarily on challenging Fulbright's analyses of U.S. intervention in Korea and Vietnam. His main criticism of the book is the senator's failure to develop a theory of foreign policy that harmonizes with his stated point of view. For a similar conclusion regarding *The Arrogance of Power,* see Charles Gati's article, "Another Grand Debate? The Limitationist Critique of American Foreign Policy," in the October 1968 issue of *World Politics.*

1079　"Rusk vs. Senators: The War Explained." *U.S. News and World Report,* 25 March 1968, 74, 76-78.

The article consists of excerpts from the testimony of Secretary of State Dean Rusk before the Foreign Relations Committee on March 11 and 12, 1968, on U.S. policies in Vietnam.

1080　"A Scattering of Doves." *Newsweek,* 14 March 1966, 26-27.

The article mentions Fulbright's vote to repeal the Tonkin Gulf resolution and also examines his speech on U.S. policy toward China.

1081　Schmidt, John William. "The Gulf of Tonkin Debates, 1964 and 1967: A Study in Argument." Ph.D. diss., University of Minnesota, 1969, 1, 4, 35, 101-6, 110-11, 120, 127-36, 145-47, 149-57, 163-64, 167, 169-70, 173, 175-76, 183-86, 201, 205, 207-8, 210-11, 213-14, 216, 227, 229, 237-38, 246-54, 259, 263, 266-67, 269-74, 276, 280.

Using principles of argumentation, the author examines the Senate debates in 1964 and 1967 on the Tonkin Gulf resolution. The study is concerned with the issues, the arguments, and the nature of the senatorial role and function in each set of debates. It also includes an assessment of Fulbright's position in the August 1964 debate, particularly his management of the Tonkin Gulf document. The final chapter reviews the reasons for the Senate's reexamination of the resolution.

1082　"The Senate Hearings." *New World Review* 34, No. 3 (1966): 9-10.

The editorial comment concerns Fulbright and the Foreign Relations Committee hearings on Vietnam.

1083　"The Senate Hearings." *Newsweek,* 21 February 1966, 27.

In hearings before the Foreign Relations Committee on U.S. policy in Vietnam, James M. Gavin and George F. Kennan oppose escalation of the war. Excerpts from their testimony follow on pages 28 and 29.

1084　"Senate: Locking a Barn Door." *Newsweek,* 23 February 1970, 19.

The item concerns the proposed repeal of the Senate's Tonkin Gulf resolution of 1964.

1085　"Senate Rift over Vietnam Widens." *Business Week,* 12 February 1966, 28-29.

In an article pertaining to the dissenters' concern over the direction of U.S. foreign policy, Fulbright defends his hearings before the Foreign Relations Committee on the Vietnam War.

1086　Sevareid, Eric. "Why Our Foreign Policy Is Failing: An Exclusive Interview with Senator Fulbright." *Look,* 3 May 1966, 23-31.

In an interview with the senator, the author examines Fulbright's ideas regarding

U.S. involvement in Vietnam and U.S. policy toward China, as well as the positions of Fulbright and Dean Rusk before the Foreign Relations Committee hearings on the war. He also explains the "paradox" of the senator's political career in terms of his Arkansas origins and constituency.

1087 Sherrill, Robert G. "Wedge of Dissent: The Democratic Rebels in Congress." *The Nation,* 10 October 1966, 341-46.

In an article about the dissenters in Congress, the author notes the diffusion of leadership among the Senate group and Fulbright's failure to assume the role.

1088 "Sorry 'Bout That." *The New Republic,* 7 January 1967, 7-9.

The editorial examines the dearth of official statistics on civilian casualties in South Vietnam and includes Fulbright's questions for the Department of Defense, along with the department's response.

1089 "Standoff." *Time,* 22 March 1968, 20.

The article concerns the appearance of Secretary of State Dean Rusk before the Foreign Relations Committee on the subject of Vietnam and the ensuing standoff between the secretary and Fulbright. It also examines the significance of the session.

1090 "Step-up in the War—And Its Risks." *Newsweek,* 9 May 1966, 25-26.

The article mentions Fulbright's concern about the dangers of escalating the air war over North Vietnam.

1091 Stoler, Mark A. "Aiken, Mansfield, and the Tonkin Gulf Crisis: Notes from the Congressional Leadership Meeting at the White House, August 4, 1964." *Vermont History: The Proceedings of the Vermont Historical Society* 50, No. 2 (1982): 80-94.

The article concerns the notes taken by Walter Jenkins at the congressional leadership meeting with President Johnson on August 4, 1964, on the Tonkin Gulf resolution and focuses on conflicts between the version prepared shortly after the meeting and a later version prepared in 1967. The 1964 notes and excerpts from the 1967 notes are included in the article. Fulbright, as chairman of the Foreign Relations Committee, was present at the meeting.

1092 Stone, I.F. "Fulbright: From Hawk to Dove (Part 2)." *The New York Review of Books,* 12 January 1967, 8, 10, 12. (Reprinted in Stone's *In a Time of Torment.* New York: Random House, 1967, 337-45.)

The writer continues his critique of Tristram Coffin's *Senator Fulbright: Portrait of a Public Philosopher* with an incisive analysis of the senator's position on Vietnam prior to his break with Lyndon Johnson in 1965. The Fulbright series concludes in the January 26, 1967, issue on pages 10, 12, and 13. For annotation of the first article, see chapter 2.

1093 ———. "Fulbright: The Timid Opposition." *The New York Review of Books,* 26 January 1967, 10, 12-13. (Reprinted in Stone's *In a Time of Torment.* New York: Random House, 1967, 345-54.)

In the final installment of a three-part series on Fulbright, the author critiques the record of the Foreign Relations Committee as an effective curb on the executive and the ability of Fulbright as chairman to lead the opposition. Special attention is given to the Vietnam War hearings. Stone incorrectly cites the dates of the senator's appointment to the committee as 1945 and his elevation to the chairmanship as 1958. The correct dates are 1949 and 1959.

1094 ———. "International Law and the Tonkin Bay Incidents." In *The Viet-Nam Reader: Articles and Documents on American Foreign Policy and the Viet-Nam Crisis,* edited by Marcus G. Raskin and Bernard B. Fall, 307-15. New York: Random House, 1965.

Stone takes Fulbright to task for not addressing the issues raised by Wayne Morse during debate on the Tonkin Gulf resolution on August 5 and 6, 1964.

1095 ———. "McNamara and Tonkin Bay: The Unanswered Questions." *The New York Review of Books,* 28 March 1968, 5-6, 8, 10-12. (Reprinted in Stone's *Polemics and Prophecies, 1967-1970.* New York: Random House, 1970, 312-26.)

The article concerns the Foreign Relations Committee's investigation of the August 1964 incidents in the Tonkin Gulf and focuses on Secretary of Defense Robert McNamara's testimony. In a penetrating account of information revealed and not revealed, the author urges the committee to recall McNamara for the purpose of clarifying unanswered questions in the record of the February 20, 1968, hearing.

1096 ———. *Polemics and Prophecies, 1967-1970.* New York: Random House, 1970, 83, 312-39, 368, 377n. (The two Fulbright selections in this collection of Stone writings first appeared in *The New York Review of Books,* 28 March 1968, 5-6, 8, 10-12, under the title "McNamara and Tonkin Bay: The Unanswered Questions"; and 13 February 1969, 3-4, 6, under the title "The Supineness of the Senate.")

This collection of Stone writings from the period 1967-1970 includes two articles concerning Fulbright and the Foreign Relations Committee investigation of the Tonkin Gulf episode. For annotations of the Stone articles, see entries under their respective titles in this chapter.

1097 ———. "The Supineness of the Senate." *The New York Review of Books,* 13 February 1969, 3-4, 6. (Reprinted in Stone's *Polemics and Prophecies, 1967-1970.* New York: Random House, 1970, 326-39.)

The author criticizes Fulbright's handling of the Foreign Relations Committee's five-year intermittent investigation of the Tonkin Gulf episode and the committee's failure to issue a final report.

1098 "Students' Rights." *The Nation,* 16 May 1966, 573.

The editors argue that the issue of students' rights should be considered within the context of the evolving political climate of the Vietnam crisis. They refer to Fulbright's remarks in an April 28 speech about the growing "war fever" in the country.

1099 Sundquist, James L. *The Decline and Resurgence of Congress.* Washington, D.C.: Brookings Institution, 1981, 106n, 116n, 119-23, 239-45, 247n, 248, 252, 256, 445, 461.

The author notes Fulbright's role in the passage of the Tonkin Gulf resolution and also looks at his efforts to reassert the role of the Senate in policy making, particularly regarding the war power. The senator's national commitments resolution of 1969 is mentioned.

1100 "Suspicions of a Moonless Night." *Time,* 1 March 1968, 12.

The article concerns Secretary of Defense Robert McNamara's testimony before a closed session of the Senate Foreign Relations Committee about the August 1964 events in the Gulf of Tonkin and Fulbright's insistence that the Pentagon release the transcript.

1101 T.R.B. "Dealing with Fulbright." *The New Republic,* 16 April 1966, 4.

The item concerns *Time's* explanation of President Johnson's trip to Honolulu to meet with Premier Nguyen Cao Ky and its impact on Fulbright's Foreign Relations Committee hearings on Vietnam.

1102 ———. "'Morale Has Improved.'" *The New Republic,* 16 April 1966, 4.

The item concerns *Time's* February 18 cover story about Premier Nguyen Cao Ky. It focuses on President Johnson's trip to Honolulu to meet the premier shortly after Fulbright's hearings on Vietnam began.

1103 ———. "A Peace to Endure." *The New Republic,* 4 February 1967, 6.

This item previews the forthcoming foreign policy hearings before the Foreign Relations Committee and spotlights Fulbright's formula for a lasting peace in Vietnam.

1104 ———. "Snap, Crackle." *The New Republic,* 12 December 1970, 4.

This column about the exchange in the Senate between Robert Dole and Edward Kennedy regarding the attempted rescue of American prisoners at Sontay includes remarks by Fulbright on the military-industrial complex and the Defense Department's role in the conduct of foreign policy.

1105 ———. "Something in the Wind." *The New Republic,* 14 October 1967, 4.

The column includes an exchange between Fulbright and Everett Dirksen in the Senate on the objective of U.S. involvement in Vietnam.

1106 Tuchman, Barbara W. *The March of Folly: From Troy to Vietnam.* New York: Alfred A. Knopf, 1984, 316, 333-36, 352, 375.

In the section on Vietnam, the author examines Fulbright's role in the passage of the Tonkin Gulf resolution and the significance of the Senate Foreign Relations Committee war hearings held in the winter of 1966.

1107 Turesky, Stanley Fred. "A Time to Talk and a Time to Listen: A Study of the Relationship Between the Chairman of the Senate Foreign Relations Committee and the President of the United States." Ph.D. diss., Brown University, 1973.

This study of the interaction between the president and the Foreign Relations Committee chairman focuses on Fulbright's tenure, specifically his performance style, and highlights the change which occurred in 1965. The author employs two constructs, the consulting model and the dissenter model, to explain the change in performance. Special attention is given to the Fulbright-Johnson break and the development of the senator's dissent.

1108 "Two Key Senators Who Question LBJ's Policy on Vietnam." *U.S. News and World Report,* 3 May 1965, 17.

Senators Fulbright and Mike Mansfield express their concern about the Johnson policy in Vietnam leading to an expansion of the war in Asia.

1109 "Vietnam: A Period of Trial." *Newsweek,* 2 May 1966, 17-18.

The article includes quotations from Fulbright's Johns Hopkins University lecture on "The Higher Patriotism" and also mentions the senator's Foreign Relations Committee hearings on the Johnson administration's foreign aid bill.

1110 "Vietnam: The Lull Hits Home." *Newsweek,* 3 November 1969, 23-24.

The article mentions Fulbright's decision to delay the Vietnam War hearings until after President Nixon's foreign policy speech on November 3.

1111 "Vietnam: The Pause Comes to an End." *Newsweek,* 7 February 1966, 15-17.

The article concerns the debate over the bombing respite in the Vietnam War. It notes Fulbright's position regarding the lull and his relentless questioning of Secretary of State Dean Rusk before the Foreign Relations Committee.

1112 "Voices of Dissent: Gavin and Kennan." *Newsweek,* 21 February 1966, 28-29.

In hearings before the Senate Foreign Relations Committee on U.S. policy in Vietnam, James M. Gavin and George F. Kennan argue against intensifying the war. The article consists of excerpts from their testimony.

1113 "The War: More Men, More Doubts." *Newsweek,* 4 March 1968, 19-20.

The article notes the Senate Foreign Relations Committee's clash with Secretary of Defense Robert McNamara over the August 1964 incidents in the Tonkin Gulf.

1114 "What U.S. Should Do About Vietnam: Survey of Key Senators." *U.S. News and World Report,* 10 February 1969, 29-32.

The article concerns a survey conducted by *U.S. News and World Report* of key members of the Foreign Relations Committee and the Armed Services Committee regarding troop disengagement, truce terms, and peace prospects. It includes a summary of the majority opinion as well as Fulbright's position.

1115 "When Rusk Was Challenged on Vietnam Policy . . . " *U.S. News and World Report,* 25 March 1968, 75.

The article examines Secretary of State Dean Rusk's appearance before the Foreign Relations Committee hearings on U.S. policy in Vietnam and notes his exchange with Fulbright on the Tonkin Gulf resolution.

1116 "Who's Nervous?" *The Nation,* 6 June 1966, 666.

The editors examine President Johnson's denunciation of opponents of his Vietnam policy, including his use of the epithet "nervous Nellies," and conclude that he himself is nervous.

1117 "Why the U.S. Fights: Rusk and Taylor." *Newsweek,* 28 February 1966, 19-20.

The article consists of excerpts from the testimony of witnesses Dean Rusk and Maxwell Taylor before the Senate Foreign Relations Committee on Johnson administration policy in Vietnam.

1118 Windchy, Eugene G. *Tonkin Gulf.* Garden City, N.Y.: Doubleday and Company, 1971, 21, 34-35, 40-50, 52-53, 56, 139, 152, 174, 188, 212, 217, 287-88, 299, 315, 324, 326, 335, 337.

The author discusses Fulbright's role in the passage of the Tonkin Gulf resolution, his breach with President Johnson, and the Foreign Relations Committee hearings in 1966 and 1968 on the August 1964 Tonkin Gulf incidents.

1119 Wise, David. "Remember the Maddox!" *Esquire* 69 (April 1968): 123-27, continues on pages 56, 60, 62.

In an article about the August 1964 incidents in the Tonkin Gulf, the author notes Fulbright's role in the passage of the Tonkin Gulf resolution and his subsequent dissent from Johnson administration policy in Vietnam.

1120 Witze, Claude. "Is the Enemy in Hanoi?" *Air Force and Space Digest* 53 (July 1970): 12-13.

Citing Gordon L. Allott's Senate speech praising Fulbright's early ideas regarding the role of the president in the foreign policy realm, the author draws attention to the reversal of Fulbright's belief that the president should have more control over foreign policy than Congress. Senator Allott's remarks were inspired by a Fulbright speech of January 22, 1951, a Senate debate on August 17, 1961, and an article in the fall 1961 issue of the *Cornell Law Quarterly*, all sources in which the Arkansas senator advocated a strong presidential role in the conduct of foreign policy.

1121 ———"Who's on Our Side?" *Air Force and Space Digest* 50 (April 1967): 29-31.

The author discusses the Senate debate inspired by the authorization bill giving the Department of Defense the means to conduct the Vietnam War. He includes Fulbright's position concerning U.S. disengagement.

1122 Wolk, Herman S. "Vietnam and the Warfare State Complex." *Air Force and Space Digest* 50 (April 1967): 39-43.

The author mentions Fulbright's position on the military.

1123 "A Word from Zephyr." *Newsweek,* 16 May 1966, 31-32.

The article notes President Johnson's reference to Fulbright's "arrogance of power" lectures at Johns Hopkins University in his encounter with the senator at a White House reception.

1124 "Worldgram: From the Capitals of the World." *U.S. News and World Report,* 19 September 1966, 63-64.

The item concerns Fulbright's plans to investigate national commitments and military presence in Thailand.

1125 Zaroulis, Nancy, and Gerald Sullivan. *Who Spoke Up? American Protest Against the War in Vietnam, 1963-1975.* Garden City, N.Y.: Doubleday and Company, 1984, 22-24, 26-27, 70-77, 82-84, 116, 144, 154-59, 250, 281, 338, 361, 368.

This year-by-year chronicle of the history of the Vietnam War protest movement includes information regarding the role of Fulbright as dissenter.

1126 Zelman, Walter Arnold. "Senate Dissent and the Vietnam War, 1964-1968." Ph.D. diss., University of California, Los Angeles, 1971, 7, 10-11, 54, 68-73, 77-79, 81-83, 85-87, 91-96, 98-99, 101-6, 109-10, 112, 114-15, 123, 126-28, 132, 134, 138, 140-42, 144, 146, 150, 159, 161, 165-66, 172-73, 181-82, 187-89, 191, 194, 197, 202-58, 263, 267, 270, 275, 292-93, 307, 324, 326, 328-29, 343-44, 358, 378.

Fulbright figures prominently in this study of the development of Senate dissent from U.S. policy in Vietnam and its impact on the Johnson administration and the public. The author treats the senator's role in the passage of the Tonkin Gulf resolution, the Foreign Relations Committee hearings of January and February 1966, the subsequent committee investigation of the August 1964 Tonkin Gulf incidents, the senator's transition from an administration supporter to war critic, and his national commitments resolution. In an assessment of the impact of Fulbright's dissent on colleagues, the administration, and the public, the writer concludes that the senator's service was in making the war a constitutional issue by placing it within the context of executive-legislative relations.

7
Election Campaigns, 1942-1974

1127 "Alumni Figure Prominently in Primary Victories; Fulbright, McMath, Gordon Win." *Arkansas Alumnus,* n.s. 4 (September 1950): 8.

The article notes Fulbright's reelection to a second term in the U.S. Senate.

1128 "Anti-Anti-American?" *Newsweek,* 27 November 1961, 49.

British newsman Kingsley Martin covers Fulbright's reelection campaign in Arkansas for the *New Statesman.* A profile of Martin is included.

1129 "Arkansas Winners: Faubus and Fulbright." *U.S. News and World Report,* 13 August 1962, 16.

The article notes the Democratic primary victories of Governor Orval Faubus and Fulbright.

1130 Atkinson, J.H. "Personal Notes." *The Arkansas Historical Quarterly* 4 (Spring 1945): 78.

The item announces the swearing-in of the junior senator from Arkansas on January 3, 1945. He was the junior senator for his thirty-year tenure, serving with John L. McClellan, who was in the Senate from 1942 until 1977.

1131 "Back in Arkansas." *Newsweek,* 13 November 1961, 24-25.

The article previews Fulbright's 1962 reelection campaign in Arkansas.

1132 "Bumpered." *Newsweek,* 10 June 1974, 25-27.

The article concerns Dale Bumpers's Arkansas primary victory over Fulbright and the effects of the senator's defeat in Washington.

1133 "Candidate Fulbright." *Newsweek,* 25 March 1968, 36.

The story concerns Fulbright's campaign for reelection in Arkansas.

1134 "Decisions, Decisions . . . " *Newsweek,* 8 January 1962, 16-18.

The article concerns the effects of certain political decisions on the future of national figures in Connecticut, New York, and Arkansas. It includes a section on Congressman Dale Alford's announcement to enter the governor's race against Orval Faubus in the July primary and what the move means for Fulbright in his reelection bid.

1135 "Dinner at the National Gallery Honors French Foreign Minister." *The Department of State Bulletin,* 21 October 1974, 541-42.

Henry Kissinger recalls the reception that he attended earlier for Fulbright's retirement from the Senate. Reflecting on the special role of the senator in national government, the secretary of state notes that Fulbright's dealings with the State Department resemble France's relationship with the United States.

1136 "'Doves' in Trouble? Their Problem in '68—." *U.S. News and World Report,* 5 June 1967, 78-79.

This is a report on seven leading "doves" facing reelection in 1968: J. William Fulbright, Wayne Morse, Frank Church, Gaylord Nelson, Joseph Clark, Ernest Gruening, and George McGovern.

1137 Edwards, Basil. "'A Damned Good Politician.'" *Lithopinion* 10, No. 1, Issue 37 (1975): 22-23.

In a thoughtful assessment of Fulbright's political career, the writer makes several interesting observations about the senator and his state. "Stereotypical" Arkansas aside, he concludes that the two are not so contradictory as people may think.

1138 "The Fall of Fulbright." *The New Republic,* 8 June 1974, 7.

The editors acknowledge Fulbright's contributions as chairman of the Foreign Relations Committee, following his loss to Governor Dale Bumpers in the Arkansas Democratic primary.

1139 "Ford Wields a Broom." *Time,* 16 September 1974, 20.

The article mentions President Ford's offer of the ambassadorship to Great Britain to Fulbright.

1140 "Fulbright: Hard Fight Ahead." *Newsweek,* 12 August 1968, 10.

The article notes Fulbright's victory in the Democratic primary against Jim Johnson and his upcoming contest with Republican Charles Bernard in the general election.

1141 "Gentleman in Arkansas." *Time,* 24 August 1942, 15.

This is a short profile of Fulbright after his victory in the Democratic congressional primary, a victory which sent him to Washington as U.S. Representative from the Third Congressional District in Arkansas.

1142 "The Giant Killer." *Time,* 10 June 1974, 26, 29-30.

The article concerns Fulbright's loss in the Arkansas Democratic primary to Governor Dale Bumpers. It includes a profile of the senator titled "The Professor of Restraint."

1143 Healy, Paul F. "Seven Sitting Doves." *The New Republic,* 3 June 1967, 8-10.

The article concerns the upcoming reelection campaigns of seven Democratic doves in the Senate in 1968: Frank Church, Joseph Clark, J. William Fulbright, Ernest Gruening, George McGovern, Wayne Morse, and Gaylord Nelson. The author assesses their positions with their local constituencies and their prospects for returning to the Senate.

1144 "In Need of Polishing." *Time,* 10 November 1961, 26-27.

The article concerns President Kennedy's week of stumping for Democratic candidates and mentions his stop in Fort Smith, Arkansas, to endorse Fulbright.

1145 "An Irreparable Loss." *Middle East Perspective,* June-July 1974, 2.

This is an editorial lamenting the senator's defeat by Governor Dale Bumpers in the Arkansas primary. It praises his Middle East position, particularly regarding the Israeli lobby.

1146 Johnson, Willie Stephen. "The Bumpers-Fulbright Senate Race: A Rhetorical Analysis." Ph.D. diss., University of Illinois at Urbana-Champaign, 1981.

The author examines the role of personal rhetoric in Fulbright's and Dale Bumpers's campaign strategies, specifically the harmony of discourse with strategy. Using content analysis, analysis of arguments, and quantitative research, he evaluates three dimensions of their rhetoric: content of campaign discourse, verbal style, and nonverbal communication. Johnson concludes that images, more than issues, were the determining factor in the outcome of the election.

1147 "Just Plain Bill." *Newsweek,* 12 August 1968, 27-28.

The article concerns Fulbright's victory in the Democratic primary and his race in the general election against Republican Charles T. Bernard.

1148 "Just Plain Bill." *Time,* 3 November 1961, 24.

The article concerns the senator's early campaign for reelection. Fulbright remarks emphasize his service to Arkansas.

1149 "Just Plain Bill." *Time,* 26 July 1968, 24.

This is an assessment of Fulbright's prospects for reelection in the face of voter discontent and three opponents in the Democratic preferential primary.

1150 "Last of the First." *Time,* 7 August 1944, 19.

The article concerns election results, specifically the defeat of Senator Hattie Caraway in the Arkansas primary and the appearance of Fulbright as the leading candidate for her Senate seat.

1151 "Latest Signal from Voters: A Rough Year for the 'Ins.'" *U.S. News and World Report,* 10 June 1974, 40.

The article notes Fulbright's defeat by Governor Dale Bumpers in Arkansas's Democratic primary.

1152 Lippmann, Walter. "J. William Fulbright." In Lippmann's *Public Persons,* edited by Gilbert A. Harrison, 173-75. New York: Liveright, 1976.

Written on the eve of the senator's 1962 campaign, this column is a tribute to Fulbright's vision and wisdom in international affairs. Lippmann expresses concern for the upcoming Arkansas senatorial campaign, which he views as a conflict between a traditional conservative and reactionary radicals espousing political conservatism. An adapted version of this article appears as the preface in Karl E. Meyer's *Fulbright of Arkansas: The Public Positions of a Private Thinker.*

1153 "The Local Scene: Where the Pork Barrel Still Rules." *Newsweek,* 10 July 1967, 39.

The article includes a report from *Newsweek* correspondent Philip Carter on Fulbright's prospects for reelection in Arkansas.

1154 Lomax, Louis E. "Two Millionaires, Two Senators, and a Faubus: The Curious

Constellation of Arkansas Politics." *Harper's Magazine* 220 (March 1960): 73-76, 82-84, 86.

The author reviews Orval Faubus's career in Arkansas politics and examines the pivotal role that he may play in the political future of the senators from Arkansas, John McClellan and Fulbright. The writer also looks at Faubus's prospects of running for a fourth term for governor against New York millionaire Winthrop Rockefeller. The other millionaire profiled in the article is financier Witt Stephens.

1155 McCord, Robert S. "Can Fulbright Be Re-elected?" *The Progressive* 31 (November 1967): 13-16.

In an article about the senator's upcoming election, the writer examines the conjecture regarding opposition, campaign strategy, and the impact of Fulbright's criticism of the Vietnam War. Assessing his relationship with his constituency, McCord concludes that the people of Arkansas consider the senator to be "a sort of natural resource."

1156 *"Mountaineer's* Stand on November Elections." *The Ozarks Mountaineer* 10 (October 1962): 15.

In this editorial the *Mountaineer* supports the reelection of Senator Edward V. Long of Missouri and Senator J.W. Fulbright and Congressman James W. Trimble of Arkansas.

1157 Neil, Jerry. "They're Out to Get Fulbright: Arkansas' Internationalist Is in Trouble Back Home." *The New Republic,* 9 October 1961, 9-10.

The author discusses the upcoming Senate race in Arkansas and predicts that the senator will have serious opposition, possibly Governor Orval Faubus or Congressman Dale Alford. He ponders the aftereffects of Fulbright's silence during the Little Rock school integration crisis in 1957.

1158 "The New Senate." *Time,* 13 November 1944, 21.

The article concerns the senatorial election results and the implications for the new Senate in international affairs. It notes the victory of Fulbright in Arkansas.

1159 "Out of the Woods." *Time,* 9 August 1968, 21.

The article reviews the results of the Arkansas primaries and notes Fulbright's successful renomination.

1160 "The Penalties of Virtue." *The Nation,* 14 October 1961, 238-39.

Expressing concern for Fulbright in the 1962 election, the editors review the reasons for his troubles with the right-wing constituency.

1161 "Political Notes." *The New Republic,* 7 August 1944, 149.

The *New Republic* endorses Fulbright in his run-off election for the Senate.

1162 Rakow, Michael Gerard. "Southern Politics in the United States Senate: 1948-1972." Ph.D. diss., Arizona State University, 1973, 91, 128, 138-39, 199-200, 219, 226, 230, 275, 277, 307, 313, 319, 325, 376.

This study of southern senators includes incidental references to Fulbright and election statistics for each of his races from 1950 through 1968.

1163 Reed, Roy. "Raspy Statesmanship Against Earnest Politics: Fulbright vs. Bumpers." *The New York Times Magazine,* 26 May 1974, 26-28, 30-33, 35.

In a profile of Fulbright and Dale Bumpers, the writer examines the problems facing Fulbright in the campaign for the Democratic senatorial nomination. He concludes that the major issue may have been one of attitude: the senator's somewhat pessimistic outlook, in the southern tradition, versus the governor's more optimistic approach to problem solving. Bumpers defeated Fulbright in the May 28 primary.

1164 "Rose Between Thorns." *Newsweek,* 13 August 1962, 19.

The article concerns Fulbright's victory in the Arkansas primary against Winston G. Chandler.

1165 "Season on Doves." *Newsweek,* 7 October 1968, 43-44.

The article concerns leading Senate doves' chances of surviving the upcoming general election: J. William Fulbright, Wayne Morse, George McGovern, Frank Church, Joseph Clark, and Gaylord Nelson. The survey by *Newsweek's* political correspondents reveals that Fulbright has the safest margin of all the doves.

1166 "Senate Scorecard." *Time,* 26 October 1962, 26-27.

The article lists Fulbright's Senate seat as one of nine in question on the Democratic side and notes the presence of a vigorous Republican opponent in Kenneth G. Jones.

1167 "The Senate: Small Gains for the GOP." *Newsweek,* 11 November 1968, 40-42.

The article presents the results and analyses of the major races, including Fulbright's reelection to a fifth term.

1168 "The Shape of Things." *The Nation,* 5 August 1944, 143.

The item includes a note about Fulbright's showing in the Arkansas senatorial race. The editors predict a victory in the run-off primary against Homer Adkins.

1169 Smith, Harold T. "J. William Fulbright and the Arkansas 1974 Senatorial Election." *The Arkansas Historical Quarterly* 44 (Summer 1985): 103-17.

The article concerns the 1974 senatorial election in Arkansas, particularly the emergence of Dale Bumpers as a force in state politics. The author describes the campaign as one in which personalities figured more prominently than political issues and the positions of the candidates. Bumpers defeated Fulbright in his bid for a sixth term.

1170 Terry, Bill. "Fulbright's Last Stand; Along Came Bumpers." *The New Republic,* 27 April 1974, 11.

The article concerns Governor Dale Bumpers's announcement of his candidacy for the Senate seat held by Fulbright.

1171 "To Recess or Not Recess." *Newsweek,* 17 July 1950, 23-24.

The article focuses on a needed congressional recess for senators facing primaries and includes a Fulbright quotation.

1172 "Tough Fight for Fulbright." *Newsweek,* 29 July 1968, 16.

Fulbright faces strong opposition from Jim Johnson in the Arkansas primary.

1173 "Traveler's Perils." *Time,* 25 March 1974, 24.

The article concerns Fulbright's upcoming senatorial campaign against Governor Dale Bumpers for a sixth term.

1174   "The Uphill Fight for Republicans." *U.S. News and World Report,* 29 April 1974, 19-20.

The article includes a segment on upcoming key primaries in eight states, including Arkansas's contest between Fulbright and Dale Bumpers.

1175   "Washington Whispers." *U.S. News and World Report,* 7 October 1974, 13.

This item concerns the senator's reasons for turning down the offer of the ambassadorship to Great Britain.

1176   "What Will Governor Faubus Do?" *U.S. News and World Report,* 8 January 1962, 19.

The article concerns the political plans of Fulbright, Orval Faubus, and Dale Alford.

1177   White, Mel. "Arkansas Politics: Pierre and Chickens on the Campaign Trail." *Arkansas Times* 4 (May 1978): 20-24, 29-39.

This is an irreverant recollection of Fulbright's 1974 campaign against Dale Bumpers and the gubernatorial contest between Orval Faubus and David Pryor. The author remembers the candidates, their aides, and the press, including Pierre Salinger and Roger Mudd, in Nashville, Arkansas, for the Southwest Arkansas Poultry Festival.

1178   "Who'll Challenge Fulbright?" *Newsweek,* 27 November 1967, 15.

The article mentions Orval Faubus and Sidney S. McMath as possible opponents in Fulbright's upcoming Democratic primary in Arkansas.

1179   Witcover, Jules. "Fulbright's Prospects." *The New Republic,* 10 June 1967, 4-5.

The author evaluates Fulbright's position with the Arkansas constituency and discusses two possible opponents, Sidney S. McMath and Orval Faubus.

1180   Yergin, Daniel. "Fulbright's Last Frustration." *The New York Times Magazine,* 24 November 1974, 14-15, 76-78, 80, 82, 87-88, 90, 93-94.

Stating that Fulbright may well be the best remembered senator of his time, the author describes his career in terms of its close connection with the course of postwar U.S. foreign policy. He discusses the senator's character as a legislator in both the domestic and foreign policy realms. Included is a penetrating assessment of his role as dissenter.

8
Constituency, 1942-1974

1181 Adams, Harvey. "Agricultural Council of Arkansas." *Cotton Farming* 5 (March-April 1961): 30, 32.

The article includes extensive remarks by Fulbright regarding U.S. reciprocal trade agreement policy and the foreign aid program and their effect on domestic markets. His remarks also concern the importance of foreign markets, particularly for agriculture.

1182 "AEA Convention Speakers." *The Journal of Arkansas Education* 34 (October 1961): 6-11.

This is an article introducing the speakers for the ninety-third convention of the Arkansas Education Association in Little Rock in November 1961 and includes a short profile of the senator.

1183 "Arkansas." *Retirement Life* 42 (November 1967): 21.

This is an announcement of Fulbright's talk before the twelfth annual convention of the Arkansas Federation of Chapters of the National Association of Retired Civil Employees in Little Rock in September. *Retirement Life* is the official magazine of the national organization.

1184 Faubus, Orval Eugene. *Down from the Hills*. Little Rock, Ark.: Democrat Printing and Lithographing Company, 1980, 17, 20, 31, 55, 68-69, 87, 96-97, 107, 119, 126, 128, 145, 147, 184, 363, 424-25.

Governor Faubus includes several references to the senator in the first volume of his reminiscences, particularly Fulbright's signature on the Southern Manifesto in the spring of 1956.

1185 ———. *Down from the Hills—II*. Little Rock, Ark.: Democrat Printing and Lithographing Company, 1985, 7, 34, 59, 64-66, 86, 89, 92, 102, 104-5, 125, 135, 144-55, 157, 160, 162, 169, 172-74, 181, 190, 201, 203-5, 208-12, 215, 218-19, 240, 269, 273, 290, 295, 305, 318, 321, 325, 377, 414, 423, 437, 439, 478, 480, 486-87.

Fulbright references in the second volume of Faubus reminiscences primarily concern civil rights issues, Fulbright's dissent from Vietnam War policy, the senatorial election of 1962, the gubernatorial campaign of 1970 and the senator's support of Dale Bumpers, and the Bumpers-Fulbright senatorial campaign of 1974.

1186 "Fulbright Deplores U.S. Tendency to Direct Others." *The Arkansas Publisher,* no volume number, January 1968, 3.

This article concerns the senator's comments at the Arkansas Press Association's midwinter meeting in Hot Springs. He directs his attention to several contemporary issues, including the seizure of the U.S. intelligence ship *Pueblo* by North Korea.

1187 "Fulbright Gets Tribute from Poultry Industry." *Turkey World,* February 1961, 62d.

The article concerns the Institute of American Poultry Industries' recognition of Fulbright's efforts to reverse protectionist trade policies and open foreign markets to U.S. poultry products.

1188 "Fulbright Presses Italian Trade." *Broiler Industry* 23 (August 1960): 40.

The article pertains to Fulbright's efforts in behalf of the poultry industry, including the arrangement of an industry conference with the secretary of agriculture to explore the possibility of reducing trade barriers between Italy and the United States.

1189 "Game Festivities." *Arkansas Alumnus,* n.s. 4 (November 1950): 5.

The article includes a report of homecoming ceremonies at the University of Arkansas on November 11, 1950, including the senator's crowning of Betty Jo Simmons with a red baseball cap before the game when the crown bearer failed to appear. A picture is included.

1190 "Good Will to Men: Senator Fulbright Speaks on Peace; Spirit Shown in Services, Plays." *The Christian Advocate,* 10 January 1946, 52.

The article includes a report on Fulbright's address, "What We Can Do to Implement Peace and Good Will Around the World," at the Central Methodist Church in the senator's home town of Fayetteville, Arkansas, on December 23, 1945.

1191 Hamm, Don M. "Senator J. William Fulbright Writes Concerning Dental Legislation." *Arkansas Dental Journal* 32, No. 3 (1961): 12.

The article includes a letter from Fulbright regarding the Senate Appropriations Committee's recommendation of an appropriation for the National Institute of Dental Research.

1192 Jinske, Henry W. "Impressive Christmas Service." *Arkansas Methodist,* 10 January 1946, 14.

The article includes a report of Fulbright's address, "What We Can Do to Implement Peace and Good Will Around the World," at the Central Methodist Church, Fayetteville, Arkansas, on December 23, 1945. Among the issues discussed are the control and use of atomic energy, the United Nations Organization, and restrictions on national sovereignty.

1193 Kennedy, Jon. *Look Back and Laugh: 38 Years of Arkansas Political Cartoons.* Little Rock, Ark.: Pioneer, 1978, 7-8, 14-15, 51, 56, 77, 83, 89, 96, 102, 111, 118, 122, 126, 138.

Fulbright figures prominently in this book of political cartoons covering the author's thirty-eight years with the *Arkansas Democrat* newspaper in Little Rock. The cartoons and text cover the administrations of eight Arkansas governors, from Homer Adkins through David Pryor.

1194 "Mid-Winter Convention: Program to Include Prominent Speakers." *The Arkansas Publisher* 18 (January 1948): 3, 9.

The article announces the program for the 1948 midwinter convention of the Arkansas Press Association. Fulbright was one of the principal speakers.

1195 "Mid-Winter Sessions Set in Spa: APA Meet to Hear Fulbright." *The Arkansas Publisher,* no volume number, December 1967, 3.

This article announces the program for the ninety-sixth annual midwinter meeting of the Arkansas Press Association in Hot Springs in January 1968 and includes Fulbright as a featured speaker.

1196 "Millers Seek Expansion of Markets, Disposal of CCC-Held Rice Stocks: Rice Millers' Association Elects Lloyd A. Villeret Chairman of Board at 56th Annual Meeting." *The Rice Journal,* 1 June 1955, 14-16, 39-40.

The article notes Fulbright's address supporting reduction of foreign trade barriers, particularly in the sugar and rice markets.

1197 "$990 Million Asked." *Construction News Monthly,* November 1955, 119.

The item concerns Fulbright's request for $990 million in the federal budget for flood control and hydroelectric projects in Arkansas. *Construction News Monthly* is a publication covering industry news in the Lower Mississippi Valley.

1198 "People of the Week." *U.S. News and World Report,* 23 July 1954, 14, 16.

The article focuses on Fulbright's support of the Truman administration's plan for construction of a private power plant in West Memphis, Arkansas.

1199 "Quiet Reappraisal." *Newsweek,* 29 October 1962, 80-81.

The article concerns a reevaluation of the American National Theatre and Academy's supervisory role in the government's International Cultural Exchange Program. The reappraisal resulted when Fulbright protested a decision by ANTA not to send a University of Arkansas choral group abroad. Traveling independently, the choir subsequently won an international competition in Italy.

1200 "Senator Fulbright Supports Federal Aid." *The Journal of Arkansas Education* 22 (April 1948): 34.

The article concerns Fulbright's position on federal assistance to education.

1201 "Senator Fulbright Talks on Farming." *The Arkansas Union Farmer* 38 (November 1961): 6-7.

In an interview with *Union Farmer,* Fulbright discusses the role of government in stabilizing agriculture. He also responds to questions about the broiler industry, rice acreage, federal aid to education, and medical care for the elderly.

1202 "Speak Up Citizen! Your Washington Representative Wants—And Needs—Your Views About Public Affairs." *The Link* 25, No. 5 (1960): 9.

The article includes Fulbright remarks regarding the importance of constituent correspondence. It appeared in the *Link,* the bimonthly publication of Humble Oil and Refining Company.

1203 Teter, Park. "Chicken Feed." *The New Republic,* 5 October 1963, 5.

This item is a tongue-in-cheek look at the merits of attaching a rider to the nuclear test ban treaty making the agreement contingent upon Soviet purchase of U.S. poultry.

1204 "They Face the People." *Time,* 2 August 1943, 22-23.

The article pertains to congressmen returning home to constituents after the close of the session. Fulbright is featured, among others, and finds his Arkansas constituents concerned about the young congressman's role in postwar peace planning.

1205 "Two Distinguished Citizens." *Arkansas Alumnus,* n.s. 5 (December 1951): 27.

This is an interesting picture of Fulbright and Lewis Webster Jones, former president of the University of Arkansas, in the fine arts center theatre just before Dr. Jones left to become president of Rutgers University.

1206 "University to Award Five Honorary Degrees in June: Miss Jobelle Holcombe and Senator Fulbright Among Those Honored." *University of Arkansas News* 6, No. 8 (1947): 1, 4.

The article includes the announcement of the senator's honorary degree from the University of Arkansas on its seventy-fifth anniversary.

1207 Untitled. *The Arkansas Publisher* 18 (October 1948): 2, 7.

The article concerns a travelogue presented by the senator to the Little Rock Ad Club regarding his recent European trip.

1208 Untitled. *Education Newsmagazine* 5 (April 1967): cover.

The issue includes a picture of Fulbright with two representatives of the fifth annual Senate Youth Program in Washington.

1209 Untitled. *Education Newsmagazine* 6 (July 1968): 15.

The issue includes a picture of Fulbright with two representatives of the sixth annual Senate Youth Program in Washington.

1210 "A World Statesman Takes a Look at His Home Town." *Arkansas Alumnus,* n.s. 9 (November 1955): 30-31.

This short article and photograph concern a visit by the senator to his hometown of Fayetteville in late summer of 1955. The photograph shows him taking a walk around the town square, now Fulbright Square, named in his honor at a homecoming in September 1989.

9

Fulbright Exchange Program

1211 "Blackboard Exercises." *Newsweek,* 14 August 1961, 68.

The article includes President Kennedy's remarks praising the Fulbright scholarship program on its fifteenth anniversary.

1212 Bray, Charles W., III. "Helping Americans Understand World Affairs." *The Department of State Bulletin,* 26 September 1977, 402-4.

The article includes a cogent quotation by Fulbright regarding the benefits of educational exchange.

1213 Burns, Arthur F. "The Human Side of German-American Relations." *The Department of State Bulletin* 83 (June 1983): 32-36. (The publication changed from a weekly to a monthly format in January 1978.)

The author includes a Fulbright quotation in which the senator forcefully describes the purpose of the Fulbright exchange program.

1214 "Charge of the 600." *Pathfinder,* 1 June 1949, 34.

The article concerns Fulbright's academic exchange program three years after the passage of the Fulbright Act and includes remarks by the senator.

1215 "Class Notes of 1925—Senator J.W. Fulbright." *Arkansas Alumnus,* n.s. 2 (June 1949): 14.

The article notes the senator's activities and interests, including the signing of the Fulbright educational exchange agreement with the Netherlands.

1216 "Class of 1925—Senator J.W. Fulbright." *Arkansas Alumnus,* n.s. 2 (October 1948): 15.

This is a report of a tour of Europe in the fall of 1948, a trip which included the Inter-Parliamentarian Union Conference in Rome and the ceremony for the formal signing of the Fulbright educational exchange agreement with the United Kingdom.

1217 Cook, Donald B., and J. Paul Smith. "The Philosophy of the Fulbright Programme." *International Social Science Bulletin* 8, No. 4 (1956): 615-28.

This scholarly article examines the Fulbright program in its first decade, particularly the conceptual components of the philosophy underlying the program.

1218   Crawford, Clare. "Bill Fulbright Looks Back on 30 Years of the Scholarships That Bear His Name." *People Weekly*, 14 June 1976, [93]-94.

In an article commemorating the thirtieth anniversary of the Fulbright program, the senator comments on the significance of the academic exchange for the advancement of world peace.

1219   "First Fulbrights." *Time*, 2 February 1948, 35.

The article announces the opening of the first Fulbright scholarship program for study in China and Burma. The senator introduced legislation shortly after World War II which authorized an academic exchange for students, teachers, professors, and research scholars.

1220   "Free Trade in Scholars?" *Time*, 31 December 1945, 46.

This article concerns the senator's proposal for making funds from the sale of U.S. surplus war properties in foreign countries available for academic exchanges.

1221   "Fulbright Joins AMIDEAST Board." *AMIDEAST Report*, No. 26 (1978): 1-2.

The article introduces Fulbright as a member of AMIDEAST's board of directors and includes a biographical sketch. *AMIDEAST Report* is a quarterly newsletter concerning educational activities in the Middle East and North Africa.

1222   "The Fulbright Pilgrims." *Newsweek*, 27 May 1957, 102.

The article concerns the Fulbright program and includes comments on the support of the program abroad, especially in Europe, and funding problems at home. It also includes Fulbright remarks on the value of the exchange.

1223   Jeffrey, Harry P. "Legislative Origins of the Fulbright Program." *The Annals of The American Academy of Political and Social Science* 491 (May 1987): 36-47.

The author emphasizes the importance of Fulbright's early experiences as a Rhodes scholar, a professor, and a university president and his subsequent experiences as a member of Congress during and immediately following World War II in shaping his concept of an international academic exchange program. He focuses on the strategy employed by Fulbright to secure passage of the legislation in both houses of Congress and concludes with a discussion of the reasons for his success. The article is adapted from a paper presented at a Fulbright Institute of International Relations special symposium at the University of Arkansas in Fayetteville commemorating the fortieth anniversary of the Fulbright program.

1224   Johnson, Walter, and Francis J. Colligan. *The Fulbright Program: A History.* Chicago: University of Chicago Press, 1965.

This is a history of the Fulbright program from its inception under the Fulbright Act in 1946 to the consolidation and reorganization of exchange program activities under the Fulbright-Hays Act in 1961. The authors emphasize the special features of the program, including the role of the Board of Foreign Scholarships and the cooperating agencies in its administration. Although their focus is on the U.S. side of the operation, they feature some educational activities in a few countries: the United Kingdom, Italy, Greece, Egypt, India and Southeast Asia, the Philippines, Japan, Colombia, Chile, and the East African Wildlife Project. Included also is a bibliographical essay. The foreword is by the senator.

1225   Jones, Allen. "An Interview with J.W. Fulbright: AMIDEAST Board Member

Comments on International Education, Fulbright Program." *AMIDEAST Report,* No. 28 (1978): 1-3.

In an interview with the editor of AMIDEAST, Fulbright talks about the significance of his Rhodes scholar experience in the establishment of the Fulbright program; the program's purposes, strengths, and weaknesses; and the importance of keeping it apolitical. He also discusses his association with AMIDEAST and the rivalry between the United States and the Soviet Union. AMIDEAST is an organization cooperating in the administration of Fulbright-Hays grants for students from the Middle East.

1226 Kemler, Edgar. "The Fulbright Fellow: An Arkansas Traveler." *The Nation,* 20 February 1954, 146-49.

The author profiles the senator, focusing on the Fulbright scholar program and Fulbright's clashes in the Senate with Joseph R. McCarthy over the program. Fulbright responds in a letter to the editor on page 248 of the March 20 issue in which he corrects several statements in the article.

1227 Kostelanetz, Richard. "In Darkest Fulbright." *The Nation,* 13 June 1966, 725-26.

A former Fulbright scholar discusses shortcomings in the academic exchange and offers a five-point proposal for improving the program. Among the proposed reforms are increasing stipends, installing a new selection procedure to encourage mature scholars, and abolishing the educational commissions and selection committees.

1228 Lindley, Ernest K. "Rhodes Reunion." *Newsweek,* 6 July 1953, 54.

In an article about the first fifty years of the Rhodes scholarships, the author notes that Fulbright is the only Rhodes scholar to be elected to the U.S. Senate. He also mentions the Fulbright scholarships as an example of international exchange inspired by the Rhodes scholarships.

1229 Marks, Leonard H. "Commission Comments." *International Educational and Cultural Exchange* 10 (Spring 1975): inside cover and page 32.

The article is a tribute to the senator as the author of the Fulbright scholarship program.

1230 Mueller, Marti. "Fulbright Program: Retrenchment Is the Word." *Science* 161, No. 3844 (1968): 870-71.

The writer discusses the unexampled thirty per cent reduction in funds for the Fulbright program, including the reasons for the cut, and traces the legislative history of the program from 1946.

1231 Oberdorfer, Don. "Common Noun Spelled f-u-l-b-r-i-g-h-t." *The New York Times Magazine,* 4 April 1965, 79-80, 82, 84, 87.

In an article about the Fulbright scholar program initiated by the senator in 1946, the writer notes the personal accomplishments of several grantees, including soprano Anna Moffo and sculptress Lee Bontecou. He also discusses the origin of the Fulbright idea and the strategy employed by the senator to get the legislation passed. The definition of the word "fulbright" as a synonym for the scholarship, taken from *Webster's Third International Dictionary,* introduces the article.

1232 Odegaard, Charles E. "The Fulbright Exchange Program in Operation." *The ACLS Newsletter* 1 (December 1949): 1-14.

In an evaluation of the Fulbright program in its first year, the writer discusses its administrative apparatus, including the role of the Board of Foreign Scholarships; the purpose of the binational foundations; the role of the cooperating agencies; and selection procedures. He also discusses problems and limitations associated with the program. The senator praised the article as "one of the best on the subject" when he placed it in the *Congressional Record* on February 14, 1950.

1233 O'Grady, Joseph Patrick. "J.W. Fulbright and the Fulbright Program in Ireland." *The Arkansas Historical Quarterly* 47 (Spring 1988): 47-69.

The author recounts Fulbright's role in negotiations with the Irish government in 1954 to execute an agreement for a Fulbright scholar program in Ireland.

1234 "One World by Surplus." *Newsweek,* 31 December 1945, 73.

The story outlines Fulbright's Senate Bill 1636 proposing an educational exchange program funded by the sale of U.S. surplus war property abroad. It also notes General Omar Bradley's support of the bill.

1235 Peterson, Avery F. "Senator J. William Fulbright." *The American Foreign Service Journal* 28 (February 1951): 18-19.

The author presents a profile of Fulbright, focusing on the educational exchange program that he initiated shortly after the war. The senator acknowledges the significance of his own experience as a Rhodes scholar and discusses the benefits and advantages for participants on both sides of the exchange.

1236 "Return of the Fulbright." *Newsweek,* 31 May 1971, 80.

The article notes the new focus of the revamped Fulbright scholar program toward the underdeveloped countries.

1237 "Rhodes Reunion." *People Weekly,* 11 July 1983, 61-64.

The article concerns the eightieth anniversary of the Rhodes scholarships and features prominent Oxford scholars, including Fulbright, Carl Albert, and Daniel Boorstin. The Fulbright scholarship program is mentioned.

1238 Riedel, Richard Langham. *Halls of the Mighty: My 47 Years at the Senate.* Washington, D.C.: Robert B. Luce, 1969, 47, 111, 214-16, 243.

The author presents his impressions of Fulbright and relates an interesting account of behind-the-scenes strategy associated with the passage of the Fulbright Act authorizing the academic exchange program that bears the senator's name. The story involves the role that Walter Reynolds, Fulbright's legislative assistant, played in persuading Congressman Clare Hoffman of the soundness of the program. The author was liaison between the senators and the media.

1239 "Rules of Exchange." *Newsweek,* 1 November 1948, 78.

The article reviews the recommendations of the advisory commission report on educational exchange under the Fulbright Act.

1240 Schlesinger, Arthur M., Jr., ed. *The Dynamics of World Power: A Documentary History of United States Foreign Policy, 1945-1973.* Vol. 1, *Western Europe.* Edited by Robert Dallek. New York: Chelsea House Publishers in association with McGraw-Hill Book Company, 1973, 36-37. (Also published in *The Department of State Bulletin,* 11 August 1946, 262-63, under the title "Bill Authorizes Use of Proceeds from Surplus Sales for Educational Purposes: Statement by Assistant Secretary Benton"; and *The*

Journal of Arkansas Education 20 [November 1946]: 24, under the title "Fulbright Bill Is of World Significance.")

This is a statement by Assistant Secretary of State William Benton announcing the signing of the Fulbright Act by President Harry Truman. Benton outlines the educational activities authorized by the act and describes the role of the Board of Foreign Scholarships.

1241 "Scholarship Honors Senator Fulbright: Annual Award Is Designated for a College Sophomore." *The Journal of Arkansas Education* 38 (January 1966): 24.

The article pertains to an annual scholarship established by the Institute of European Studies for an Arkansas undergraduate to study at designated European study centers during the junior year.

1242 "Scholarships from Surplus." *Newsweek,* 28 July 1947, 83.

The article concerns the educational exchange program authorized by the Fulbright Act.

1243 "Senator Fulbright." *The New Yorker,* 10 May 1958, 31-32.

In New York for a preview of an exhibition of applied arts by Fulbright designers at the Museum of Contemporary Crafts, Fulbright talks about the Fulbright scholar program, the arts, and the University of Oxford.

1244 "Special Centennial Event Features Sen. Fulbright." *Arkansas Alumnus,* n.s. 25 (October 1971): 2.

This is a report of the senator's participation in a special University of Arkansas program on October 11, 1971, marking the twenty-fifth anniversary of the Fulbright Act and the centennial of the university. The report includes statistical information about the scope of the educational exchange program.

1245 "Tanks into Scholars." *Newsweek,* 19 August 1946, 85-86.

The article examines the Fulbright Act establishing an academic exchange funded by the sale of U.S. surplus war property abroad and the apparatus that will administer the program. Assistant Secretary of State William Benton is quoted.

1246 "Twenty-fifth Anniversary of the Educational Exchange Program." *The Department of State Bulletin,* 11 October 1971, 386.

This announcement includes a short statement by Fulbright regarding educational exchange in its twenty-fifth year.

1247 "United States and Israel Sign Educational Exchange Agreement." *The Department of State Bulletin,* 6 August 1956, 224-26.

The announcement includes a statement by Fulbright.

1248 Vogel, Ralph H. "The Making of the Fulbright Program." *The Annals of The American Academy of Political and Social Science* 491 (May 1987): 11-21.

In a profile of the Fulbright program, the author notes the special features that have contributed to its longevity. He emphasizes the binational approach of the program and the role of the Board of Foreign Scholarships, noting the early historical decisions reached by the board. His concluding remarks address the issues crucial for the future operation of the program. Ralph Vogel is long-time staff director of the Board of Foreign Scholarships, now called the J. William Fulbright Foreign Scholarship Board.

1249　Woods, Randall Bennett. "Fulbright Internationalism." *The Annals of The American Academy of Political and Social Science* 491 (May 1987): 22-35.

The writer discusses the experiences and circumstances which influenced the senator's introduction of legislation creating the Fulbright scholarship program: his early educational activities at Oxford University and travels in Europe, the revival of the internationalist movement in the United States during the war, Fulbright's ideas about internationalism, and his disenchantment with the political and diplomatic leadership of the country in postwar efforts to achieve collective security. The article appeared in the issue commemorating the fortieth anniversary of the academic exchange program.

1250　"World Scholars." *Newsweek,* 24 October 1949, 80-81.

The article reviews the Fulbright program.

10

The Postsenatorial Years, 1975-1990

1251 "Arts and Sciences Embodying the Fulbright Philosophy." *Arkansas Alumnus,* n.s. 32 (October 1982): 18, 20-21.

This article concerns a seven-point program undertaken by the University of Arkansas's Fulbright College of Arts and Sciences to be funded by private endowments. Dean John C. Guilds prefaces his remarks about his hopes for the college with a consideration of the senator's philosophy regarding the importance of an educated electorate in a democratic society. Fulbright's picture is on the cover.

1252 Buchanan, Patrick. "Fulbright Terms Media Muckrakers National Danger." *TV Guide,* 29 November 1975, A5-A6.

The writer concurs with views by Fulbright in an article in the November-December 1975 issue of the *Columbia Journalism Review* regarding the new style of investigative journalism in the United States since Watergate.

1253 Burnett, Henry B., Jr. "Interview with J. William Fulbright." *Skeptic,* No. 12 (March-April 1976): 8-11, 52-53.

Fulbright discusses his views on a variety of issues pertaining to the conflict in the Middle East: his recommendation of a solution based on UN Resolution 242, the Palestinian Arabs, the weight of the pro-Israeli lobby in Congress, his recommendation of a U.S. security guarantee for Israel, Israeli domestic politics, parallels in our foreign policy in Vietnam and the Middle East, and his position on the creation of Israel in 1948. *Skeptic* is a journal of the Forum for Contemporary History.

1254 Greenberg, Paul. "Fulbright Persists in His Delusions." *Arkansas Times* 11 (April 1985): 35-36.

Columnist Greenberg critiques the senator's views concerning the Soviet Union. He charges the foreign policy realists with failure to recognize the affinity between freedom and peace and to appreciate the threat of totalitarian systems to the peace process.

1255 Howe, Russell Warren, and Sarah Trott. "J. William Fulbright: Reflections on a Troubled World." *Saturday Review,* 11 January 1975, 12-16, 19.

In an interview following his loss in the Democratic senatorial primary to Governor Dale Bumpers, the senator discusses the prospects for a long stretch of peace, the future role of the United Nations, arms control, U.S.-Chinese relations, U.S.-Cuban relations, Soviet-Chinese discord, his position on the Middle East, and his views on civil rights.

1256 "Inside Story: Foreign Grab for Influence in Washington." *U.S. News and World Report,* 22 November 1976, 30-32, 35-36.

The article about foreign lobbyists in Washington mentions Fulbright's association with the law firm of Hogan and Hartson and his position as a registered agent for the United Arab Emirates and Saudi Arabia.

1257 Keerdoja, Eileen. "Fulbright: A Critical Elder Statesman." *Newsweek,* 8 August 1983, 10.

The article is an update of Fulbright's postsenatorial activities and interests and includes remarks regarding the Fulbright scholar program and U.S.-Soviet relations.

1258 "Secretary Names Five to Board of Governors for East-West Center." *The Department of State Bulletin,* 7 July 1975, 14.

This announcement pertains to the appointment of five Americans, including Fulbright, to the board of governors of the East-West Center in Hawaii.

1259 Sherrill, Robert. "Nothing off the Record." *Lithopinion* 10, No. 1, Issue 37 (1975): 19-22.

In an interview with Robert Sherrill, Fulbright discusses the harmonizing of his role as world leader with his position as senator from a state primarily concerned with domestic issues. Other subjects include myths in foreign policy, loss of congressional power, anti-intellectualism, the promise of the United Nations, the Tonkin Gulf resolution, the Fulbright program, the senator's tendency toward pessimism, and his 1974 senatorial race.

1260 "Three Views of J.W. Fulbright." *Lithopinion* 10, No. 1, Issue 37 (1975): 17-23.

This is a set of three articles honoring Fulbright following his departure from the Senate in December 1974. They are annotated separately under the following titles: "'Our Ultimate Defense Against Tyranny,'" noted in the publication history of the senator's article, "The Neglect of the Song"; "Nothing Off the Record," an interview with Fulbright by Robert Sherrill; and "'A Damned Good Politician'" by Basil Edwards. *Lithopinion* is a publication of Local One, Amalgamated Lithographers of America (New York).

1261 "Truth Hurts." *Time,* 24 November 1975, 78.

Fulbright expresses his concerns about the new style of investigative reporting, particularly the distrust exhibited among journalists toward public officials. Fulbright quotations are drawn from his article, "Fulbright on the Press," in the November-December 1975 issue of the *Columbia Journalism Review.*

1262 "University News: Pledge of $1 Million from Stephens Charitable Trust Made to Arts and Sciences Honoring Senator Fulbright." *Arkansas Alumnus,* n.s. 31 (December 1981): 2.

The article concerns the one-million-dollar pledge from the Stephens Charitable Trust to launch a full-scale development program for the College of Arts and Sciences at the University of Arkansas in Fayetteville. Included are statements by Jackson

T. Stephens and Fulbright. The college was subsequently renamed for the senator at dedication ceremonies in July 1982.

1263   Williams, Paul H. "Look Out, Harvard: Here Comes the UA's Fulbright College." *Arkansas Times* 10 (February 1984): 58-61, 98, 100, 102, 104.

The article concerns the behind-the-scenes strategy employed by university deans and Fulbright backers to secure support for a development proposal for the College of Arts and Sciences at the University of Arkansas in Fayetteville. It recounts their efforts, from drafting the plan to convincing the senator, and finally, raising funds from private endowments for the proposed programs.

11
Fulbright Family

1264 "ANW Pay Tribute to Mrs. Fulbright." *The Arkansas Publisher* 20 (February 1950): 7.

This short article notes the Arkansas Newspaper Women's recognition of Roberta Fulbright's birthday on February 14. She was honorary lifetime president of the ANW.

1265 "Arkansas Oak with a New Accent." *House and Garden,* June 1951, 98-99.

The article features furniture designed by architect Edward D. Stone and manufactured by Fulbright Industries, Fayetteville, Arkansas.

1266 Campbell, William S. *One Hundred Years of Fayetteville, 1828-1928.* Fayetteville, Arkansas, 1928, 14, 18, 32, 35, 39, 41, 77-78, 81, 87, 97, 105, 115.

This history of the senator's hometown mentions his father Jay, his mother Roberta, and his brother Jack.

1267 Davis, Wanda. "The Story of Jay Fulbright, Arkansan." *The Guild Ticker* 11 (January 1948): 6-7, 22.

This is a biographical sketch of the senator's father as a force in Fayetteville.

1268 Dew, Stephen Herman. "The New Deal and Fayetteville, Arkansas, 1933-1941." Master's thesis, University of Arkansas, 1987, 16, 18-19, 32-33, 42, 61-62, 68, 122, 186, 195-96, 202, 204-5, 207-9, 212-14, 218-21, 223-26, 239-47, 252-54, 259, 265-66, 268.

In a treatment of the senator's hometown during the New Deal, the author discusses the role of Roberta Fulbright and her newspaper in city, county, and state politics.

1269 "Fulbright Accepts Sweepstakes Award for Fayetteville *Times.*" *The Arkansas Publisher* 25 (March 1955): 3.

This article announces the presentation of the Arkansas Livestock Show Sweepstakes Award to the *Northwest Arkansas Times* of Fayetteville. The senator is pictured on the cover with the award.

1270 Fulbright, Grace G. *Wagon Train, 1829-30.* Batesville, Ark.: Guard-Record Company, 1969, 74.

This genealogy mentions the senator's family.

1271 Fulbright, Roberta. *As I See It.* Fayetteville, Arkansas, 1952.

This collection of columns written by Roberta Fulbright for the *Fayetteville Daily Democrat,* later the *Northwest Arkansas Times,* covers the period from 1932 until 1952. Mrs. Fulbright, long-time civic leader and publisher of the local newspaper, writes about an assortment of topics, including gardening, travel, and civic responsibility.

1272 "Fulbrights Establish Scholarship at U of A." *The Arkansas Publisher* 20 (August 1950): 5.

The article announces the establishment of a journalism scholarship at the University of Arkansas by the senator's family. Named for the Fulbright family newspaper, the *Northwest Arkansas Times* Scholarship provided an annual award of three hundred dollars to a senior in journalism.

1273 Gilbert, Allan. *A Fulbright Chronicle (Having to Do with Jay and Roberta Fulbright, Their Kinfolks and Their Progeny).* Fayetteville, Ark.: Fulbright Investment Company, 1980.

This collection of notes, reminiscences, genealogical charts, illustrations, and photographs records the history of the Fulbrights of Northwest Arkansas.

1274 "Honorary President Mrs. Fulbright Was Unable to Attend." *The Arkansas Publisher* 21 (January 1951): 8.

This news item reports the absence of Roberta Fulbright from the annual meeting of the Arkansas Newspaper Women.

1275 "Leaders in the Industry." *Furniture Manufacturer,* May 1951, 46.

The article features Fulbright as president of Fulbright Industries, Fayetteville, Arkansas, and highlights the company's line of furniture designed by architect Edward D. Stone.

1276 "The Love, Lewis, and Fulbright Families." *The Independence County Chronicle* 8 (July 1967): 22-25.

This genealogy mentions the relationship of the senator's family to the Springfield, Missouri, branch of the Fulbrights.

1277 "Lucile Fulbright Gilbert Dies." *Arkansas Alumnus* 2 (April 1925): 6.

The item announces the death of Lucile Fulbright Gilbert on April 8, 1925. She was the senator's sister.

1278 "Mrs. Fulbright Is Placed on Committee." *The Arkansas Publisher* 10 (September 1939): 6.

The article announces Roberta Fulbright's appointment to the editorial committee of the National Federation of Press Women.

1279 "Mrs. Roberta Fulbright." *The Arkansas Publisher* 23 (January 1953): 4.

This is the obituary of Roberta Fulbright, who died on January 11, 1953, in Fayetteville.

1280 Read, Lessie Stringfellow. "Arkansas Women Publishers." *The Arkansas Publisher* 16 (December 1946): 3.

The author presents a profile of Roberta Fulbright, long-time Fayetteville newspaper columnist and publisher, civic and business leader, and mother of the senator.

1281 ——, ed. *Sea (See) Foam: Travel Notes by Roberta Waugh Fulbright.* Siloam Springs, Ark.: John Brown University Press, 1949.

This is a compilation of travel notes by Roberta Fulbright, in verse form, concerning her trips to Europe in 1926 and 1928 when her son was at Oxford.

1282 "Roberta Fulbright Hall." *Arkansas Alumnus,* n.s. 13 (November 1959): 2-7.

This article concerns the opening and dedication on October 11 of a dormitory for freshman women on the University of Arkansas campus. The senator was the principal speaker at the dedication honoring his mother.

1283 "The Roberta Fulbright Memorial Bookshelf at University of Arkansas Is Displayed." *The Arkansas Publisher* 23 (August 1953): 6.

This caption and photograph concern the Roberta Fulbright Memorial Bookshelf in the journalism department at the University of Arkansas. The bookshelf was established to honor the memory of the long-time newspaper columnist and mother of the senator. Daughter Helen Fulbright Douglas and Professor Walter Lemke are in the picture.

1284 Rose, F.P. "The Springfield Wagon Company." *The Arkansas Historical Quarterly* 10 (Spring 1951): 95-103.

The article is a history of the Springfield Wagon and Trailer Company of Springfield, Missouri. It includes a note on the purchase in 1941 by the Fulbright family of the company's wagon department and its subsequent transfer to Fayetteville, where it became a unit of the Phipps Lumber Company. Fulbright was president of Phipps at the time.

1285 Rothrock, Thomas. "A History of the Washington County Press." *Flashback* 16 (February 1966): 1-15.

The article includes a brief history of the *Fayetteville Daily Democrat,* later the *Northwest Arkansas Times,* and includes an account of its ownership by the Fulbright family, dating from about 1913 when Jay Fulbright, the senator's father, purchased it. It incorporates a chronology of the staff through the years and information concerning the role of Roberta Fulbright, the senator's mother.

1286 "Russellville Paper Purchased by Brown, Fulbright, Palmer." *The Arkansas Publisher* 21 (May 1951): 2.

This article announces the purchase of the *Russellville Daily and Weekly Courier-Democrat* by Fulbright, Clyde Palmer, and Edgar Brown.

1287 *Sumner, Missouri, 1882-1982.* Marceline, Mo.: Walsworth Publishing Company, n.d., 147.

The volume includes information on the Fulbright Museum in Sumner, Missouri. Fulbright was born in Sumner on April 9, 1905.

1288 T.R.W. "Mrs. Roberta Fulbright." *The Arkansas Publisher* 23 (January 1953): 7.

This is a tribute to Roberta Fulbright following her death on January 11, 1953.

1289 "There's Increasing Evidence of America's Own Style." *House Beautiful* 93 (June 1951): 94-95.

The article features a photograph of architect Edward D. Stone's oak furniture, manufactured by Fulbright Industries, Fayetteville, Arkansas.

1290 Untitled. *Arkansas Alumnus,* n.s. 7 (September 1953): 5.

This is a short article regarding the Roberta Fulbright Memorial Bookshelf in the journalism department at the University of Arkansas, established to honor the memory of the long-time newspaper columnist and publisher. Daughter Helen Fulbright Douglas and Professor Walter Lemke are in the picture.

Index

The index includes both author and subject entries. The numbers following the headings and subheadings refer to bibliographic entry numbers, not page numbers.

About the Compiler

BETTY AUSTIN has worked in the Special Collections Division of the University of Arkansas Library for the past 18 years where she manages the J. William Fulbright archives. She is a member of the Society of Southwest Archivists, associate member of the Fulbright Association, and has participated in the Modern Archives Institute at the National Archives and Records Administration in Washington, D.C.

ISBN 0-313-26336-1

9 780313 263361